Biblical and Theological Studies on the Trinity

Edited by
Paul Petersen and Robert K McIver

Biblical and Theological Studies on the Trinity

Edited by
Paul Petersen and Robert K McIver

Adelaide
2014

Text copyright © 2014 remains with all authors.

All rights reserved. Except for any fair dealing permitted under the Copyright Act, no part of this book may be reproduced by any means without prior permission. Inquiries should be made to the publisher.

National Library of Australia Cataloguing-in-Publication entry : (pbk)

Author:	Petersen, Paul 1952-
Title:	Biblical and theological studies on the Trinity / Paul Petersen ; Robert K McIver.
ISBN:	9781921511394 (pbk.)
Notes:	Includes index.
Subjects:	Trinity. Appropriation (Christian theology) God (Christianity)

Other Authors/Contributors:
    McIver, Robert K. (Robert Kerry), 1953-

Dewey Number: 231.044

An imprint of the ATF Ltd
PO Box 504
Hindmarsh, SA 5007
ABN 90 116 359 963
www.atfpress.com

Avondale Academic Press
PO Box 19
Cooranbong
NSW 2265

Contents

List of Contributors ix
Introduction xi

PART 1 Biblical Studies

1. Some Aspects of the Christology of the Fourth Gospel
   Relevant to Contemporary Christological Controversy 3
   Robert K McIver
2. Jesus—the 'One and Only', or 'Only Begotten': The Meaning
   of *Monogenes* 29
   Paul Petersen
3. Worshipping Jesus—the 'eternally blessed God!' (Romans 9:5) 35
   Paul Petersen
4. A Study of Paul's Concept of the Saving Act
   of 1 Corinthians 15:27–28 47
   Roland D Meyer
5. The Firstborn in Colossians 1:15 65
   Ekkehardt Mueller

PART 2 Historical and Theological Studies

6. Trinity: Toward a (Somewhat) Postmodern Perspective 89
   Ray CW Roennfeldt
7. The Trinitarian Basis of Christian Community 101
   Richard Rice

8. Alexandrian School and the Trinitarian Problem   113
    Darius Jankiewicz
9. The Holy Spirit: His Divinity and Personality   127
    Frank M Hasel
10. Trinity and Tawhid In Islam—An Appraisal   145
    Børge Schantz

PART 3   Studies in Seventh-day Adventist History and Theology

11. The Influence of Restorationism on Early Seventh-day Adventism and the Emergence of a Trinitarian Perspective   165
    Karl Arasola
12. The Trinitarian Issue in Seventh-day Adventism   181
    Gunnar Pedersen
13. John Harvey Kellogg's Concept of the Godhead   193
    John Skrzypaszek

Appendix: Consensus Statement   219

Index of Persons and Authors   221

Index of Subjects   227

Index of Christian Scriptural References   237

Index of Islamic Scriptural References   251

"In the past God spoke to our forefathers through the prophets at many times and in various ways, but in these last days he has spoken to us by his Son, whom he appointed heir of all things, and through whom he made the universe. The Son is the radiance of the God's glory and the exact representation of his being, sustaining all things by his powerful word. After he had provided purification for sins, he sat down at the right hand of the Majesty in heaven."

Hebrews 1:1-3 NIV

List of Contributors

	At time of conference	At time of publication
Kai Arasola	Mission College, Thailand [Asia-Pacific Adventist University]	Finland Union Conference
Frank M Hasel	Bogenhofen Seminary, Austria	Bogenhofen Seminary, Austria
Darius Jankiewicz	Fulton College, Fiji	Seventh-day Adventist Theological Seminary, Andrews University, United States
Robert K McIver	Course Coordinator, Faculty of Theology, Avondale College, Australia	Head of School of Ministry and Theology, Avondale College of Higher Education, Australia
Roland D Meyer	Dean of the Seventh-day Adventist Theological Seminary, Salève Adventist University, France	Dean of the Seventh-day Adventist Theological Seminary, Salève Adventist University, France
Ekkehardt Mueller	Biblical Research Institute, General Conference of Seventh-day Adventists, United States	Biblical Research Institute, General Conference of Seventh-day Adventists, United States

Gunnar Pedersen	Department of Theological Studies, Newbold College, United Kingdom	Department of Theological Studies, Newbold College, United Kingdom
Paul Petersen	Field Secretary, South-Pacific Division of Seventh-day Adventists, Australia	Chair of Department of Religion & Biblical Languages, Andrews University
Richard Rice	School of Religion, Loma Linda University, United States	School of Religion, Loma Linda University, United States
Ray CW Roennfeldt	Dean of Faculty of Theology, Avondale College, Australia	Principal, Avondale College of Higher Education, Australia
Børge Schantz	Allied Health Studies, Loma Linda University, United States	Allied Health Studies, Loma Linda University, United States
John Skrzypaszek	Ellen G White/SDA Research Centre, Avondale College, New South Wales	Ellen G White/SDA Research Centre, Avondale College of Higher Education

Introduction

The Trinity has long been a standard topic in theological education. Students either revel or tolerate the complexities of the development of the doctrine, but until quite recent years, the topic is one that largely remained as a historical study in the professional life of pastors and academics. A dramatic change has taken place in recent years. As will be documented in the following chapters, the doctrine of the Trinity has emerged as a 'hot topic' within academic circles both within the academic sphere, and within the theological topics of greatest controversy amongst the laity of Churches of all denominations, including the Seventh-day Adventist churches of the South Pacific.

The controversy surrounding the doctrine of the Trinity made it a natural topic to choose as the theme of a theological consultation that took place at the offices of the South-Pacific Division of Seventh-day Adventists, between 1 and 4 May 2008.

The chapters in this book were commissioned as part of the proceedings of the May 2008 consultation. They are shared here in the hope that they may be of interest to a wider audience.

Paul Petersen and Rob McIver
December 2012

PART 1
Biblical Studies

Some Aspects of the Christology of the Fourth Gospel Relevant to Contemporary Christological Controversy

Robert K McIver

The Issue

The Gospel of John has been at the heart of christological debate from earliest times. As TE Pollard observed,

> At the turn of this century, FC Conybeare ... wrote: 'If Athanasius had not had the Fourth Gospel to draw texts from, Arius would never have been confuted.' This is however only part of the truth, for it would also be true to say that if Arius had not the Fourth Gospel to draw texts from, he would not have needed confuting. Without in any way diminishing the importance of other biblical writings in the development of the church's doctrine, it is St John's Gospel—and the First Epistle of St John—that brings into sharpest focus the problems which created doctrinal controversy in the early church and which indeed still perplex the church today.[1]

This observation is also pertinent to the modern discussions swirling around the topic of Christology in both academic and lay circles. John provides the raw material for orthodox and heterodox alike. Nor is this surprising, given the fact that John contains some of the most profound thinking about Jesus in the New Testament. The Gospel leads the reader/listener[2] into a deeper understanding of Jesus by posing a set of paradoxes

---

1. TE Pollard, *Johannine Christology and the Early Church* (London: Cambridge University Press, 1970), 3. Pollard references the citation from FC Conybeare as coming from *Hibbert Journal* 7 (1903): 620.
2. Manuscripts were usually read aloud in the ancient world, as is pointed out by Paul J Achtemeier, '*Omne Verbum Sonat*: The New Testament and the Oral Environment of

and playing off the readers' preconceptions. Yet this method has its attendant risks, and sometimes the way the statements about Jesus are formulated on the Fourth Gospel can lend themselves to misunderstanding. For example, while 'The evangelist takes for granted that he is interpreting the life of a fully human figure,'[3] so much emphasis is placed on the divinity of Jesus that no less scholar than Ernst Käsemann has charged John with a tendency to a naïve docetism. Nor is this a position that can be dismissed out of hand. As Käsemann says,

> ... we must also ask: in what sense is he flesh, who walks on the water and through closed doors, who cannot be captured by his enemies, who at the well of Samaria is tired and desires a drink, yet has no need of drink and has food different from that which his disciples seek? He cannot be deceived by men, because he knows their innermost thoughts even before they speak. He debates with them from the vantage point of the infinite difference between heaven and earth. He has need neither of the witness of Moses nor of the Baptist. He dissociates himself from the Jews, as if they were not his own people, and he meets his mother as one who is her Lord. He permits Lazarus to lie in the grave four days in order that the miracle of his resurrection may be more impressive. And in the end the Johannine Christ goes victoriously to his death of his own accord.[4]

> ... One can hardly fail to recognise the danger of his Christology of glory, namely, the danger of docetism. It is present

---

Late Western Antiquity', in *Journal of Biblical Literature* 109 (1990): 3–27. Furthermore, Catherine Hezser, *Jewish Literacy in Roman Palestine* (Tübingen: Mohr, 2001), estimates that literacy rates in Palestine were likely to be much lower than the 10–15% estimated for the Roman world in general; although this perhaps should be balanced somewhat by the work of Alan R Millard, *Reading and Writing at the Time of Jesus* (Sheffield: Academic Press, 2000). The implication, being, that works like the Fourth Gospel were usually read aloud to a circle of listeners, not all of whom were literate. Thus it is probably more appropriate to speak of the those who heard the Gospel rather than those who read it.

3. Andrew T Lincoln, *The Gospel According to St John* (Peabody, MA: Hendrickson, 2005), 59.
4. Ernst Käsemann, *The Testament of Jesus* (London: SCM, 1968), 9.

in a still naïve, unreflected form and it has not yet been recognised by the community.[5]

Anyone who has given close attention to the Fourth Gospel will find Käsemann's remarks challenging and difficult to refute, although an attempt will be mounted later in this chapter.

The issues raised by Johannine Christology are not just confined to its strong emphasis on the divinity of Christ. As well as recording the claim of Jesus that 'I and the Father are one' (John 10:30), this is the Gospel that records Jesus as saying, 'The Father is greater than I (John 14:10), and of himself and his mission that, 'The son is able to do nothing of himself except what he sees the Father doing' (John 5:19).[6] In recent times these latter texts, and others like them in the Gospel, have been used in evangelical circles to argue the eternal subordination of the Son to the Father.[7] The strong emphasis on Jesus' divinity, together with those texts in John which speak of Jesus' subordination to his Father are but two examples of a range of texts in John that have proved the focus of intense theological controversy, from some of the earliest debates in Christianity, right through to the contemporary resurgence of interest in Christology.

---

5. *Ibid*, 26.
6. Scripture references are either the author's translation from the Greek New Testament, or taken from the Revised Standard Version.
7. For example, see the case made by Craig S Keener, 'Is Subordination Within the Trinity Heresy?: A Study of John 5:18 in Context', in *Trinity Journal*, 20 ns (1999): 39–51. Keener concludes that 'one can make a case for the Son's subordination to the Father, probably even in some sense for his eternal subordination' (51), but wishes to decouple this insight from contemporary debates about gender roles within evangelicalism. See also Kevin Giles, *Jesus and the Father: Modern Evangelicals Reinvent the Doctrine of the Trinity* (Grand Rapids, MI: Zondervan, 2006), *passim*, for extensive documentation of the terms of this debate within evangelicalism, particularly within Australian Anglicanism. Giles categorises subordinationism together with Modalism and tritheism as three extremes which surround orthodox trinitarianism (see convenient diagram at 74). He has written his book as 'a plea from the heart to my fellow evangelicals who in growing numbers in recent years have begun arguing for the eternal subordination in function and authority of the Son to the Father. I say to them, "Go back, you are going the wrong way".' (9).

Three Approaches to Johannine Christological Paradoxes

John includes data that can be used to reconstruct apparently contradictory views of Jesus. One set of texts appears to present a very human Jesus who gets tired and feels human emotions. Another set, those highlighted in the citation from Ernst Käsemann above, portray a fully divine Jesus who lives far above the mundane concerns of other humans. As Paul N Anderson has observed, scholars have used these variations in several ways:

1. An approach adopted until the beginning of the nineteenth century was 'to diminish or ignore the apparent contradictions' by 'attempting to harmonise the christological tensions'. Anderson observes, though, that 'to overlook the tensions in John without addressing the problems they present is not an option for contemporary and serious study of the Fourth Gospel'.[8]
2. 'A second option is to acknowledge John's christological tensions, but to ascribe them to literary sources *external* to the thinking of the evangelist.'[9] This approach to the Gospel uses the differences in Christology as a significant clue to enable the reconstruction of the various literary layers of John. A well-known example of this approach is the five-stage development of the Fourth Gospel proposed by Raymond Brown.[10] Brown then uses this reconstruction to discern the history of the Johannine Community. According to Brown, the Gospel reveals that what was originally a group of Jewish Christians with a rather 'low' Christology were joined by second group with a higher Christology. The Gospel reveals itself as the product of the fertile interac-

---

8. Paul N Anderson, *The Christology of the Fourth Gospel: Its Unity and Disunity in the Light of John 6* (Valley Forge, PN: Trinity, 1996), 2, 4.
9. Anderson, *Christology*, 4.
10. First there was a body of traditional material, similar to, but independent of the traditions that ended up in the Synoptic Gospels. Second the traditional material was moulded into the style of discourses that became part of the Fourth Gospel under the guidance of a master preacher (the evangelist). Third, the master preacher organised his materials into a first edition of his Gospel. Fourth, the evangelist preacher published a second edition, to take into account issues raised by Jewish Christians and others. Finally, the whole Gospel was edited by somebody other than the evangelist. At least so is the reconstruction put forward by Raymond Brown in, *The Gospel According to John (i–xii)* (Garden City, NI: Doubleday, 1966), xxxiv–xxxix. Brown himself provides a very helpful summary of the ways other scholars have reconstructed the literary history of the Gospel using the clues provided by the differences in theology, apparent discontinuities in the flow of the text, etc (see xxiv–xxxiv).

tion between these two groups, and those external to the community. By the time the Johannine epistles appeared, though, this community has split asunder over Christology.[11] Anderson criticises such reconstructions (he analyses that of Rudolf Bultmann in some detail) on the risk that their very complexity makes them vulnerable to misjudgments.[12] It may be argued that the very multiplicity of incompatible reconstructions of the literary history of the Gospels that have been published by various scholars argues against the likelihood of such a methodology bearing long-term fruit. While Brown, Bultmann and others clearly demonstrate a serious engagement with the text, their whole work depends on a highly vulnerable literary reconstruction of sources. If the underlying reconstruction is not accepted, and few accept that of Brown or Bultmann today, then much of their writing becomes tendentious, if not irrelevant.

3. A third approach is to treat 'John's christological tensions . . . as tensions *internal* to the thinking and writing of the evangelist'.[13] This chapter suggests that an approach similar to this is the best way to understand John's Christology, though, as will emerge, I will argue that some of the tensions are deliberately created by the evangelist, and used by him to play on the expectations of his readers.

Examples of John's Play on Reader's Expectations

The Fourth Gospel uses several different ways to lead the reader to a deeper understanding of Jesus. The work divides naturally into two main parts, often described as the Book of Signs (chapters 1 – 12), and the Book of Glory (chapters 13 – 21).[14] In the Book of Signs, the reader is lead to

---

11. Raymond Brown, *The Community of the Beloved Disciple* (London: Chapman, 1979), *passim*.
12. 'The weakness of assuming distinct literary sources on the basis of theological judgments, however, is obvious. It rests upon at least three layers of judgment: a) a correct and singular interpretation of what the text both says and means, b) an accurate assessment that meanings are genuinely incompatible with each other within the text as they stand, and c) a superior reassignment of material to other sources which creates fewer problems—or at least preferable ones. If any of these layers of judgment be flawed, *in any way*, the validity of one's interpretation is correspondingly weakened.' Anderson, *Christology*, 10.
13. Anderson, *Christology*, 10.
14. For example, Derek Tovey divides the Gospel into the Book of Signs and the Book of Glory. He points out that 'There is a definite epilogue to the Book of Signs at 12:36b–50 where Jesus' public ministry comes to a close, and the narrator assesses its impact'.

meditate on the meaning of several of Jesus important miracles, which are described as signs. These include the turning of water into wine at Cana (the beginning of Jesus' signs, John 2:11), the healing of the royal official's son (the second sign, John 4:54), the feeding of the 5000 (a sign Jesus had performed, John 6:14), and the raising of Lazarus from the dead (John 12:17-18). Interspersed with these miracles or attached to them, are a series of extendend discourses during which Jesus is reported to have introduced the key ideas about himself to the crowd, playing on their preconceptions, and expressing them in increasingly confrontational terms, until the individuals that have heard him bring positive or negative judgment upon themselves because they either believe or reject Jesus' claims (for example. John 3:18; 5:24). This may be illustrated by looking at two of the christiological titles used by Jesus, the title 'I am', and the title Christ.

The Title 'I am' (ἐγώ εἰμι)

The 'I am' (ἐγώ εἰμι) sayings in the Fourth Gospel fall into two categories: those without predicates and those with predicates. The phrase 'I am' (ἐγώ εἰμι) occurs without a predicate in John 4:26; 6:20; 8:24, 28, 58; 9:9; 13:19; 18:5-6, 8.[15] In Johannine usage it is clear that the phrase can have a mundane meaning. The man who received back his sight identified himself by saying 'I am' (ἐγώ εἰμι; 9:9). When Jesus was talking to the woman at the well he indicated that he was the Christ by saying 'I am (ἐγώ εἰμι; 4:26). In 6:20, where Jesus was walking on the water, the phrase could again merely be self-identification, as it could be also in 18:5, 6, 8. Yet at times the phrase takes on a meaning that is more than just mundane self-identification. It is definitely used as a title in 3:24, 28 and 13:19, where the phrase is the subject of the verb 'to believe' (πιστεύειν). Even in 4:26, 6:20, and 18:5-8 the context is anything but mundane. In 18:6, when Jesus said 'I am' (ἐγώ εἰμι) those that had come to arrest him fell to the ground.

In, *Jesus: Story of God: John's Story of Jesus* (Adelaide: ATF, 2007), 41-67. The citation is found on 42.

15. This group of texts is discussed by B Harner in *The 'I Am' of the Fourth Gospel* (Philadelphia, PA: Fortress, 1970), and David Mark Ball, *'I Am' in John's Gospel: Literary Function, Backgronud and Theological Implications* (Sheffield: JSNT, 1996), 176-203. See also CH Dodd, *The Interpretation of the Fourth Gospel* (Cambridge: University Press, 1955), 93-96; David Daube, *The New Testament and Rabbinic Judaism* (London: Athlone, 1956), chapter 9, 'The "I Am" of the Messianic Presence' (325-29); and the more general discussion in Brown, *John*, 1:533-58, and Rudolf Schnackenburg, *The Gospel According to John* (New York: Herder & Herder, 1968), 2:79-89.

In 6:20 it is Jesus who is walking on water who says 'I am' (ἐγώ εἰμι), and in 4:26 Jesus is identifying himself as the Messiah.

There are few clearer supra-mundane uses of the phrase 'I am' (ἐγώ εἰμι) than that found in John 8. In the discourse recorded in that chapter, Jesus tells his listeners that they will die in their sins unless they believe that 'I am' (ἐγώ εἰμι; 8:24). Thus, this title embodies within it a conception of the person of Jesus that is a necessary part of saving faith. His hearers are surprised at this, and ask, 'Who are you?' (8:25). Jesus answers in terms of the one who sent him, his Father, and then tells his listeners that when they see the Son of Man lifted up, then they will know (8:28). It is the cross that more than any other thing reveals the true nature of Jesus.[16] Later in the same chapter Jesus tells his listeners that Abraham rejoiced to see his day. The Jews immediately questioned this statement because Jesus was not yet fifty years old. Jesus then solemnly declared that before Abraham was, ἐγώ εἰμι ('I am'; 8:58). At this the Jews pick up stones to throw at him—not only because Jesus had made a clear claim to re-existence, but presumably because his listeners were reminded of some of the uses of this phrase in the Old Testament, particularly those found in Isaiah and Exodus.[17] The following is a relatively literal translation of the LXX of some of these crucial passages (the Greek text may be found in the footnotes):

Isaiah 43:10: 'Become witnesses for me . . . so that you may know and believe and understand that 'I am' [ἐγώ εἰμι], before me other Gods did not come into existence, and there will be none after me.'[18]

Isaiah 41:4: Who produced and made these things? [Who is] the one who called these from the beginning of generations[?]. I [am] God [the] first, and to those who are coming, 'I am' [ἐγώ εἰμι][19]

---

16. See JE Morgan-Wynne, 'The Cross and the Revelation of Jesus as ἐγώ εἰμι in the Fourth Gospel (John 8:28)', in *Studia Biblica* 2 (1978): 219–26.
17. Passages from Isaiah are particularly highlighted by Ball, *'I Am' in John's Gospel*, 177–203.
18. γένεσθε μοι μάρτυρες . . . ἵνα γνῶτε καὶ πιστεύσητε καὶ συνῆτε ὅτι ἐγώ εἰμι, ἔμπροσθέν μου οὐκ ἐγένετο ἄλλος θεὸς καὶ μετ' ἐμὲ οὐκ ἔσται. This and the following LXX citations are taken from Alfred Rahlfs, ed, *Septuaginta*, fourth edition (Stuttgart: Privilegierte Württembergische Bibelanstalt, 1950).
19. τίς ἐνήργησεν καὶ ἐποίησεν ταῦτα; ἐκάλεσεν αὐτὴν ὁ καλῶν αὐτὴν ἀπὸ γενεῶν ἀρχῆς, ἐγὼ θεὸς πρῶτος, καὶ εἰς τὰ ἐπερχόμενα ἐγώ εἰμι.

Isaiah 51:12: I am, I am the one who comforts you [ἐγώ εἰμι ἐγώ εἰμι ὁ παρακαλῶν σε] ... God who made you, the one who made the heavens and the foundations of the earth ...[20]

Exodus 3:13–14: And Moses said to God, 'Behold, I will go to the Children of Israel and I will say to them, "The God of your fathers sent me to you". They will ask me, "What is his name?" What will I say to them?' And God said to Moses, 'I am the one who is ['Εγώ εἰμι ὁ ὤν]'. And thus you will speak to the sons of Israel, 'The one who is ['Ο ὤν], he sent me to you.'[21]

In all these instances the phrase 'I am' (ἐγώ εἰμι) is an important self-designation of the One God. Thus, when Jesus says, before Abraham was, I am (πρὶν 'Αβραὰμ γενέσθαι ἐγὼ εἰμί) in John 8:58, he is using the phrase 'I am' (ἐγώ εἰμι) in a manner that cannot really be confused with a mundane self-identification. Its use constitutes nothing less than a serious claim to divinity. But once the reader has realised this, the phrase becomes a double entendre each time it is met on the lips of Jesus in the Fourth Gospel. It sometimes means nothing more than 'I am' in the mundane sense. But each use has the potential to mean something more, and usually does. As the reader notes the reply of Jesus to the soldiers in the garden, there is no surprise when the rabble falls to the ground, as they would when confronted with the divinity of Jesus. When he hears Jesus admit to the woman at the well that he is the Messiah by saying 'I am' ἐγώ εἰμι, the reader cannot but help hearing a distant echo of divinity in his mind. At the same time, though, this can at times be but an intriguing echo.

Nor does this exhaust the use made of the phrase 'I am' in the Gospel. There are seven 'I am' (ἐγώ εἰμι) sayings with a predicate:

> I am the bread   - of life (6:35, 48)
>   - which has come down from heaven (6:41)
>   - the living bread (5:51)
> I am the light of the world (8:12)
> I am the door (10:7, 9)

---

20. ἐγώ εἰμι ἐγώ εἰμι ὁ παρακαλῶν σε ... θεὸν τὸν ποιήσαντά σε τὸν ποιήσαντα τὸν οὐρανὸν καὶ θεμελιώσαντα τὴν γῆν.
21. καὶ εἶπεν Μωυσῆς πρὸς τὸν θεός Ἰδοὺ ἐγὼ ἐλεύσομαι πρὸς τοὺς υἱοὺς Ισραηλ καὶ ἐρῶ πρὸς αὐτούς Ὁ θεὸς τῶν πατέρων ὑμῶν ἀπέσταλκέν με πρὸς ὑμᾶς, ἐρωτήσουσίν με Τί ὄνομα αὐτῷ; τί ἐρῶ πρὸς αὐτούς; καὶ εἶπεν ὁ θεὸς πρὸς Μωυσῆν Ἐγώ εἰμι ὁ ὤν· καὶ εἶπεν Οὕτως ἐρεῖς τοῖς υἱοῖς Ισραηλ Ὁ ὤν ἀπέσταλκέν με πρὸς ὑμᾶς.

> I am the good shepherd (10:11, 14)
> I am the resurrection and life (11:25)
> I am the way, the truth and life (14:6)
> I am the true vine (15:1, 5)

Together, these seven sayings encompass a large proportion of the first half of the Fourth Gospel. They are significant summary statements of the meaning the reader is to place on the signs (σημεῖα) chosen by the fourth evangelist. The restoration of the sight of a blind man (9:1–7) shows that Jesus is indeed the light of the world (8:12). Jesus can raise Lazarus to life again (11:1–44) precisely because he is the resurrection and the life (11:25). The significance of the feeding of the five thousand (6:1–15) is that Jesus is the bread of life that has come down from heaven (John 6:22–58 *passim*, for example verse 33).

Jesus' use of the title 'I am' in John is but one illustration the subtlety with which titles and other theologically charged language is used in John. One could argue that there is an inherent contradiction in the use made of 'I am'. If it can be a mundane self-designation, then how could it be a claim to divinity? Or, if it is a claim to divinity, how could it every be used in a mundane sense? But it is used both ways, and I do not think that this indicates two separate theological streams in John that should be identified with separate stages in the development of the Johannine community, or as associated with different source documents within the Gospel. On the contrary, the play on reader's expectations is deliberate. The reader is expected to be held in suspense each time the term, 'I am' (ἐγώ εἰμι) is read. The double entendre is intentional.

The Title 'Christ' (Χριστός)

Another example of John's play on reader's expecations is his use of the title 'Messiah' or 'Christ' (εὑρήκαμεν τὸν Μεσσίαν, ὅ ἐστιν μεθερμηνευόμενον Χριστός; 'We have found the Messiah, which is interpreted Christ'; 1:41). The term Χριστός occurs in the Fourth Gospel at 1:17, 20, 41; 3:28; 4:25, 29; 7:26, 27, 31, 41, 42; 9:22; 10:24, 31; 11:27; 12:34; 17:3; 20:31.[22] The crucial importance of this title in the thinking of the Fourth

---

22. It is omitted from John 4:42 and 6:69 in the best MSS. On John 6:69, see Bruce M Metzger, *A Textual Commentary on the Greek New Testament* (London: United Bible Societies, 1971), 215; John 4:42 does not warrant a comment in Metzger because it is not listed as a variant in the UBS Greek New Testament.

Evangelist is shown by its use to summarise the kernel of what the Gospel is intended to convey—that 'Jesus is the Christ, the Son of God' (20:31). Nor should it be overlooked, that the very first time the name Jesus is found in the Gospel it is in the form, 'Jesus Christ' (διά' Ἰησοῦ Χριστοῦ; 1:17). The title is naturally applied to the name of Jesus (cf 17:3).

Moving through the Gospel, the reader slowly becomes introduced to the various possibilities inherent in the title, and which are those that belong to Jesus. For example, from John 1:17 the reader already knows that Jesus is the Christ when John the Baptist denies the title for himself (1:20, 25; 3:28). Questions about the nature and function of the Messiah are raised by the question directed at John the Baptist, but not answered in John 1:19–28. He is asked why he is baptising if he is not the Christ (1:25). It also appears significant that at 1:41 a translation is given. Andrew, immediately after meeting Jesus, finds his brother Simon and tells him, 'We have found the Messiah'. The Hebrew title Messiah is immediately translated into the Greek title Christ or anointed one. This is an indication that the etymology of the word had not lost its force.[23] The Messiah-Christ was the anointed one. John the Baptist bore witness that he saw the Spirit descend upon Jesus. John recognised that he could only baptise with water, but the one who was to come (Jesus) was to baptise with the Holy Spirit. Jesus is the Christ in part because of his unique endowment of the Spirit.[24]

More of the expectations surrounding the term Messiah current in the first century are revealed in John 7. For example, John 7:27 reveals that it was expected that the Christ would have an unknown origin. Jesus informs his hearers that they might think they know his origins, but in reality, they do not (7:28).[25] Then 7:31 shows that it was also expected that the Christ would be a wonder worker. After Jesus' teaching about the water, there is again speculation about the Messianic status of Jesus. Some would

---

23. WC van Unnik, 'Jesus the Christ', in *New Testament Studies* 8 (1961/62): 113. Van Unnik concludes: 'However, it is important for our investigation to see what was the essential element in the Messiahship of Jesus for those early Christians: this *was not the outward activity of a king*, but *the person possessed by the Spirit*' (115).
24. Cf the remarks made by S Mowinckel about the anointing of the Kings of Israel *in He that Cometh* (Oxford: Basil Blackwell, 1959), 63–74.
25. Warren Carter states, 'Many of these features of irony are evident, for instance, in 6:42 and 7:27–28'. *John: Storyteller, Interpreter, Evangelist* (Peabody, MA: Hendrickson, 2006), 119. The irony he highlights in John 7:27–28 is the misunderstanding of Jesus' origins by the crowd. The crowd think they know of the origin of Jesus, but Jesus says they do not. The attentive reader of the Gospel also knows that Jesus' true origin is 'from above'.

understand Jesus as Prophet, others as Christ (7:40). This is ironic[26] because, as is already clear to the reader, Jesus is both Prophet (4:44; 6:14[27]) and Christ (1:17, etc). Another objection is raised in John 7:41–42 against the identification of Jesus as the Christ. The Christ does not come from Galilee, but is a descendant of David, from the village of David.[28] Here, I believe, is an ironic situation that creates a very strong play on the expectations of all readers of the Gospel. The reader knows that Jesus was, in fact born in Bethlehem, the village of David, and thus fits this aspect of the concept of Messiah. But this information is given nowhere in John! A little thought persuades the reader that this omission is deliberate. As emerges from the perspective of the Fourth Gospel, Jesus true origin is that he comes from above. Thus his earthly place of birth is of no relevance to the discussion in the as to whether or not Jesus is the Christ.

In the Fourth Gospel Jesus is portrayed as Messiah, and this role implies his kingship. Yet the Messianic kingship of Jesus is a paradoxical kingship. Jesus explained to Pilate that his kingdom is not of this world

---

26. As Derek Tovey says, 'The use of irony is a device much used by the writer-witness. Irony occurs when a deeper level of meaning lies below the surface of the plain meaning of the words. Irony often involves a form of communication between the writer-witness and the readers, whereby the readers understand the words spoken by characters, for instance, or the event described, to have a significance that is lost on those within the story world.' In *Jesus: Story of God*, 69.
27. The expectation that the title prophet could appropriately be ascribed to Jesus is aroused by the fact that John the Baptist denies that he is the Christ and denies that he is the prophet (John 1:21). On the other hand, the title 'Prophet' is not applied to Jesus without ambiguity. It is usually a title given to Jesus by those who have an inadequate understanding of him, such as the woman at the well (John 4:19) and the people who had concluded from the miracle of the feeding of the 5000 that they should force Jesus to become king (John 6:14).
28. This reflects the Old Testament prophecies concerning the Davidic king. In 2 Samuel 7:8–16 is recorded the oracle of Nathan to David. In the oracle, David is promised that when he dies the Lord will raise up offspring after him, and God will establish his kingdom. God will be his Father, and he shall be God's son (cf the Father/Son motif in the Fourth Gospel). The throne will be established forever. This theme finds expression in several places in the Old Testament. For example, Isaiah 11:1–16 talks of the shoot from the stump of Jesse. The Spirit of the Lord will rest upon him. He will judge in righteousness, and the wicked will be slain by his breath. The edenic state will be restored—the wolf will lie with the lamb. The remnant of the Lord's people will be gathered in, and the enemies of Israel destroyed. Curiously enough, while Jesus is called 'Son of David' freely in the Synoptic Gospels (for example Matt 1:1; 9:27; 15:22; 21:9; Mark 10:47; 11:10; Luke 1:27; 2:11; 18:38–39; etc), he is not so designated in the Fourth Gospel at all. Probably because in John his sonship is more located in the terms Son of Man and the Son of God.

(18:36). He avoided any involvement in a political move to make him king by popular acclamation (6:14–15). In hanging the placard on the cross, Pilate indicated the nature of the kingship of Jesus. Jesus on the cross was king of the Jews. The cross was his throne. If he was lifted up on the cross, not only would this cast out the ruler of this world, it would draw all men to Jesus (12:31–32). It is the cross, then, which is the judgment of the world; it is the cross which gains the victory over the Devil; it is the cross which is the focal point of Jesus' kingdom.

The title, 'Christ', like the title 'I am' illustrates how John plays on the readers expectations. Irony, double entendre and theologically charged symbolism is the stock in trade of this Gospel. The paradoxes in the way Jesus is portrayed in the Gospel is an essential part of the way the reader is led into a fuller understanding of Jesus. The end result, though, is that none of the elements that make up the total picture of Jesus can be studied in isolation from the others. Nor is it legitimate for modern Christians to seize on one aspect of John's portrayal of Jesus and construct their understanding of Jesus from just this aspect of John. John's Christology is complex, and must be understood in the light of the whole development of his christological ideas. It cannot be understood apart from his wider symbolic universe.

Keys to the Johannine Symbolic Universe

The genius of the Fourth Gospel lies in its ability to use simple language and simple ideas to convey very profound thinking about who Jesus is. Using simple spatial and temporal concepts, the Gospel invites the reader to enter into a new symbolic universe. Two schema operate simultaneously. The first is a spatial schema, and expressed by the simple language of above/below. The second, a temporal schema, implies the blessings of the future (judgment, eternal life, etc) have come into the present.[29]

Above / below

A simple spatial schema dominates much of the dialogues in the book of signs (chapters 2 –12). Indeed, the whole Gospel abounds with pairs of terms or images: God/devil; heaven/earth, life/death, light/darkness,

---

29. The spatial schema will be explored in this chapter. On the temporal schema, see Robert McIver, *The Four Faces of Jesus* (Boise, ID: Pacific Press, 2000), 225–35.

truth/lying, spirit/flesh. Each of these are encompassed in the rubric, above / below:

ABOVE	God	heaven	life	light	truth	spirit
BELOW	devil	earth	death	darkness	lying	flesh

The important role played by the schema represented by these pairs might be illustrated in the dialogue between Jesus and Nicodemus in John 3:1–21, 31–36, particularly those of light and darkness, above and below, and flesh and spirit, together with a new pair, the verbs ascend and descend (ἀναβαίνω and καταβαίνω). Well before the introduction of Nicodemus, the reader has been prepared to understand the symbolic importance of some of these terms. Indeed, light and darkness dominate the first verses of the Gospel. John 1:1 begins with the word (λόγος) that was with God and was God, and eventually is said to have became 'flesh' (1:14). This word was 'light' (1:4), a 'light' that shone in 'darkness', but which the darkness could not comprehend[30] (1:5).[28] In the light was 'life' (1:4). The light was said to be the 'true' light (1:9). Thus truth and light are contrasted with darkness right from the beginning of the Gospel. What, then, should be made of the fact that Nicodemus came to Jesus by night (3:2)?[31] It turns out that while there may be eventual hope that this 'ruler of the Jews' (3:1) may eventually become a disciple of Jesus—after all, he was the one that defended Jesus to the chief priests and Pharisees (7:50–51) and who

---

30. The word καταλάμβανω, whose aorist (κατέλαβεν) is found in John 1:5, has several possible meanings: one clustered around the concepts of attack, overtake, overcome; another clustered around the concepts of understanding, comprehending; yet another clustered around the idea of obtaining, or making something one's own. Given John's delight elsewhere in double entendre, it is tempting to think that this word was chosen exactly because it could encompass several layers of meaning, each of which has theological import.
31. 'The image of darkness surrounding Nicodemus reinforces the universal dimensions of his character. Nicodemus first approached Jesus "by night" (3:2), and by the end of the discourse their nocturnal meeting becomes a microcosm of the encounter between Jesus and the world ... (3:19-21).' In Craig R Koester, *Symbolism in the Fourth Gospel* (Minneapolis, MN: Fortress, 1995), 47

provided an appropriate burial for Jesus (19:39–40)[32]—clearly in John 3 Nicodemus fundamentally misunderstands Jesus.[33]

At the beginning of his interchange with Nicodemus, Jesus abruptly informs him that it is not possible for anyone to see the kingdom of God unless he is born ἄνωθεν (3:3). The term ἄνωθεν is ambiguous. While its primary meaning was probably something like 'from above' (see John 19:11, 23; cf Matt 27:51; Mark 15:38), it could also mean 'again, a second time'. Nicodemus takes the word in this secondary sense, and asks how it is possible to be born a second time, because an adult is too large to enter a womb a second time (verse 4), and thus fundamentally misunderstands what has just be said to him. Jesus further explains himself using another of the paired concepts—that of flesh and spirit. He explains to Nicodemus that what is born of flesh is flesh, and what is born of spirit is spirit. Therefore, Nicodemus should not be surprised that he is told that it is necessary for him to be born ἄνωθεν (3:6–7). Jesus goes on to say that he knows of what he speaks, because he bears witness to what he has seen (3:11). He introduces yet another pair that also contrasts the realm of the above from the realm of the below. He contrasts the things of heaven with the things of earth (verse 12). Jesus then further expands his observation by taking up a theme that will dominate several of the dialogues found in later chapters in John, the theme of ascent and descent (ἀναβαίνω and καταβαίνω). Jesus tells Nicodemus that no one will ascend to heaven except the Son of Man, who has come down from heaven (3:13). Verse 14 introduces another aspect of the theme of ascent. It is necessary for the Son of Man to be 'lifted up', so that all who believe in him might have eternal life. Here the double meaning of the expression is clear. Jesus is to be lifted up on the cross, like the serpent in the wilderness (3:14); but in the back of the mind of the reader must be the rest of the context of this chapter. The Son of Man is to be lifted up, he is to ascend again to his Father, from whence he came. His cross is his exaltation.

---

32. I am struck by the fact that Nicodemus remains an ambiguous figure to the end in the Gospel—he is only associated with the dead Jesus, not the risen Jesus.
33. 'The first and primary message of the dialogue is thus simply that Jesus is incomprehensible to Nicodemus. They belong to two different worlds, and, despite Nicodemus' initial good intentions (v 2), Jesus's world seems quite opaque to him.' So Wayne A Meeks, 'The Man from Heaven in Johannine Sectariansm', in *Journal of Biblical Literature*, 91 (1972): 54. Cf the words of Craig R Koester: 'Jesus acknowledges Nicodemus's representative status by calling him "the teacher of Israel" (3:10), but he indicates that the Jewish teacher's primary trait is an inability to understand the ways of God', in *Symbolism in the Fourth Gospel*, 46.

The descending-ascending motif is further explored in the discussion between Jesus and the Jews following the multiplication of the loaves and fishes. The Jews asked Jesus for a sign, citing the example of Moses who brought bread down from heaven. Jesus answers that it was not Moses who gave them bread from heaven, but his Father, who gives the true bread which comes down out of heaven and gives life to the world (6:31-33). Jesus is the bread of life who has come down from heaven (6:35, 41, 48, 58). No one has seen the Father except he who was with (παρά) God, he has seen the Father (6:46). He who believes has eternal life (6:47). The Jews grumble at the idea that Jesus has come down from heaven because they know his origins, they know his parents (6:42). This same idea is brought up again in 7:25-31 in the discussion as to whether or not Jesus is the Christ. The crowd reasons that Jesus cannot be the Christ because they know from whence he comes; when the Christ comes, they will not know from whence he comes. This is ironic because, in fact, they do not know from whence Jesus has come. As Jesus points out, they do not know who sent him, but he knows for he is from him (παρ' αὐτοῦ) and he sent him (7:29). As has already been pointed out, this irony is even stronger in 7:40-44. The crowd reasons that Jesus cannot be the Christ because the Christ is to come from Bethlehem. This sets up an expectation in the mind of the reader of the gospel who know that Jesus was in fact born at Bethlehem. But the Fourth Gospel never points this out; this is not the ultimate point of Jesus' origins. Jesus originates in heaven.

In 8:21-29 Jesus begins to tell his disciples that he is going where they cannot follow. His remark is misunderstood by the crowd and even by his disciples (13:33, 36-37). It is explained clearly only after the resurrection. Jesus sends a message to the disciples (via Mary) that he is going to his Father (and their Father), to his God (and their God) (20:17).

Much more material in the gospel could be used to illuminate the descent/ascent motif,[34] but what has been discussed here is perhaps sufficient to illustrate the dynamic involved, and how it is used to draw the reader into a greater understanding of who Jesus is.

---

34. For example, the motif also appears in 9:29, 33; 10:36; 11:29; 13:1,3; 14:2-3, 12, 28; 15:5; 16:16-17, 27-30; 17:8, 11; 20:17. It is probably also worth noting an important point made by Wayne Meeks: 'The motif [of ascent / descent] belongs exclusively to discourse, not to narrative' [in italics in original]. 'Man from Heaven', 50.

Father/Son, Sender/Sent in Johannine Christology

A dominant motif in the Christology of the Fourth Gospel is the motif of the Father/Son, Sender/Sent.[35] The theme is introduced in the prologue. The Logos became flesh and dwelt among us, and we have seen his glory, 'a glory as the only-begotten from the Father' (δόξαν ὡς μονογενοῦς παρὰ πατρός; 1:14). There is something unique about the relationship between Jesus and God. He is the 'only begotton from the Father' (μονογενοῦς παρὰ πατρός), he is the word (λόγος) that was not only with God, but was God (θεὸς ἦν ὁ λόγος; 1:1). No one has seen God but the only begotten God (μονογενὴς θεὸς[36]) who was in the bosom (εἰς τὸν κόλπον) of the Father, who has made him known (1:18). That Jesus is sent from the Father, and has such a unique relationship to the Father, means that he is uniquely qualified to act as the agent of the Father.[37]

The discussion that follows Jesus' healing of the man at the pool Bethzatha allows a further development of this theme. The Jews were incensed because Jesus had not only healed the man on the Sabbath but had also told him to take up his pallet and walk. Jesus retorts that his Father is working still, and he is working. The Jews understand this as a claim that Jesus is equal with God (5:11–18). Jesus goes on to explain the relationship between himself and the Father. The Son does nothing, except what he sees the Father doing. But Jesus will do greater works so that they might marvel, even raising the dead and giving life. The Father judges no man but has given all judgement to the Son. Their identity is such that all who honour the Son, honours the Father (who sent the Son) as well. The Father has life in himself and has given the Son to have life in himself; in fact, there is an hour coming in which all who are in the tomb will hear the voice of the Son of Man and come forth. The Father has given the Son authority to execute judgement, because he is the Son of Man (5:25–29).

---

35. 'The Gospel of St John is pre-eminently the Gospel of "the Father and the Son"'. Pollard, *Johannine Christology*, 15. Cf Also Warren Carter, *John and Empire* (New York, London: Clark, 2008), 235.
36. The reading μονογενὴς θεὸς is to be preferred rather than μονογενὴς υἱὸς (contra Bart D Ehrman, *The Orthodox Corruption of Scripture* [Oxford: Oxford University Press, 2003], 78–82). See also Craig S Keener, *The Gospel of* John (Peabody, MA: Hendrickson, 2003), 425–26; Bruce M Metzger, *A Textual Commentary on the Greek New Testament* (London: United Bible Societies, 1971), 198; and Raymond E Brown, *The Gospel According to John I–XII* (Garden City, NI: Doubleday, 1966), 17.
37. See the helpful discussion of the motif of agency in Keener, *Gospel of John*, 310–20.

Jesus goes on to cite a list of witnesses to himself: John the Baptist, the Father, his works, and scripture (5:30–47).

When the Jews were amazed at the teaching of Jesus and asked how he had received 'learning' seeing that he had not been educated, Jesus replied that the teaching was not his, but 'his who sent me' (7:15–18).

John 8:31–58 records a discussion between Jesus and some Jews who believed in him. The Jews were incensed at the implication that they were slaves. They were descendants of Abraham and had never been enslaved. Jesus answered in terms of their actions. If they sin, they are slaves to sin; if they were Abraham's seed, then they would do the works of Abraham (who would have believed Jesus). Their works show who their true Father is; he is the Devil. If they had God as their Father, they would have loved Jesus (verse 42). If Jesus glorifies himself, then his glory is nothing; but his Father glorifies him, whom the Jews call their God (verse 54). After the statement that Jesus existed before Abraham, the Jews took up stones to throw at Jesus.

John 10:31–39 records another incident in which the Jews wished to stone Jesus, and they explain their reasons for wishing to do so. The Jews assure Jesus that they do not wish to stone him because of his good works, but because he, a man who makes himself to be God, commits blasphemy. This is what the Jews understood when Jesus said, 'I and my Father are one'. In reply, Jesus cited Psalm 82:6 which calls judges 'gods'. It is an argument *a minori ad maius*.[38] If God himself could call those πρὸς οὓς ὁ λόγος τοῦ θεοῦ ἐγένετο (cf 10:35, 1:14) gods, then how much more can he whom the Father consecrated (ἡγίασεν) and sent into the world call himself the son of God. The sum of Jesus' argument is this, that as the one sent from God, the Father is in him and he is in the Father. He was, as it were, God's personal ambassador (or special envoy), and thus dealing with him was in effect dealing with God. Expressed in personal terms this means that Jesus had the right to call himself Son of God.

In the Fourth Gospel the final meeting of Jesus and the disciples is prefaced by the comment that Jesus knew that his hour had come to depart from this world to the Father. He knew that the Father had given all things into his hand, that he had come out from God and was going to God (13:1–3). Thus this motif of sender/sent combined with that of descent/ascent is to provide the key to understanding the rest of the scenes before the betrayal and arrest.

---

38. Brown, *John (i–xii)*, I:410; Rudolf Bultmann, *The Gospel of John* (Oxford: Basil Blackwell, 1971), 389.

In his conversation Jesus says that no one comes to the Father except by (διά) him; he is the way, the truth, and the life (14:6). When Philip asks him to show them the Father, he replies, 'He who has seen me has seen the Father' (14:9). The Father loves the disciples because they love Jesus (16:27-28). Jesus' Father is also the disciples' Father by virtue of their relationship to Jesus.

Much more of the gospel could profitably be canvassed to illustrate this theme,[39] but enough material has been covered to enable conclusions to be drawn about the way the Fourth Gospel intend it to be understood.

The motif of Father/Son used in the Fourth Gospel describes the unique relationship between Jesus and God. He is from God. The Father is in him, and he is in the Father to such an extent that they are one. He that has seen the Son has seen the Father, and he who honors the Son honors the Father. The Son exercises the functions of divinity: he judges, he raises the dead to life. The Sender/Sent aspect of this motif also describes this. 'An emissary is not simply someone who is sent, but also an envoy, a plenipotentiary; he speaks and acts in the name of the one who has sent him. The perfect emissary identifies himself entirely with the sender.'[40]

But as well as this strong note of equality with God, there is at the same time a definite subordination of the Son to the Father.[41] Jesus is dependent on the Father for his message (7:16; 14:24), his life (5:26; 6:57), his power (5:30), his authority to execute judgement and give life (5:21-29), his disciples (6:37, 44), and his glory (17:1). This is not restricted to just the occasional saying, it is widespread throughout the whole Gospel. Both the equality with God, and his subordination to him are expressed by the motif of the Father/Son.

---

39. For example the motif is also present at 3:16, 35; 6:29, 37–40, 44, 46, 57; 7:28–29; 8:16–18, 26–27; 9:4; 10:25; 11:40; 12:26, 44–45, 49–50; 14:2, 7–8, 11, 20–24, 28, 31; 15:21, 23, 26; 16:15; 17:2; 18:11. This list is not complete.

40. M de Jong. 'The Son of God and the Children of God in the Fourth Gospel', in *Saved by Hope*, edited by JI Cook (Grand Rapids, MI: Eerdmans, 1978), 48; the article is reprinted in de Jong's book, *Jesus: Stranger from Heaven and Son of God* (Missoula, MT: Scholars Press, 1977).

41. This is so much so that CK Barrett, after quoting the Quicumque vult, asks provocatively: 'On this basis, does the Fourth Evangelist qualify for salvation?'. '"The Father is greater than I" (John 14, 28): Subordinationist Christology in the New Testament', in Herausgegeben von Joachim Gnilka, *Neues Testament und Kurche*, Herausgegeben von Joachim Gnilka (Freiburg: Herder, 1974), 144. For subordination in John see the whole of this article (144–59), and the more detailed exposition in J Ernest Davey, *The Jesus of St John: Historical and Christological Studies in the Fourth Gospel* (London: Lutterworth, 1958), 90–157.

The question as to Jesus' divine status is not foreign to the concerns of the Gospel. One of the charges brought by the Jews at the trial of Jesus was that he made himself the Son of God (19:7); and twice the Jews wanted to stone Jesus because of his claim to a special relationship to God (5:18, 10:33). It is undeniable that the Fourth Gospel ascribes to Jesus the designation 'God'.[42] One of the first statements of the Gospel is that the Logos is God (1:1); and the Gospel works towards the climax where Thomas confesses 'My Lord and my God' (20:28). This confession is immediately followed by the statement of purpose: The Gospel had been written that the reader might believe that Jesus is the Christ, the Son of God (20:31). Thomas has seen and believed, but it is better to believe without seeing. The Fourth Evangelist has no quarrel with the statement of Thomas. On the contrary, he would have all his readers make the same statement of belief, on the basis of his testimony as an eyewitness. Thus in the Fourth Gospel, Jesus is portrayed as fully divine, as the μονογενὴς θεός, but also as one who is subordinate to the Father.

Son of Man in the Christology of the Fourth Gospel

The title 'Son of Man' has a somewhat different locus to the title 'Son of God', although (as is seen) the two are related. The title 'Son of Man' has generated a large body of secondary literature and little consensus. For example, Geza Vermes bases his understanding of the title on the fact that ὁ υἱός τοῦ ἀνθηώπου is not a genuine Greek idiom. Therefore, if the phrase is to have any meaning, it must be an Aramaic meaning. He concludes from his study of Aramaic that *bar nasha* usually meant 'man', in general, but that at times it is used as a circumlocution for the personal pronoun; it was never used as a title.[43] While supported by Matthew Black, Vermes' ideas have not gained wide support.[44] Most scholars would still

---

42. On this, see BA Mastin, 'A Neglected Feature of the Christology of the Fourth Gospel', in *New Testament Studies* 22 (1975): 32–51; and Oscar Cullmann, *The Christology of the New Testament* (London: SCM, 1959), 306–10.
43. Geza Vermes, 'The 'Son of Man' Debate', in *Journal for the Study of New Testament* 1 (1978): 20.
44. Matthew Black, 'Jesus and the Son of Man', in *Journal for the Study of New Testament* 1 (1978): 4–18. See also: Joseph A Fitzmyer, 'Another View of the "Son of Man" Debate', in *Journal for the Study of New Testament* 1 (1978): 58–68; John P Brown, 'The Son of Man: "This Fellow"', in *Biblica* 58 (1977): 361; Francis J Maloney, 'The Johannine Son of Man', in *Biblical Theology Bulletin* 6 (1976): 182–83; Barnabas Lindars, 'Jesus as Advocate: A Contribution to the Christology Debate', in *Bulletin, John Rylands*

agree that in the Gospels the expression must be understood to be a title in some of its uses.

Another problem with the title 'Son of Man' is its background. Within the Old Testament, the background is generally agreed to be Daniel 7, where the Son of Man is an heavenly being associated with the Ancient of Days, and to whom was given glory and everlasting kingdom.[45] The use in Ezekiel, where Ezekiel is addressed as Son of Man, does not have the same sort of relevance. Most agree with this, but the problem lies with First Enoch. In Enoch there is a personal, heavenly Son of Man, very like the Christian concept.[46] But it is impossible to determine the relative dating between the New Testament and the Similitudes of Enoch.[47] It is perfectly possible that the use of the title in Enoch is a derivative from Christianity. The other extra-New Testament parallel that could be cited as background is 2 Esdras 13:1–3.[48] A this document is to be dated to the last decade of the first century, it is a valuable insight into how some contemporary Jews were thinking about the Messiah, but it can hardly be said to be influen-

---

Library 60 (1980): 479; Barnabas Lindars, 'Re-enter the Apocalyptic Son of Man', in *New Testament Studies* 22 (1976): 53; Merril C Tenney, 'The Concept of Sonship in the Fourth Gospel', in *New Testament Studies*, edited by HL Drumwright and Curtis Vaughen (Waco, TX: Markham, 1975), 48; William O Walker, 'The Son of Man: Son Recent Developments', in *Catholic Biblical Quarterly* 45 (1983): 585, who all refer to the Son of Man as a title.

45. AJ Ferch, *The Son of Man in Daniel 7* (Berrien Springs, MI: Andrews University Press, 1979) has a full discussion of Daniel 7.

46. 1 Enoch 46:3–4 reads: 'And I asked the angel who went with me and showed me all the hidden things, concerning that Son of Man, who he was, and whence he was, (and) why he went with the Head of Days? And he answered and said unto me: this is the Son of Man who hath righteousness, with whom dwelleth righteousness, and who revealeth all the treasures of that which is hidden, because the Lord of Spirits has chosen him, and whose lot hath the pre-eminence before the Lord of Spirits in uprightness for ever. And this Son of Man whom thou hast seen shall raise up the kings and the mighty from their seats, and the strong from their thrones and shall loosen the reins of the strong, and break the teeth of sinners.' (*The Apocrypha and Pseudepigrapha of the Old Testament in English*, edited by CH Charles [Oxford: Clarendon, 1964], 2:214–15).

47. For a discussion of relative dating, etc, see James DG Dunn, *Christology in the Making* (Philadelphia, PA: Westminster, 1980), 75–78; see also, CFD Moule 'Neglected Features in the Problem of "the Son of Man"', in *Neues Testament und Kirch*, Herausgegeben von Joachin Gnilka (Freiburg: Herder, 1974), 414; JC Greenfield and ME Stone, 'The Enochic Pentateuch and the Date of the Similitudes', in *Harvard Theological Review* 70 (1977): 51–65; CL Mearns, 'Dating the Similitudes of Enoch', in *New Testament Studies* 25 (1979): 360–69.

48. Jacob M Myers, *I and II Esdras*, Anchor Bible (New York: Doubleday, 1974), 126–29; Dunn, *Christology in the Making*, 79–81.

tial in the formation of the way the Son of Man title is used in the Fourth Gospel.

Within the Fourth Gospel the term 'Son of Man' is found in 1:51; 3:13–14; 5:27; 6:27, 53, 62; 8:28; 9:35; 12:23, 34; 13:31. The title is first used at 1:51 as the climax of the introductory section. Others attribute titles to Jesus (Messiah, King of Israel, etc), but Jesus calls himself 'Son of Man'. He assures Nathaniel that he will see greater things, he will see the heavens opened, and the angels of God going up and coming down upon the Son of Man. Jesus, as Son of Man, is the bridge between the heavenly and earthly realms.[49]

In 3:14–15 the Son of Man is seen as a heavenly figure. No one has ascended into heaven except the one who has come down out of heaven, the Son of Man. Just as Moses lifted up the serpent in the desert, so it is necessary for the Son of Man to be lifted up. Jesus is to be again exalted to heaven, he is to be lifted up; but paradoxically this is by means of his suffering and death, by being lifted up on the cross. John 12:23 and 13:31 both speak of the glorification of the Son of Man in terms that clearly mean his death on the cross. Thus, exaltation through suffering is inherent in the Fourth Gospel's use of the Son of Man.

In 5:27 the title is used without the definite article. The Father has given the Son authority to execute judgement, because he is a Son of Man.[50] It is possible that the title is anarthrous because it is emphasising that the humanity of Jesus makes him uniquely qualified to judge humanity, but this is less likely than the possibility that the LXX text of Daniel 7:13 (in which the Son of Man is anarthrous) is reflected here.[51] What is clear is that in 5:27 the Son of Man is eschatological judge. It is he who will raise the dead at the last day.

---

49. CH Dodd quote from *Bereshith Rabba* 70:12 where the ladder is identified by some rabbis as Joseph himself, in which case Jesus could be substituting himself in the place of Joseph, and thereby making a comparison between himself and Joseph. *The Interpretation of the Fourth Gospel* (Cambridge: University Press, 1955), 245. However, Raymond E Brown finds 'No one of these variations is particularly convincing. However, in the theme that they have in common they are probably correct . . . Jesus as Son of Man becomes the locus of divine glory, the point of contact between heaven and earth', *John*, 91.
50. Translation by author.
51. So CK Barrett, *The Gospel According to John*, second edition (London: SPCK, 1978), 262; and Brown, *John*, 1:215. Marsh, 265, takes both options, while Bultmann, *John*, 260–61, and Schnackenburg, *John*, 2:112–13, cast doubt on the authenticity of the saying.

Chapter 6 also emphasises the heavenly nature of the Son of Man. It is the Son of Man who will give the true bread from heaven (6:27); in fact, it is the Son of Man himself who is the true bread from heaven (6:53, cf 6:51). Jesus asks his disciples if they are scandalised by the statement that he is the true bread from heaven, what will they be when the Son of Man goes up to where he was before (6:62).

In the Fourth Gospel the Son of Man is almost exclusively a self-designation of Jesus. It conveys the fact that he is the bridge between the earthly and heavenly realms. It denotes his exaltation, the exaltation of the cross. As the Son of Man he is eschatological judge (cf Dan 7:9-10, 13-14).

Full Humanity of Jesus in the Fourth Gospel

The quotation of Ernst Käsemann at the beginning of this chapter has presented the problem of the humanity of Jesus in the Fourth Gospel with disturbing clarity. Nor has the analysis thus far provided much counter evidence for his claims that John reveals a naïve docetism. As might be expected, Käsemann's remarks have not gone unchallenged. Leon Morris, for example, has devoted a whole paper to analysing the above comments phrase by phrase.[52] Jesus does not customarily walk on water, he only walks through doors after the resurrection (which coincides with the Synoptic view of the resurrected Jesus), and so on. In fact, at times the Johannine portrayal of Jesus emphasises his humanity to a greater extent that the synoptics. The father, mother, and brothers of Jesus are known (6:42; 7:2). He experiences human emotions such as love (11:5) and anger (11:33), and he even wept at the death of Lazarus (11:35). He can grow weary (4:6), and he bleeds (water and blood) when a spear is thrust into his side (19:33-34). Even his resurrection body has a form which can be touched (20:27).[53] CFD Moule is probably correct when he said:

> There is no denying that the fourth evangelist allows himself sometimes to draw a very docetic picture; but then he also contradicts it. The truth seems to be that he simply states both facts—Jesus is the pre-existent Son of God, the unique Son who shares God's glory; yet also, Jesus is the one who

---

52. Leon Morris, 'The Jesus of Saint John', in *Unity and Diversity in New Testament Theology*, edited by RA Guelich (Grand Rapids, MI: Eerdmans, 1978), 37–53.
53. James McPolin gives a good discussion of the real humanity of Jesus in his article, 'The Word Was Made Flesh', in *The Way* 21 (1981): 22–33.

accepts human limitations; and he does not bring them into anything like a unified system.[54]

What is most significant to the present investigation is that the Fourth Gospel allows itself to portray Jesus in ways which are so open to a docetic misinterpretation that

> . . . the total weight of the material makes certain that the writer was blissfully unconcerned about the Docetic heresy. He goes as freely as he pleases in the direction of Docetism, although, for practical reasons, he does not embrace entirely the idea that his subject is merely an appearance. But he is at no point anti-Docetic, and seems plainly unaware that a problem of the kind exists for Christianity.[55]

On the whole, this is probably a true assessment of the presentation of the humanity of Jesus in the Fourth Gospel. There is debate about the nature of Jesus, but it tends to be carried out in terms that would emphasise the divinity of Jesus rather than his humanity. Over and over the Jews are antagonistic towards Jesus because of his high claims. There seems to be little debate about whether or not Jesus was fully human. This is assumed.[56] What is clearly most controversial is that this man could be divine, that his man could be from heaven.

John's Contribution to Contemporary Christological Debate

While John works with great subtlety and sophistication to bring his readers/hearers to a greater understanding of Jesus, there are several themes relating to Jesus to which he frequently returns. For example, Jesus as Son is often portrayed as having equality or oneness with the Father (1:1, 18; 5:18; 8:16-23, 58; 10:29–30, 33, 38; 12:41; 14:10; 20:28). Yet at the same

---

54. CFD Moule, 'The Manhood of Jesus in the New Testament', in *Christ, Faith and History*, edited by SW Sykes and JP Clayton (Cambridge: University Press, 1972), 100.
55. Guy M Davis, Jr, 'The Humanity of Jesus in John', in *Journal of Biblical Literature* 70 (1950): 105–12. For a contrary viewpoint see Udo Schnelle, *Antidocetic Christology in the Gospel of John* (Minneapolis, MN: Fortress, 1992), who argues that 'The Johannine letters restrict themselves to polemic and a defence of correct beliefs, while the Gospel undertakes a comprehensive theological combat with Docetism' (228).
56. Lincoln, *John*, 59.

time, and often in the same passage, Jesus as Son is portrayed as dependent on God (5:26, 21–30; 6:37, 44, 57; 7:16; 14:24; 17:1). While the Jesus of the Fourth Gospel is from the realm of the above (John 3:31; 8:33), and claims an relationship with God that belongs to no other human, his is at times portrayed as fully human (4:6; 6:42; 7:2; 11:5, 33, 35; 19:33–34). These paradoxes are deeply embedded in the Johannine text as it unfolds. Most importantly, John's paradoxes are deliberate. They serve the purpose of leading the reader/listener into a deeper understanding of Jesus, and we should be reluctant to too quickly explain them away. The reader/hearer of the Gospel remains intrigued by who Jesus is. So many questions remain to be thought through. There is an open-ended wonder about Jesus. Yes, one knows enough to call him Lord, to believe that he is the one who comes from God and has returned to God. He is the one whose crucifixion is at the same time his uplifting that brings salvation to all. He is the Messiah, the Son of Man, and the Son of God. Yet at the same time, there remains a mystery about Jesus. One cannot but wonder at who he is and what he has done.

It is somewhat disorienting to move from the symbolic universe of the Fourth Gospel to modern christological controversies, as while the same issues are at the fore, both the tone and content of contemporary debate belong to a different domain of discourse. The Fourth Gospel has the raw material for centuries of Christian reflection on Jesus, true enough. Yet that reflection, refined by controversy and expressed in carefully worded creeds, is expressed in language that is much less open-ended than the Fourth Gospel.

One cannot un-think the questions posed by Arius, nor ignore the hard-won consensus of the various creeds. Nor should one consider that the issues of Christology have been solved finally in the words of the Nicene Creed and the Chalcedon definition.[57] The nature of Jesus and salvation is, after all, one of the central mysteries of Christianity, and must be thought through anew by every generation. Over the past centuries the Fourth Gospel has provided much of the raw material to these ongoing reflections about Jesus, and no doubt will continue to do so in the coming

---

57. Just as one cannot be now be free of the types of christological questions raised in the early centuries of the Christian Church, one cannot ignore the further issues raised by such systematic theologians as Friedrich Schleiermacher, *The Christian Faith* (Edinburgh: Clark, 1928), 391–417.

years. It continuously brings us back to the mysteries of Jesus, to ponder the paradox of God who becomes man, a man whose death has provided the opportunity for the entire world to be saved.

Jesus—the 'One and Only', or 'Only Begotten': The Meaning of *Monogenes*

Paul Petersen

One of the most beloved texts of the Bible is John 3:16. Let me quote from three major translations: 'For God so loved the world that he gave his one and only Son, that whoever believes in him shall not perish but have eternal life (NIV).' 'For God so loved the world that He gave his only begotten Son, that whoever believes in Him should not perish but have everlasting life (NKJ).' 'For God so loved the world that he gave his only son . . .' (RSV).[1]

Which is it? Is Jesus the 'the only' or 'one and only', or is he 'the only begotten'? What is the meaning of the Greek word '*monogenēs*'? And what difference does it make?

Let me begin by dispelling a common misunderstanding. However way the word *monogenēs* is to be translated, it does not denote a literal birth in our modern sense of the word. Such language imposes upon the Bible our modern culture, and such a claim would presuppose that there is a mother with whom the Father God had intercourse! That would be the meaning if the expressions are to be understood literally. A typical rhetorical question from modern anti-trinitarians goes like this, 'do you believe that Jesus literally was the only begotten Son of the Father?'[2] But

---

1. The article by Dale Moody in the wake of the 1952 translation of the Revised Standard Version provided a significant evangelical summary of the main arguments for the meaning of *monogenēs* as 'unique', 'The Translation of John 3:16 in the Revised Standard Version', in *Journal of Biblical Literature* 72 (1952): 213–219.
2. I have encountered several anti-trinitarians who struggle with this point. They misunderstand the meaning of metaphor, as if it is in opposition to reality, and they fear that acknowledging the metaphorical use of our human language about God will take away the the historical facts of God's intervention to save humankind. It remains, however, a fact that God is not a father exactly in our sense of the word—he is for instance a father who never himself had a father. Similarly, the Son is not a son exactly in our human sense of the word—as a divine being he had for instance no mother.

we are not speaking about humans, we are speaking about God, and our language is in this case metaphorical and has clear limitations.[3]

Moreover, we have of course to understand the expressions used in the biblical texts against the background of the culture into which the Bible was spoken, not in light of our present culture. 'Fatherhood' and 'Sonship' had different connotations both in Semitic and Indo-European cultures of biblical times from what these concepts carry today. In the Bible a 'son' may of course mean a 'son', but also a descendant, a successor (like Belshazzar in Daniel 5:2), students (like the sons of the prophets), or a representative (like the King of Israel, cf Psalm 2:7).

So, what is the meaning of the *monogenēs* in John 3:16?[4] The prefix mono means one or only one as in words like *monogamy* and *monotheism*. In this case the prefix is combined with *genes*. Greek scholars have proposed two origins for this word. One theory has been that the word stems from the verb *gennaō*, which means 'to beget' and is generally used only about males, as in the genealogy in Matthew 1. In that case the meaning of the term *monogenēs* would be 'the only one born to/begotten'.

This view has, however, for a long time been rejected by Greek scholars.[5] Rather, the origin of the word is understood as *genos*, which means 'kind, type'. The term *monogenēs* in John 3:16 (and in 1:18 and other New Testament texts) therefore means 'the only one of its kind' or as said in

---

3. Reading the discussion of the Trinity in the Church Fathers, not least in the Cappadocian Fathers of the fourth century, it is striking how many pages they used on semantics. Basil of Caesarea, his brother Gregory of Nyssa, and Gregory of Nazianzus all spent considerable time reflecting on how we are able to speak about God, and what language we can use. They realised that in speaking about God we are limited by our human language, and we should not impose upon God meanings derived just from our human experience. They reacted to the extreme rationalistic approach by 'arians' like Eunomius who believed in the human ability to understand and explain God. Their interpretation of the Nicene Creed is described by, among others, Lewis Ayres, *Nicaea and Its Legacy* (Oxford: Oxford University Press, 2004). A splendid introduction to Gregory of Nazianzus is found in Christopher A Beeley, *Gregory of Nazianzus on the Trinity and the Knowledge of God*, Oxford Studies in Historical Theology (Oxford: Oxford University Press, 2008).
4. For a very recent discussion and a good summary of this question, see Kevin Giles, *The Eternal Generation of the Son: Maintaining Orthodoxy in Trinitarian Theology* (Downer's Grove, IL: InterVarsity Press, 2012), 63–65. See also Michael Peppard, 'Adopted and Begotten Sons of God: Paul and John on Divine Sonship', in *Catholic Biblical Quarterly* 73 (2011): 92–110, especially the second part of the article from 102–110.
5. See for instance, James Hope Moulton and George Miligan, *The Vocabulary of the Greek New Testament* (Grand Rapids, MI: Eerdmans, 1930), 416–17.

NIV, 'the one and only'.[6] In this view the meaning could, but does not have to include the sense 'only one born to/begotten'. Any 'only begotten' son is of course unique, but being unique does not necessarily mean that you are the only one born.[7]

How is this view substantiated? Let me mention three supporting arguments. One is a little technical and requires some understanding of Greek grammar; one, however, is based on the usage of the word and easily checked also without any training in Ancient Greek. First, the natural way to form a participle from the verb *gennaō* creates the word *monogennetos*, not *monogenēs*. Second, the use in Hebrews 11: 17 of the word *monogenēs* about Isaach as the unique son of Abraham makes the meaning 'only begotten' impossible as Abraham in a literal sense had more sons (Gen 16:11; 25:1-2).[8]

Third, when one studies the context of several passages where *monogenēs* is found along with forms of the verb *gennaō*, to beget, it seems evident that it cannot mean 'only begotten/only one born to'. Such passages are found in both the Gospel of John (1:13–14) and the first epistle of John (4:7-9).[9] In John 1:13, for instance, the Gospel writer uses the verb *gennaō* to describe believers who have been 'born' by God. Next he in

---

6. This meaning is, by the way, supported by the usage of *monogenēs* in other contexts. Clement wrote around 100 to the Christian Church in Rome and mentions the mythical bird the phoenix and describes it as unique by the term *monogenēs* (1 Clement 25:2), obviously not meaning 'the only begotten'. Moulton and Miligan also lists a third century use of the word about God and a passage from a fourth century papyrus where the Holy Spirit is called *monogenēs*. Peppard lists other examples of the occurrence of *monogenēs* in the sense of 'unique', from Josephus, Wisdom (7:22: the 'unique spirit'), and Plutarch in describing Plato's cosmology (106).
7. As expressed by Peppard, 'Adopted and Begotten Sons of God,' 106: 'It *can* refer to an only son, but that is because an *only* son fits into the category of unique; it can also refer to a unique son that is *not* the only-begotten son (for example Isaac)'.
8. At times anti-trinitarians argue that Hebrews 11:17 is to be understood as saying that Isaac was 'the only son begotten by the promises'. Such reading is, however, grammatically impossible. The Greek relative clause 'who had received the promises' can only refer to Abraham and does not qualify the adjective *monogenēs*. The biblical narratives in Genesis speaks about not only Hagar's son Ishmael, but later also of Abraham's son's through Keturah, his second wife (see Gen 25:1–5). It is true, as often emphasised by anti-trinitarians that Isaac when he was born was Abraham's only legitimate son, but as Peppard points out, 'to call him an "only-begotten" son would stretch the boundaries of what "begetting" normally means' (106).
9. The word *monogenēs* is only used about Christ in the writings of John; Luke employs it about an only and therefore unique son in 7:12 and 9:38, the sons of the widow from Nain and the moon sick son, respectively, and about a unique and only daughter in 8:42, the daughter of Jairus.

verse 14 moves on to state that Jesus is the *monogenēs*. But if believers are 'born' by God, Jesus cannot in the same context be said to be the only one born by God—the meaning must be different, that is 'unique'. The fact is that Prologue of John only speaks about the children of God as 'begotten' children, not Jesus.[10] The similar conclusion is evident from 1 John 4:7 which says that 'love is from God, and everyone who loves, has been born by God'. The verse uses the verb *gennaō* when speaking about the birth of believers and immediately moves on to mention Jesus as *monogenēs* (verse 9). Obviously John does not contradict himself by saying that Jesus was the '*only* one born/begotten' when he has just told that the believers are all 'born/begotten' by God.[11]

Furthermore, it is possible quite clearly to trace the origin of the meaning 'only begotten' as the understanding of *monogenēs*. The misunderstanding grew out of translation from Greek to Latin during the fourth and the fifth century. Early or old Latin translations (Vetus Latina) read John 1:14's *monogenēs* as 'unicus' (unique).[12] When Jerome in the late fourth century translated the New Testament into Latin, he used Hilary of Poitiers' Latin rendering of the Nicene Creed which contained the word *monogenēs*, resulting in the Latin expression in Vulgate, 'unigenitus'. From there the term became dominant in the Western Church though the Greek Fathers throughout the fourth century's christological and trinitarian discussions clearly maintained the meaning of *monogenēs* as 'unique', not 'only begotten'.[13]

The claims at times made for defenders of the NKJ translation's 'only begotten' do, therefore, not hold. The RSV's 'only' or NIV's 'one and only' are

---

10. Cf Peppard's conclusion, 'no divine begetting is expressed in the Prologue, except that of Christians in vs. 13' ('Adopted and Begotten Sons of God,' 107).
11. Donald W Burdick expresses it clearly: '. . . it is generally agreed that this (only begotten) is not the meaning of the word . . . (it) is always used to speak about uniqueness rather than origin.' *The Letters of John the Apostle: An In-Depth Commentary* (Chicago, IL: Moody Press, 1985), 321.
12. The oldest Latin translation known of John 1:14 is Codex Vercellensis is dated to the mid-fourth century and reads unicus'.
13. It has been claimed that Athanasius and the Cappadocian fathers mistakenly believed that *monogenēs* originally meant 'only begotten', so for instance, Wayne Grudem, 'Appendix 6', in *Systematic Theology: An Introduction to Biblical Doctrine* (Grand Rapids: Zondervan, revised edition, 2000), 1233–34 and RL Reymond, *A New Systematic Theology of the Christian Faith* (Nashville: Thomas Nelson, 1998), 325. However, the recent comprehensive analysis by Giles in *The Eternal Generation of the Son* clearly establishes that they also in the fourth century were well aware of the difference between *gennaō* and *monogenēs*.

not examples of 'dynamic equivalents of sorts',[14] but on the contrary providing the exact original meaning of the word *monogenēs*. Furthermore, it is a common misunderstanding[15] that the expression 'born, not made' in the Nicene-Constantinople Creed of 381 is referring to *monogenēs*. Also here 'born' comes from the Greek verb *gennaō*.[16]

So, the meaning 'one and only' or 'unique' is the natural and obvious meaning of the word *monogenēs*. Does that imply that Jesus had a beginning? The answer is no, unless you claim that Jesus is a different God and entertain a pagan view of the divine. Jesus is the unique representative of the Godhead to all creation. This is what he has always been.

The final aspect I want you to notice is that when the New Testament speaks about the Father and the Son, it describes a unique relationship. God is mentioned as a Father in only eighteen texts of the Old Testament. In the Gospel of John alone, Jesus mentions his Heavenly Father more than 100 times in direct speech. We know the Father because we know the Son. As Son, so Father. Their relationship is unique in part because it is eternal. There never was a time when it did not exist. If there was a time when the Son was not, there would have been a time when God would not have been the Father. The unique unity and intimate relationship between the two presupposes, that the persons within the Godhead are 'co-eternal'

This short article began by asking the question, not only what *monogenēs* means, but also what difference it makes. The unique relationship between Father and Son is exactly that difference. To Arius the term applied a beginning in time for the Son and consequently a subordinate position in rank and power. To many modern anti-trinitarians, *monogenēs* is taken dogmatically as meaning 'the only begotten' and employed almost as a battle cry in a very literalistic manner about the 'birth' and beginning in time of the Son, implying that he is a created being.

But the doctrine of the Trinity has as its foundation the eternal divinity of Jesus. As indicated by the meaning of *monogenēs*, he is the unique rep-

---

14. As expressed in the preface to The Holy Bible NKJV Version (Nashville: Thomas Nelson, 1982), iii.
15. *Ibid*.
16. In the creed the phrase is usually rendered *gennethenta, ou poiethanta*, 'born, not made/created'. At times the verb *ginomai* (to become) was used in the discussion in place of *poieo*. In that case the meaning of the creed was expressed by the phrase *gennetos, ou genetos*, the only difference being the present of an extra letter 'n', see for instance Robert Letham, *The Holy Trinity In Scripture, Theology, and Worship* (Phillipsburg, NJ: P&R Publishing), 121). While it most likely created some confusion, it also made a good pun!

resentative for God, the eternal Son. We know God as a person through the crucified Savior, and we know Jesus through the Holy Spirit who inspired the Bible and illuminates our minds to see Jesus.

Worshipping Jesus—the 'Eternally Blessed God!' (Romans 9:5)

Paul Petersen

'They are Israelites . . . to them belong the Patriarchs, and from them, according to the flesh, comes the Messiah, who is overall, God blessed forever. Amen.' Romans 9:4–5 [NRSV]

From Worship Towards Theology

The foundation for the doctrine of the Trinity is the divinity of Jesus, and this chapter will outline the main theological arguments for that foundation. The Church Fathers argued for his divinity from three sources: the biblical texts, the drama of salvation, and the devotion to Jesus.

Worship directed towards Jesus played a major role in the development of what is now known as the doctrine of the Trinity. In the ancient world, the first Christians' all-decisive commitment to Jesus did not go without notice. Pliny the Younger, governor of the province of Bithynia, wrote to the Roman Emperor Trajan that they 'sing hymns to Christ as to a God'.[1] Everywhere they willingly testified to the divinity of Jesus and some even died as martyrs because of that confession. On the floor in one of the earliest Christian church buildings excavated in Palestine, burned into stone in Megiddo in the early third century, we read the words of dedication 'to our God and Saviour Jesus Christ.'

The Christian pioneers ventured into the world with the Gospel and proclaimed the risen and divine Saviour. But as they carried forth their witness to the Jesus they worshipped, questions and challenges arose.

---

1. Or 'chant antiphonically a hymn to Christ as to a god' in *Epistles*, 10.96. English translation in *A New Eusebius: Documents Illustrative of the History of the Church to AD 337*, edited by J Stevenson (London: SPCK, 1974), 13–15. Pliny the Younger was governor in Bithynia from 111–113 A.D.

How can you say that Jesus is God?[2] What does it mean that he is? Reflecting on and responding to these challenges, the Church developed its thinking and its theology—that is, speaking systematically about God.[3] Let us, therefore, follow the process and look at the biblical foundation upon which the Church built its doctrine of the Trinity when it faced the challenges in its mission to the world.[4]

Jesus—God in Person!

The basis of the doctrine of the Trinity was and is the Bible. The belief that Jesus is God was not a late invention of the fourth century in order to hide the real truth about Him, as claimed in 'The Da Vinci Code' and similar conspiracy theories. Neither is the Bible nor the New Testament in particular only calling Jesus the 'Son of God' as if that title makes him

---

2. Celsos or Celsus in Latin spelling was a significant Roman critic of the Christian Church and wrote about 177 AD against the Christians and ridiculed them, among other things, for the perceived inconsistency of being monotheists, yet worshipping Jesus as God, *On the True Doctrine: A Discourse Against the Christians* (New York: Oxford University Press, 1987), 116.
3. It is important to note that the enterprise of doing theology in a sense is a secondary activity of the church. Theology is developed as a response to the needs of the church in worship and mission which are the primary activities of the Christian church.
4. A number of scholars have recently described this development. Fairly brief, but helpful introductions are found in Roger E Olson and Christopher A Hall, *The Trinity, Guides to Theology* (Grand Rapids, MI: Eerdmans, 2002), 5–49; Veli-Matti Kärkkäinen, *The Trinity: Global Perspectives* (Louisville/London: Westminster John Knox Press, 2007), 3–64; and Declan Marmion and Rik Van Nieuwenhove, *An Introduction to the Trinity* (Cambridge: Cambridge University Press, 2011), 29–95. Slightly more comprehensive overviews can be found in Robert Letham, *The Holy Trinity In Scripture, History, Theology, and Worship* (Philipsburg, NJ: PR Publishing Company, 2004), 17–200, and Allan Coppedge, *The God who is Triune: Revisioning the Christian Doctrine of God* (Downers Grove, IL: InterVarsity Press, 2007), 23–110. A description of the development after Nicaea as well as a comprehensive guide to the background is found in Frances M Young with Andrew Teal, *From Nicaea to Chalcedon: A Guide to the Literature and Its Background*, second edition (Grand Rapids, MI: Baker, 2010). From a specific Seventh-day Adventist perspective, Woodrow W Whidden, Jerry Moon, and John W Reeve, *The Trinity: Understanding God's Love, His Plan of Salvation, and Christian Relationships* (Hagerstown, MD: Review and Herald, 2002) presents both biblical reasons (pp 21–119) and a historical survey of the early church (pp 122–160). The entry on 'Doctrine of God' by Fernando L Canale in *Handbook to Seventh-day Adventist Theology*, Commentary Reference Series, edited by George W Reid and Raoul Dederen (Hagerstown, MD: Review and Herald, 2000), 12:105–59, is profound, but more theological than historical in character.

less divine, implying that he had a beginning. The claim to the full divinity of Jesus stems from the Bible itself. It arises first from a number of explicit statements. These are not few, nor are they difficult texts to comprehend. They are straight forward and permeate all of the New Testament. The following verses proclaiming Jesus to be God, may be taken as representative:[5]

- In the beginning was the Word, and the Word was with God, and **the Word was God** (John 1:1, NRSV).[6]
- No one has ever seen God. It is **God the only Son** who is close to the Father's heart, who has made him known (John 1:18, NRSV).[7]
- To them belong the patriarchs, and from their race, according to the flesh, is the **Christ who is God over all, blessed forever.** Amen (Romans 9:5, ESV).
- . . . waiting for our blessed hope, the appearing of the glory of **our great God and Savior Jesus Christ** (Titus 2:13, ESV).[8]

---

5. Norman Young lists these New Testament texts as well as John 20:28 and Hebrews 1:4 as seven 'umambigous texts' explicitly using the word *theos* about Jesus, 'Jesus – Divinity Revealed in Humility' in *The Essential Jesus: The Man, His Message, His Mission*, ed. Bryan W Ball and William G Johnsson (Boise, ID: Pacific Press, 2002), 103–23.
6. Anti-trinitarians like Jehovah's Witnesses attempt to explain this text away by claiming it is to be read as 'a god', indefinite because the article is not present in Greek. That argument does not hold up to scrutiny. Determination is not indicated by the presence of the article only. It is not present with *theos* in John 1:6, 12, and 18, nevertheless the determinate meaning in these verses is evident. Scholars usually refer to Colwell's rule to explain the Greek grammar, see Whidden, Moon, and Reeve, 61–65. Recent competent scholarship has, however, pointed out that Colwell's rule is unnecessary because the syntactically prominent word order, placing the object first in the sentence in John 1:1c, in itself confirms the determination, affirming beyond doubt what have always been the proper conclusion translation have concluded, so Mark Beatty, 'Colwell's Rule is No Longer Needed', paper presented at the annual meetings of Society of Biblical Meetings in Boston, November 22, 2008.

    The thesis at times proposed that *theos* is qualitative, meaning divine, runs against the Greek usage. If that were the case, the adjective *theios* would be the natural semantic choice.
7. From a grammatical point John 1:18 may be regarded as the least unambiguous of these texts.
8. Anti-trinitarians at times claim that Titus 2:13 and 2 Peter 1:1 speaks about two different persons, so that 'God' refers to the Father only, and not to Jesus Christ. However, this runs against basic Greek grammar. When the article in these and other texts (like Eph 5:5) is used once followed by two substantives, these two substantives (in this case the two genitives of *theos* and 'our Saviour Jesus Christ') belong together, see for instance F Blass and A Debrunner, *A Greek Grammar of the New Testament and Other Early Christian Literature*, translated and edited by Robert W Funk, ninth-tenth edi-

- ... by the righteousness of **our God and Savior Jesus Christ** (2 Peter 1:1, ESV).

Christians read further in the Scriptures and observed how a number of texts attribute to Jesus the prerogatives which belong to God alone, such as the authority to forgive sins, lordship over nature, and power to grant eternal life.
- When Jesus saw their faith, he said to the paralytic, 'Son, your sins are forgiven.' Now some teachers of the law were sitting there, thinking to themselves, 'Why does this fellow talk like that? He's blaspheming! Who can forgive sins but God alone?' (Mark 2:5–7, NIV).
- They were terrified and asked each other, 'Who is this? Even the wind and the waves obey him!' (Mark 4:41, NIV).
- And this is eternal life, that they may know you, the only true God, and Jesus Christ whom you have sent (John 17:3, NRSV).[9]

Proving that Jesus had the divine right of God to forgive, he healed the paralytic. The early Christians realised that if eternal life depends on knowing Jesus Christ, he must share the basic attributes of God. As the One who is sent he shares them with Him who sends. This belief, however, presented them with a decisive choice when they faced the pagan cultures of the Roman Empire—the choice between one or several gods, the choice of monotheism or polytheism.

God is One!

Accepting the clear biblical testimony that Jesus is God raised the question which came to define Christianity in contrast to all other religions. What kind of God is Jesus?

You may think that was a simple question. But in the Greek-Roman culture monotheism was not the norm. The pagans were fully accustomed

---

tion (Chicago, IL: Chicago University Press, 1961), 144–5.
9. While anti-trinitarians use John 17:3 to imply the eternal inferiority of the Son, the text actually parallels Father and Son and makes knowledge of Jesus a criterion for salvation and eternal life. Jesus is evidently here speaking from his human position in the incarnation, yet making a claim only God has the right to make. Here as in 1 Corinthians 8:6, the Father is named *theos*, yet unless you want to make an inherent conflict between these two texts and the overwhelming evidence from the rest of the New Testament, you have to read these as examples where *theos* is used as a name for the Father without denying the full divinity of the Son.

to having more than one God. To them it would not have been culturally strange if the Christians had proclaimed two Gods, a greater God called the Father, and a lesser god, namely Christ the Son. So, this question became a major challenge for the Christians. How are we to understand the deity of Jesus? And what is our basis for defining what it means to be God?

With the Alexandrian presbyter Arius as their spokesperson, in the early fourth century anti-trinitarians in reality chose a pagan understanding of 'god'. 'God' is someone or something you can become. 'Gods' may have a beginning, they are not necessarily omnipotent and all-knowing, and they don't necessarily have life in themselves. Such was their culture. Popular religion of the time taught it, and the philosophers expressed similar thoughts in more sophisticated form. To the Greeks only the world —*kosmos*—was eternal.[10] 'Gods' came into being.[11] They fought each other as they were not equally powerful, and they could be fooled as they did not know everything.[12] Some Christian philosophers, among them Arius, were influenced by this concept of the divine, which became the underlining premise of their understanding of Jesus.[13]

But in the end Christian doctrine came to be built on another basis than Greek philosophy for defining what it means to be God. The trinitarian doctrine takes God's self revelation in Jesus as presented in the Scriptures as the starting point. If I as a Christian is to tell what God is like, my first answer will always be a reference to the crucified Jesus, and if anyone makes any attempt to describe God in such a way that the portrayal is in

---

10. The word 'kosmos' had a double meaning in Greek, meaning both 'world' and 'beautiful', from which we have the word *cosmetics*.
11. The biblical creation account in Genesis 1–2 is unique in its concept of God as a person who is outside and independent of creation. To the Hellenistic culture all gods had a beginning.
12. Pierre Grimal, *The Dictionary of Classical Mythology*, translated by AR Maxwell-Hyslop (London: Blackwell, 1986) provides a comprehensive, but easily read overview of the Greek-Roman gods and the adventures as told about them in the stories of Antiquity. A shorter, but informative work on the pagan gods as they show up in the New Testament texts is Robert M Grant, *Gods and the One God*, Library of Early Christianity, edited by Wayne A Meeks (Philadelphia, PA: The Westminster Press, 1986).
13. Greek philosophers in the era of the early Christian church had long since moved away from the admittedly crude descriptions of the gods of the myths. It was not uncommon to believe in some kind of divine principle behind all material existence. This one principle, the ultimate source of *kosmos*, was, however untouchable and immovable, not the personal biblical God. It was this philosophical concept the educated early Christian apologists battled—and at times assumed. That development would cause serious problems for the church when attempting to understand what it means to be God.

its character different from what I see in Jesus as presented in Scripture, I will have to reject it.

The Bible is not silent on what it means to be God. God is the Creator. He made the world from nothing (the Latin expression *ex nihilo*, out of nothing, later came to signify that understanding), and as Creator, God is therefore independent of all that is created, he is before all, he has no beginning, and he is omnipotent, all-knowing, and for ever present. That is what God is as God, and there is no other. A text like Isaiah 44:6 summarises this basic understanding of the Old Testament monotheism, Thus says the LORD, the King of Israel, and his Redeemer, the LORD of hosts: I am the first and I am the last; besides me there is no god (NRS).

Defining the Divinity of Jesus—Yahweh!

So, the Early Church chose the God revealed in Scripture. They preferred the Old Testament to Greek and pagan philosophy. But it was not an easy battle. Major opponents wanted to get rid of much or even all of the Old Testament, and even major parts of the New, were considered by some to be too Jewish as well.[14] But the trinitarian doctrine developed on the basis of the whole Bible because Jesus clearly understood Himself as Yahweh, the God of the Old Testament. Let us look at a couple of the texts in the New Testament which make that identification.

- Do not be afraid; I am the First and the Last. I am He who lives, and was dead, and behold, I am alive forevermore. Amen. And I have the keys of Hades and of Death (NKJ, Revelation 1:17–18). In this verse Jesus quotes the Yahweh's words of Isaiah 44:6 as his own.
- I am the good shepherd. The good shepherd gives his life for the sheep (NKJ, John 10:11).

In the historical context it is evident that all Jews believed Yahweh was their shepherd (cf Psalm 23:1), and in the context of John 10, contemporaries of Jesus clearly are described as reacting in horror to the perceived

---

14. Marcion is one famous example. In the mid to late part of the second century he established his own church or religion, based on a revised set of holy writings, throwing out all of the Old Testament and quite a lot of the New as well, keeping very little along with his own material. His movement lasted for centuries. Examples of anti-Semitism abound, not least after the second Jewish revolt under Simon bar-Kokba in 132–135 AD.

blasphemy (cf vs 31–33). Jesus said to them, 'Truly, truly, I say to you, before Abraham was born, I am.' Therefore they picked up stones to throw at Him (NAU, John 8:58–59).

The language of Jesus in proclaiming Himself the great 'I AM' is a clear reference to the name of Yahweh in the Old Testament and especially to numerous texts in the second part of the book of Isaiah, using the Hebrew phrase *ani hu*', 'I am he'(eg Isa 43:10, 13; 48:12).[15]

So, the New Testament presents Jesus as one with Yahweh. He is creator (cf John 1:3; Colossians 1:15; and Revelation 3:14). This portrait reflects the clear prophetic statement by Isaiah about the eternal divinity of the Messiah to come, a 'mighty God' and an 'eternal Father.'

For unto us a Child is born, Unto us a Son is given; And the government will be upon his shoulder. And his name will be called Wonderful, Counselor, **Mighty God**, **Everlasting Father**, Prince of Peace (Isa 9:6 NKJ).

Oneness of Relationship

But how could Jesus be God and God be one at the same time? Some Christians moved toward one extreme position by identifying the Father totally with the Son—and later identifying the Son totally with the Holy Spirit.[16] Doing so would, however, destroy the personality and distinctiveness of each and conflict with the obvious New Testament description of the relationship between Father and Son, clearly two distinct persons.

The answer to the question is in part found in the Hebrew word used for 'one' in the famous text in Deuteronomy 6:4, the *Shema*—'Hear, O Israel! The LORD is our God, the LORD is one!' (NAU). It denotes a unity

---

15. The Hebrew expression is generally translated into the Septuagint as *ego eimi* which is used by John in the Fourth Gospel in 8:59 and other texts. A number scholars have investigated this phrase, for instance R Bauckham, 'Monotheism and Christology in the Gospel of John' in *Contours of Christology in the New Testament* (Grand Rapids, MI: Eerdmans, 2005), 148–66.
16. Called *modalism* in the Ancient Church, it pops up in various forms throughout history. At the time of the early Adventist movement, professing trinitarians presented this as genuine Christian doctrine, and their views were rejected by Adventist pioneers who mistakenly took it to represent the authentic Trinity doctrine. For a description of the historical development of early Adventist doctrine, see Merlin Burt, 'History of Seventh-day Adventist Views on the Trinity', *Journal of Adventist Theological Studies* 17 (2006), 125–139; and Jerry Moon, 'The Adventist Trinity Debate' part I and II, *Andrews University Seminary Studies* 41 (2003), 213–229 and 275–292.

of relationship, not necessarily a numerical or mathematical oneness, cf the use of the word, *'echad*, in texts like Genesis 2:24; 21:25; Judges 20:1. What is unique to the Christian confession of the divinity of Jesus is that it maintains the monotheism of the *Shema* by incorporating Jesus into it, as is done in for instance 1 Corinthians 8:4–6: 'yet for us there is one God, the Father, from whom are all things and for whom we exist, and one Lord, Jesus Christ, through whom are all things and through whom we exist.' (1Cor 8:6 ESV)[17]

Thus, on the one hand, in establishing the Trinity doctrine Christians had to denounce those views which questioned that there are three distinct persons or personalities in the Godhead,[18] willingly admitting that also the word 'person' is from the human sphere and falls short of fully and exactly describing God. On the other hand, the Christian Church had to distance itself from any position which presented Jesus as *substantially* different from the Father. The language used was that Father and the Son share in substance,[19] a term later used also by Ellen White when she writes, 'Jesus said, "I and my Father are one". The words of Christ were full of deep meaning as he put forth the claim that he and the Father were of one substance, possessing the same attributes.'[20]

The term 'substance' is not to be understood as some kind of 'stuff' mystical emanating energy,[21] but as the basic attributes without which

---

17. With special reference to the Gospel of John, Andreas J Köstenberger and Scott R Swain provide a good description of how early Christians were able to understand the divinity of Jesus within the framework of Jewish monotheism, *Father, Son, and Spirit: The Trinity and John's Gospel*, New Studies in Biblical Theology 24 (Downers Grove IL: Apollos/InterVarsity Press, 2008), 27–44.
18. Attempts to view God this way resulted in positions like *sabellianism* and *modalism*, positions in which the Father, the Son, and the Holy Spirit are totally identical and only modes of God. Not least *modalism* has reoccurred in various forms also in modern times.
19. The task of finding terms which most clearly expressed the thought was a major challenge for Christian theologians for centuries, not helped by the fact that terminology used in the Greek language not always matched what was said in Latin.
20. 'The True Sheep Respond to the Voice of the Shepherd', in *Signs of the Times*, November 27, 1893, 54. Gerald O'Collins likewise speaks about *substantia* as 'the common fundamental reality shared by Father, Son, and Holy Spirit', in *The Tripersonal God: Understanding and Interpreting the Trinity* (New York: Paulist Press, 1999), 105.
21. That danger exists due to the way the word 'substance' is often used as some kind of core of matter. God does not consist of matter or of anything. The danger of describing and understanding 'substance' this way and thus in a sense created a 'fourth' entity with an independent ontological existence has been pointed out by many theologians throughout history, see Olson and Hall, 34 (note 51). It was a major issue of discussion

God would not be God, such as being eternal and without beginning, independent of all created, and thus omnipotent, all knowing, and for ever present. Only that way the early Christians were able defend the true oneness of God and avoid worshiping more than one God and thus return to paganism.

Anti-trinitarians at the time of the Early Church either rejected the distinctive personalities of the Father, the Son, and the Holy Spirit, making them identical persons, or they understood Jesus as having a beginning and thus being substantially different from the Father, treating Jesus as a second god. Anti-trinitarians of today often perceive Jesus as a second and lesser god, returning to a view based on paganism or Greek philosophy.

The Trinity—Basic Argument!

Let me in short form outline the Bible based argumentation which led to the Early Church the doctrine of the Trinity.
1. Monotheism. God is one!
2. Jesus is God!
    a. Yet, the Father and the Son are two distinct persons
    b. There are at least two persons in that one God!
3. The Holy Spirit is a distinct person within the Godhead.
4. These three form a unity.

'But what about . . .'—and 'So What'?

But does not the Bible, not least the New Testament, contain a number of texts which speak about the subordination of Jesus the Son? Anti-trinitarians are quick to point this out by listing texts which do not speak about the eternal divinity of Jesus, but about his limitations, humility, and humanity. And is he not by being named the 'Son' per definition lesser and later?

Neither modern nor the early Christian theologians are silent about these questions and the biblical texts to which they relate, such as the 'Sonship' of Jesus and the term 'the only begotten' (John 1:18, 3:16 *et alia*).

---

at the Fourth Latheran Council in 1215, *ibid*, 62. Letham's definition of "substantia" as 'the 'stuff' of which something or someone consists' and as 'one identical substance of which the Father, the Son, and the Spirit all consist' is at best confusing and imprecise and tends to make the Godhead dependent on some other entity (502). The view has in general rightly been rejected by trinitarians throughout history.

What we have to remember is that all these texts speak about the role of Jesus in dealing with the created beings as the full representative of God, both before and after the origin of sin. They do not speak about, and they do not negate the nature of his eternal divinity.

Rather, they highlight the very point of the doctrine. Rightly understood, these texts help us to see why it is important because they reveal what the gospel is all about. Jesus is the slain Lamb; but he is also our divine Shepherd (Rev 7:17). The Christian message is based on the fact that the Creator of the Universe, the eternal omnipotent and all-knowing God Himself, stepped down and became a human being, even to the death on the cross. This is what we today using a Greek word, call the *agapē* love of God.[22] He was fully God, he humbled Himself and became fully human, and he is now exalted above all (Phil 2:5–11).[23]

Modern trinitarians—with the early Christian Church—reject any pagan concept of the divine and instead, based on the Bible, choose to believe in such a God of agape love. If Jesus was anything less than 'the eternally blessed God' (Rom 9:5), this love would disintegrate and become a phantom. We would no longer really know God as a person because He if that were the case in reality had sent someone else. And Jesus could no longer provide full sacrifice and atonement for our sins because he would not be eternal, and the cross would just be trading with the Devil. But the biblical God of agape love was willing to sacrifice Himself in order not to compromise or trade with sin.

That was why the doctrine mattered so much for the early Christian church.[24] Jesus Christ was able to become the perfect mediator between

---

22. The emphasis in modern theology on this term to describe this aspect of God's character was highlighted by Anders Nygren's monumental study, *Agape and Eros*, revised 1953 (London: SPCK, 1957).
23. Solid exegesis of this text can be found in commentaries like Peter O'Brien, *The Epistle to the Philippians* (Grand Rapids, MI: Eerdmans, 1991) and Gordon Fee, *Paul's Letter to the Philippians* (Grand Rapids, MI: Eerdmans, 1995). For a shorter, clear and insightful discussion, see Kevin Giles, *Jesus and the Father: Modern Evangelicals Reinvent the Doctrine of the Trinity* (Grand Rapids, MI: Zondervan, 2006), 99–107.
24. The Danish theologian and philosopher Johannes Sløk expressed it succinctly this way, 'Let us try to express this deep difference between Christian proclamation and all Ancient understanding of life by a short formula. In antique spirituality—as in pagan spirituality in general—religion is human's way to God, the attempt to break free of its despair and its boundaries to participate in a higher form of life. Christianity on the contrary is *God's way to human beings*; it is in a sense God Himself who has broken His boundaries by becoming human; He has sought out humans where we are, and He has united Himself with us in our damned condition.

God and human beings (1 Tim 2:5), not because he is somewhere in between, but exactly because he is both fully God and fully human.

It was impossible for the church to move from this fundamental view. Therefore it had so stubbornly to fight the so called *Arians*. Arius (c 320) did not believe Jesus to be God in the full sense of the word; as the Son of God he had to be created by the Father and, consequently, be subsequent to him. Therefore, he was just a lower god, a heavenly messenger, a prophet like figure. If this understanding had become dominant, the Christian understanding of life would have been lost, or it would have turned back into the Greek concept of humans' relationship to God.' 'The Unified Christian Culture', in Erik Lund, Mogens Pihl, and Johannes Sløk, *History of European Ideas*, third edition (Copenhagen: Gyldendal. 1993), 132.

A Study of Paul's Concept of the Saving Act of 1 Corinthians 15:27–28

Roland D Meyer

Introduction

This chapter will argue that though Christ's redeeming act described in 1 Corinthians 15:27–28 took place in time, it does not exclude his pre-incarnation nor his glorification. Indeed, the resurrection of the Son through the Father marks the end of death's rule. This is what the Apostle Paul attempts to assert to the Corinthians. In revealing this, he clearly distinguishes the responsibilities of God the Father from those of Christ made human. The Son's mission is to reduce all enemies and death to powerlessness: 'then the end will come, when he hands over the kingdom to God the Father.'[1] The Son's victory is complete, nothing escapes from him. He had already proclaimed this victory when he shouted: 'I have overcome the world.'[2] That is what Paul says in his own words to the Corinthians in the text dealt with here:

> For he 'has put everything under his feet.' Now when it says that 'everything' has been put under him, it is clear that this does not include God himself, who put everything under Christ. When he has done this, the Son himself will be made subject to him who put everything under him, so that God may be all in all.[3]

This surely implies that the Son, who has won the victory during his ministry on Earth, will return to his eternal position by the Father and the Holy Spirit. Paul undertakes a complex demonstration when he approach-

---

1. 1 Corinthians 15:24. All Bible quotations are from the *New International Version*.
2. John 16:33.
3. 1 Corinthians 15:27-28.

es the soteriological dimension of the saving act of the cross. For him, this work can take place only within the trinitarian dimension.

A distinction should be made between the two types of knowledge: what Xavier Léon-Dufour calls a 'historical knowledge'[4] on the one hand, and the 'knowledge of faith' on the other hand. When we say: 'Jesus healed the sick' or 'Jesus died on the cross', we express a proposition which can be historically proven. These are 'historical' facts testified to by witnesses and written about by apostles, evangelists or historians. These events took place in given places and at specific moments of time in the history of humankind. They may be verified by historical investigation.

When we say 'Christ is the end of the law' (Romans 10:4) or 'Christ died for our sins' (1 Cor 15:3), we accept the fact that these statements may be testified to by believers as real facts. In doing this we assume a certain interpretation of the historical data. This interpretation does not, however, proceed from a universal knowledge. Rather, it proceeds from faith. For the believer, these facts are not imaginary; yet it does not mean that they are 'historical'.

Likewise when we say that 'Christ was raised from the dead' (Romans 6:4), we express a fact which is quite real for the convinced believer. But, behind this reality of Christ's resurrection, lies the whole mystery of the resurrection of man and of everlasting life. Behind this act of power lies also the mystery of the Trinity. In this sense, therefore this fact relates neither to science nor to historical knowledge. No human witness was present when Christ rose from the dead; only the consequences of his resurrection were observed while the resurrected Christ was visible. Christ's resurrection and his exaltation in God's presence escape any type of investigation. We are entering here a meta-historical dimension.[5]

Through the logics of his reasoning, Paul endeavours to answer those of the Corinthians who claimed that there was no resurrection from the dead. In his development, the apostle does not take into account the Hellenistic dichotomist Greek dualistic concept of body and soul. If there is no resurrection, avers Paul, then 'our preaching is useless' (1 Cor 15:14), 'your faith is futile' (verse 17), 'we are then found to be false witnesses' (verse 15), 'you are still in your sins' (verse 17), and 'those also who have

---

4. Cf Xavier Léon-Dufour, *Résurrection de Jésus et message pascal* (Paris: Seuil, 1971), 252.
5. See Xavier Léon-Dufour's propositions, in 'La Résurrection du Christ et l'exégèse moderne,' Recherches de science religieuse 57 (1969): 618. This author speaks of 'trans-historical' events.

fallen asleep in Christ are lost' (verse 18). What reason is there then for this continuous struggle against difficulties and dangers? 'If the dead are not raised, let us eat and drink, for tomorrow we die' (1 Corinthians 15:32). To this polemical sentence he counters: 'But Christ has indeed been raised from the dead, the firstfruits of those who have fallen asleep' (1 Corinthians 15:20). For him, the Paul sees future victory has as having been won in Jesus Christ, 'the firstfruits of those who have fallen asleep [have died]'. He suggests that victory on over the hostile powers may be won because God has placed all the enemies, death included, under Christ's feet. At last, his final enthronement will take place after the destruction of the last enemy, death.

> This narrative shows that the Resurrection never was, and will never be, a concept like all other concepts. It contradicts human reason far more radically than the concept of the immortality of the soul, or even that of the reincarnation. It is so bold that it is impossible to discuss it, as could be done about God, sin, Christ or Redemption. It blows to pieces the most beautiful dogmatic constructions.[6]

Lets us explore this 'bold concept' as expressed in the Apocrypha, by other biblical writers and Paul.

The Concept of the Resurrection in Extra-biblical Texts

It was among the Alexandrine Jews, who had been influenced by Greek philosophy, that the concept of the immortality of the soul appeared, without any reference to a resurrection of the body: 'I was a well-born child indeed and had received a good soul; or rather, being good, I had entered a body without spot' (Wisdom 8:19, 20).

An obvious dualism appears is also evident in the Book of Wisdom (9:15) when it states: 'The body, subject to corruption, weighs the soul down, wraps it in earth and is a burden for the mind, appealed to from all sides.'

The *Book of Wisdom* is most likely to be dated to the first century BC, and is thought to have been written by a Hellenistic Jew in Alexandria. Concerning its thought on life after death, Emile Puech states:

---

6. Etienne Trocmé, in the foreword to the book of Roland Meyer, *La vie après la mort. Saint Paul défenseur de la résurrection* (Lausanne: Belle Rivière, 1989), 17.

> ... it seems to understand life after death according to a concept of transcendent eschatology, and not a linear eschatology ... It seems there has been a progressive evolution of the Jewish thought, shifting from a corporate eschatology to an invidual eschatology and resting upon an anthropology which is no more a Semitic one, but a Hellenistic one, strongly influenced by Plato's thought.[7]

The author of 2 Macchabees (6:18–31) had certainly accepted the belief in the resurrection for he wrote: 'As he was exhaling his last breath, he said: You scoundrel, you are excluding us from this present life; but the King of the world, because we shall die for his laws, will raise us from the dead for everlasting life.'

The author of 4 Ezra (7:32) gives an interesting vision of this life, considered as a difficult passage, then of the end of the world and of the resurrection:[8] 'The earth will give back those who are sleeping in its bosom, and the dust those who are resting in it.'

2 Baruch mentions very clearly the resurrection of the elect and of the damned.[9] Solomon's Psalms (3:11, 12) mentions the condemnation of the wicked and the resurrection of the righteous. In the eschatological description found in *Judah's Testament* (25:4), the whole of chapter 25 revolves around the concept of the resurrection. Other books, such as *Benjamin's Testament, Levi's Testament, Job's Testament,* the *Book of Biblical Antiquities,* the *Sybilline Oracles,* the *Greek Life of Adam and Eve,*[10] mention very distinctly the doctrine of the resurrection, while keeping at the same time a dualist approach to soul and body.

The same doctrines are to be found in the works of Philo of Alexandria,[11] who probably borrowed them from Plato. In his opinion, the soul is immortal if it succeeds in lifting itself above tangible things and in freeing itself from the yoke of passion.[12] Thus, in order for man to enjoy immor-

---

7. Émile Puech, 'Les croyances des Esséniens en la vie future.' In Immortalité, résurrection, vie éternelle ? Histoire d'une croyance dans le judaïsme ancien, vol. 1, La résurrection des morts et le contexte scripturaire (Paris: Gabalda, 1993), 92.
8. See also 4 Ezra 7:75–101.
9. See also 2 Baruch 50:2–4; 51:1–3; Jubilee 1:29.
10. See also Benjamin's Testament 10:5–10; Levi's Testament 18:9–14; Job's Testament 4:9; Biblical Antiquities 51:5; Sybilline Oracles 4:181, 182; Greek Life of Adam and Eve 28:4.
11. Greek-speaking Jewish philosopher (Alexandria, 13 BC – 45/50 AD).
12. Philon, *De somiis* I, 43; cf. *De opificio mundi* 40, 44, 46, 77, 135; De victimis 6.

tality already in his present life, the mind must dominate the bodily element.[13] Although Philo's thought was influenced by Plato's, it strongly emphasised the relationship of man with God. Philo was expecting an everlasting punishment for the impious or a definitive annihilation.[14] According to Philo's anthropology, the resurrection of the body is considered as a punishment. There is therefore, in Philo's thought, no place for a bodily resurrection. According to Flavius Josephus, the Essenes professed also the same ideas.[15]

The Concept of the Resurrection in the Old Testament

There are few Old Testament texts that appear to directly address the concept of resurrection. For the authors of the first Testament, man is a being who has been created by God: he *is* body, soul and spirit; he does not *have* a body, a soul and a spirit as the Greek philosophers understood it. In this part of the Bible, God reveals himself as having the power over life and death.[16] The certainty of a life beyond death is progressively testified to by the Biblical Israel. Not a life *in* death, but *after* death.[17] The Old Testament mentions two types of resurrections (or awakenings). The **first type** has to do with the national awakening of a people gone astray. The words *resurrection* and *awakening* are used to express the awakening of the people of Israel, meaning a national awakening. The text of Hosea 6:1-3 does not feature a bodily resurrection, but a national awakening and the healing of the sick people of Israel.[18] This restoration will take place mainly on a national, not individual level.[19] The hope of the Israelites was represented

---

13. Philon, *De gigantibus* 13, 14.
14. Philon, *De praemiis et poenis* 69; *De posteritate Caini* 39.
15. Flavius Josephus, *Antiquities of the Jews*, XVIII, 2; *Wars of the Jews*, II, 8, 12.
16. 1 Samuel 2:6.
17. Christian Grappe, 'Naissance de l'idée de résurrection dans le judaïsme', in *Résurrection. L'après-mort dans le monde ancien et le Nouveau Testament*, edited by Odette Mainville & Daniel Marguerat (Genève, Montréal: Labor et Fides, Médiaspaul, 2001), 45.
18. See Hans Küng, *Vie éternelle ?* (Paris, Seuil, 1985), 119-22.
19. Robert Martin-Achard, *La mort en face selon la Bible hébraïque* (Genève: Labor et Fides, 1998), 96. In his commentary of Hosea 6, the author specifies: 'What Ephraim wishes or even expects is a return to its former glorious situation: its wounds, that its failures face to Judah, have to be dressed; in other words, the territory occupied by the enemy will be re-conquered, and Israel will celebrate his victories in the presence of his God (verse 2). The vocabulary used here does express the concept of a resurrection ("to restore life" or "to revive", even "to survive", "to lift", to "lift up", "to straighten out"); but, in fact, a political restoration is meant.' The same is true for the text of Ezekiel

by the concept of a return to life, a corporate return. The text of Ezekiel (37:1–14) should be considered in this same perspective. The prophet himself gave the interpretation of this vision of the dry bones: 'Then he said to me: Son of man, these bones are the whole house of Israel. They say: our bones are dried up and our hope is gone; we are cut off'(Ezekiel 37:11).

Thus when Ezekiel the prophet saw the return to life of the dry bones, he did not mean, according to the context of this vision, the resurrection of the dead Israelites, but the return of those who had been transported to Babylone.

Second type: has to do with the passage from death to life for some individuals. The text of 1 Kings (17:17–24) narrates a miracle wrought by Elijah the prophet when he met a widow living in Sarepta. This second narrative of a resurrection may be found in 2 Kings (4:32–37); it narrates tells the story of the return to life of the son of a woman living in Shunem. 2 Kings narrates also that, as a man was being taken to be buried, his body touched the bones of Elisha the prophet, and he was restored to life (2 Kings 13:21).

Death was surely not understood as being a definitive state. A formulation of the resurrection may be found even in the ancient texts. The belief in the resurrection from the dead appears as a certainty in what may be called 'the Revelation of Isaiah' (Isaiah 26:19). Very ancient biblical texts, like *Psalm* 139, (see also Psalm 16:10, 11; 17:15) already testify of the belief in a death which is not definitive and, therefore, in a resurrection. Jacques Doukhan states that the author of this text presents the mechanism of this miracle in three steps: a) God is the Creator of the beginning of life; b) God controls life till its end; and c) God is still present at the moment of awakening.[20]

Job's unfortunate fate also led him also to reflect upon the reason of death and to expect a way out from this event that God had certainly not planned.[21] We must wait, however, till Daniel the prophet to find the testimony of an eschatological resurrection. The concept of a resurrection to be found in the book of Daniel is linked with the apocalyptic concepts

---

37:1–14.
20. Jacques Doukhan, *Aux portes de l'espérance* (Dammarie-lès-Lys: Vie et Santé, 1983), 232.
21. Job 19:25–27. See the development of Robert Martin-Achard, *Mort en la Bible hébraïque*, 114–118.

developed by the author. This awakening will take place at the time of the end (Daniel 8:19; 12:2, 4, 9). In its vision of the times of the end, the prophetic text highlights this revolutionary concept of the resurrection from the dead.

The Abode of the Dead

The Bible mentions frequently the concept of the abode of the dead. The Old Testament Hebrew uses the word *sheol*, the New Testament Greek the word *hades*. Very early in its history, the Roman Church tried to give a geographical description of the abode of the dead and to specify what was taking place in it. One of the terms used by the Roman Church to describe the abode of the dead is 'hell'. In the various civilisations, hell is almost always a subterranean place reached by the dead after a difficult and dangerous journey. The pre-Christian Germanic people called this hidden place *Hel*. The Latin countries called this place *infernum*, meaning 'the lower place'. Very early the various religions considered the world in the perspective of a cosmical dualism, and came to believe that the separation between good and evil would take place in the hereafter. This thought was dear to Zarathustra in Iran, about the seventh century BC. It should be mentioned that, within Christianity, the concept of a hell developed quickly. This concept can be found in both the apocryphal and apocalyptic literature. In the *Apocalypse of Peter*, a text written about the middle of the second century, and in the *Apocalypse of Paul*, written about the middle of the third century, can be found descriptions of the tortures, borrowed from the Eastern mythologies, inflicted to the damned that were borrowed from the Eastern mythologies.

The Concept of the Resurrection in the New Testament

The doctrine of the resurrection from the dead becomes more specific in the New Testament. The epistles, the gospels and the book of Revelation of John complement each other to give a coherent message about the resurrection. The vocabulary used gives to an easy understanding easily that the passage from death to life is not produced by a progressive and cyclical reincarnation, nor by the power of man himself. Rather, It does describes a passage from a state of unconsciousness to a state of consciousness. The expressions used are dynamical: to be raised from the dead, to stand, to stand up after sleeping, to wake up, an awakening, a resurrection, to stand up after having been in bed, to bring up, to raise, to lift oneself, to cause to live, to vivify, to give life.[22]

For Paul, there is no hope of a resurrection except that which is founded upon the resurrection of Christ.[23] The resurrection will take place at the parousia.[24] It will imply a new body, which will no more be subject to death (1 Corinthians 15:42–44). The words used by the apostle Paul to expressing the resurrection used by the apostle Paul recognise the reality of death, but, at the same time, its relativity in the face to of the power of God.[25]

This vocabulary on death and the resurrection reveals the thought of the apostle. The words he used to mean death are those which refer to sleep; those he chose to mean the resurrection refer to an awakening. The vocabulary chosen by Paul is in harmony with the vocabulary of the authors of the Old and New Testaments. The death of the righteous is always relativised by an awakening, often translated by the word 'resurrection'. In Paul's thought, death is linked with Adam's sin: 'Therefore, just as sin entered the world through one man, and death through sin, and in this way death came to all men, because all sinned'(Romans 5:12). Death is a state of total separation. But, through Christ, everlasting life is granted to those

---

22. ἐγείρω = *to be raised from the dead, to get up, to stand up after sleeping, to wake up, to raise*: Matthew 10:8; 11:5; 16:21; 17:9, 23; 20:19; 26:32; 27:52, 63, 64; 28:6, 7; Mark 12:26; 14:28; 16:6, 14; Luke 7:22; 9:22; 20:37; 24:6, 34; John 5:21; 12:1, 9, 17; 21:14. ἔγερσις (a hapax) = *awakening, resurrection*: Matthew 27:53. ἀνίστημι = *to get up, to stand after having been in bed, to cause to stand up, to raise, to raise from the dead, to stand up, to lift oneself*: Mark 5:42; 8:31; 9:9, 10; 10:34; 16:9; Luke 8:55; 18:33; 24:7, 46; John 11:23. ἀνάστασις = *resurrection*: Matthew 22:23, 28, 30, 31; Mark 12:18, 23; Luke 14:14; 20:27, 33, 35, 36; John 5:29; 11:24. ζωοποιέω = *to cause to live, to vivify, to give life*: John 5:21 (twice). ἐξυπνίζω = *to wake up*: John 11:11. Narratives of resurrections: Matthew 10:8; 11:5; 27:52; Mark 5:42; Luke 7:22; 8:55; John 5:21; 11:11, 23; 12:1, 9, 17. Christ's resurrection: Matthew 16:21; 17:9, 23; 20:19; 26:32; 27:53, 63, 64; 28:6, 7; Mark 8:31; 9:9, 10; 10:34; 14:28; 16:6, 9, 14; Luke 9:22; 24:6, 34; 18:33; 21:14; 24:7, 46. The eschatological resurrection: Matthew 22:23, 28, 30, 31; Mark 12:18, 23, 26; Luke 14:14; 20:27, 33, 35–37; John 5:29; 11:24.
23. 1 Corinthians 15:20, 21; 2 Corinthians 4:14.
24. 1 Thessalonians 4:16; 1 Corinthians 15:51, 52.
25. References having no direct link with the concept of the resurrection have been italicised. The principal words Paul uses to describe the resurrection are as follows: ἐγείρω Rom 4:24, 25; 6:4, 5, 9; 7:4; 8:11, 34; 10:9; 13:11; 1 Cor 6:14; 15:4, 12-17, 20, 29, 32, 35, 42-44, 52; 2 Cor 1:9; 4:14; 5:15; Gal 1:1; Eph 1:20; 5:14; Phil 1:17; Col 2:12; 1 Thess 1:10; 2 Tim 2:8; (Heb 11:19); ἀνίστημι Rom 15:12; 1 Cor 10:7; Eph 5:14; 1 Thess 4:14, 16; (Heb 7:11, 15); ἀνάστασις Rom 1:4; 6:5; 1 Cor 15:12, 13, 21, 42; Phil 3:10; 2 Tim 2:18; (Heb 6:2; 11:35); ἐξανάστασις Phil 3:11; ζωοποιέω Rom 4:17; 8:11; 1 Cor 15:22, 36, 45; 2 Cor 3:6; Gal 3:21.

who have accepted his grace: 'The wages of sin is death, but the gift of God is eternal life in Christ Jesus our Lord'(Romans 6:23).

The believer should not, however, fear the power of death, because it has been vanquished by the power of Christ's resurrection. Paul features death as a reality inescapable for man. For him, it is not a separation of soul and body—here he dissents from the Greek philosophers—but the annihilation of the living being. As a consequence of sin, this death is followed by the resurrection for those who believe that Jesus died and was raised from the dead for their salvation (1 Thessalonians 4:13–18). The resurrection is a transformation radically different from all that the theory of reincarnation could teach us. Here, there is no need of almost infinite cycles, nor of progressive transmigrations. Rather, it is an instantaneous act. This transformation takes place suddenly and at a specific moment. Paul uses two phrases to express the sudden character of this process:(1 Cor 15:52) ἐν ἀτόμῳ, literally in an indivisible moment, and ἐν ῥιπῇ ὀφθαλμοῦ, literally in the twinkling of an eye, in the twinkling of a look. This transformation will take place at the sound of the trumpet, an image which symbolises the change of this world (Cf Matthew 24:31; Revelation 8:2ff.).

Death and sin are closely linked together: 'Where, O death, is your victory? Where, O death, is your sting? The sting of death is sin.' (1 Cor 15:55, 56.)

As soon as death has been destroyed, it cannot destroy any more. The destruction of death implies the destruction of sin. The apostle John confirms the destruction of the author of evil: 'The devil . . . was thrown into the lake of burning sulphur.' (Rev 20:10)

In 1 Corinthians 15, Paul uses the word 'awakening' to mean 'resurrection'. This awakening after death always expresses an act of the power of God, including in the narratives of Jesus' resurrection. Man possesses in himself no power enabling him to pass from death to life; neither through knowledge, nor through science, nor through philosophy can man escape death. He needs an act of creation, or of recreation, of which man, however intelligent he may be, is thoroughly unable incapable.

The biblical statements on the resurrection describe an event that transcends the realm of history. Usually, the historical phenomena are interpreted from their context and by analogy with other events; but the resurrection cannot be explained by its context, neither by analogy with the other reality. The New Testament links the resurrection with eschatology.

For Paul, Christ's resurrection is a resurrection which delivers from sin. The whole of humankind is concerned. It offers a pledge of salvation. When Paul speaks about Christ's resurrection, he not only states that he rose from the dead, but he also expresses a logical sequence of implications which are the consequences of this event. Christ's resurrection is a foundational event, which produced the process of a general and eschatological resurrection:

- Christ is 'the first-fruits of those who have fallen asleep' (1 Cor 15:20).
- Christ's resurrection testifies of God's forgiveness: 'Christ died for our sins' (1 Cor 15:3).
- Christ's resurrection is linked with our life lives: 'In Christ all will be made alive' (1 Cor 15:22).
- Christ's resurrection is a cosmic victory on over the powers opposed to God: 'He hands over the kingdom to God the Father after he has destroyed all dominion, authority and power' (1 Cor 15:24).
- Christ's resurrection is a unique and atypical event: 'Since death came through a man, the resurrection of the dead comes also through a man' (1 Cor 15:21).
- The finality of Christ's resurrection for humankind is expressed by the fullness of God in man: 'When he has done this, then the Son himself will be made subject to him who put everything under him, so that God may be all in all' (1 Cor 15:28).

Paul's Eschatology

Resurrection is the starting point for the Christian thinking and for the reflection of upon faith. The history of Christianity begins at the same time as this event. Faith and Christian preaching rest only and totally upon this paschal event. The simple assertion *Jesus is Lord* was the gist of the most ancient Christian professions of faith. This formula may be found in some statements used by the newborn community. In a context of preparation to baptism, Paul states: 'If you confess with your mouth, "Jesus is Lord", and believe in your heart that God raised him from the dead, you will be saved'(Rom 10:9).

He proclaims, in a eucharistical context, the death of the one who is Lord: 'Whenever you eat this bread and drink this cup, you proclaim the Lord's death until he comes'(1 Cor 11:26).

To refer to Christ's resurrection, the Bible primarily uses mainly two verbs: *egeirō* and *anistēmi*. These two expressions suggest awakening or emerging from sleep. They may suggest the awakening of those who return to this earthly life as well as the universal eschatological awakening. When speaking of Christ's awakening, the New Testament expresses the concept of an eschatological event which has already begun. Christ is the *prōtotokos*. He must be the first to be raised from the dead to be the first in everything. This realisation has an aspect both eschatological and historical. Only when the whole universe has been restored, will God be *all in all* or *all in everything* (1 Cor 15:20-28). This realisation is historical in the sense that Christ was declared the Son of God by his resurrection from the dead (Rom 1:4). God raised him from the dead 'to open for the believers the possibility of a new life. His will was that men should be drawn with Christ into his glorious life'.[26] The resurrection was God's work. The New Testament seldom mentions Jesus' resurrection using active verb forms; rather, passive verb forms are used, thereby showing a God acting and intervening for his Son so that he may would be the firstborn.[27] God remains the agent of the resurrection.[28] While it is an act of God, the return to life is a creating or re-creating act. There is no separation between the event of the resurrection and the preaching of the faith. To believe in the resurrection, the intervention of faith is necessary. As Walter Kasper notes:

> Jesus' resurrection is not only God's decisive eschatological act, but also the eschatological revelation he gives of himself. Jesus' resurrection is the revelation of the realisation of the kingdom of God announced by Jesus. By Jesus' resurrection from the dead, God has shown his faithfulness in love and identified himself definitively with Jesus and his work.[29]

Through Jesus' awakening, the new world has entered history. Through it Christ has been enthroned in the with divine dignity and power.[30] Christ is standing on vantage ground and, in such a position, is interceding for

---

26. Franz-Jehan Leenhardt, *L'Epître de Saint Paul aux Romains* (Genève: Labor et Fides, 1981), 94.
27. Cf Romans 4:25; 6:4, 9; 7:4; 8:34; 1 Corinthians 15:4, 12ff; 2 Timothy 2:8.
28. Cf 1 Corinthians 6:14; Rom 10:9; 1 Corinthians 15:15.
29. Walter Kasper, *Jésus le Christ* (Paris: Cerf, 1991), 217.
30. Romans 1:2-4: 'This Gospel, already promised through his prophets in the Holy Scriptures, concerns his Son, "a descendant of David [. . .] as to his human nature [. . .] and who through the Spirit of holiness was declared with power to be the Son of God by his resurrection from the dead: Jesus Christ our Lord" (Romans 1:4).' See also 1 Corinthians 5:4; 2 Corinthian 12:9; Philippians 3:10; Ephesians 1:20f.

us before God. The cross of Christ is both a new beginning and the foundation of all hope; a new beginning that already took place in history and which is realised in each believer. It is also the foundation of hope in a future and definitive resurrection, which will unite man with God in unbreakable bonds. It is the hope of the transformation of the psychical body into a spiritual one, which will be totally dominated by the Spirit of God.

In the dynamism of Jesus' resurrection, Paul discovered the expression of divine love for humankind. God developed from all eternity his saving salvific plan (Eph 1:3, 4) through Jesus Christ. He makes us into adoptive sons and delivers us, through Jesus' blood, from our sinful state. God, as he saw all of us estranged from him through sin, gave his Son for us; he designed him designated Jesus to become the atonement through his blood. This divine love for humankind should reassure us on as to our final destiny. Paul expressed the this gratuitousness of this act of love by stating when he stated:

> All this is from God, who reconciled us to himself through Christ and gave us the ministry of reconciliation: that God was reconciling the world to himself in Christ, not counting men's sins against them. And he has committed to us the message of reconciliation. We are therefore Christ's ambassadors, as though God were making his appeal through us. We implore you on Christ's behalf: Be reconciled to God (2 Cor 5:18–21).

At the very moment of Jesus Christ's resurrection, death ceased to be the sign of Satan's power over man: it became a way of access to everlasting life. Because Christ possesses in himself the life of God, he testifies of the victory of this life upon the kingdom of death. Not only has Christ suffered the condemnation, but he has demonstrated his innocence by his triumph over death.

Christ's Pre-eminence in the Saving Act (1 Corinthians 15:20–28)

1 Corinthians 15: 20 begins with the words, 'but now, but in fact' (νυνὶ δὲ). It is a sigh of relief. Not only was Jesus raised from the dead, as the apostle has so carefully shown so far, but, even more, he was raised from the dead as the the first fruits (ἀπαρχή). The offering of the first fruits an-

nounced the harvest. Barley was harvested during the month of Nisan,[31] and, before harvesting commenced, a first feast was held, called the feast of the first fruits (Lev 23:10). It was the moment to bring to the temple the first sheaf from the harvest. This sheaf announced that the family could live throughout the year; it was a pledge that the harvest was about to take place. It would then be possible to garner and enjoy the products of the earth. Paul applies the same word to Jesus' resurrection in 1 Corinthians 15:20, 23: Christ is 'the first-fruits of those who have fallen asleep'. Paul's use of this expression underlines the apostle's reasoning on the certainty he wishes to impart to the recipients of his Epistle. By telling them that Christ is 'the first-fruits of those who have fallen asleep', he tells them that the resurrection of Christ announces, like the sheaf offered in the temple, the reality of the resurrection of the faithful when he comes in his glory. This expression qualifies an action, followed by another of the same type: first the resurrection of Christ, then the resurrection of the dead.

Christ's resurrection implies therefore the resurrection of 'those who have fallen sleep'. It was because Jesus died as men die that he was able to become 'the first-fruits of those who are fallen asleep'.[32] Faith allows us to share in the possessions he enjoys since he was raised from the dead. By accepting that he is the first-fruits, we accept the harvest, that is, the resurrection from the dead. As 'the first fruits of those who have fallen asleep', 'he includes all believers in his own resurrection and ascension'.[33] The choice of the word first fruits by Paul is deliberate.[34] Jesus is indeed, according to Paul, the firstborn, $\pi\rho\omega\tau\acute{o}\tau o\kappa o\varsigma$, from the dead. He is affirmed here as being first in rank.[35] John the Revelator also uses the expression, 'firstborn of the dead' (Rev 1:5). As Pierre Prigent affirms: 'By adding to the title of firstborn the complement of the dead, the book of Revelation,

---

31. The month of Nisan, in the Old Testament, corresponds with March-April.
32. Cf James DG Dunn, *Christology in the Making: A New Testament Inquiry into the Origins of the Doctrine of the Incarnation* (Philadelphia, PA: Westminster Press, 1980), 111.
33. Donald Guthrie, *New Testament Theology* (Leicester: InterVarsity Press, 1981), 400.
34. Ernest-Bernard Allo, *Saint Paul, première épître aux Corinthiens* (Paris: Gabalda, 1934), 405, specifies that the choice of the word first fruits 'implies a necessary link with the "bulk" of the other dead, from which Jesus emerged first, so that the others might follow'.
35. André Feuillet, *Le Christ sagesse de Dieu d'après les épîtres pauliniennes* (Paris: Gabalda, 1966), 261, mentions that 'the formula "the firstborn from among the dead" in Colossians 1:18 is the very equivalent of 'the firstfruits of those who have fallen asleep' in 1 Corinthians 15:20.

(just as Colossians 1:18) means to underline a very specific point: after this resurrected one, many brethren will be born to a new life.'[36]

In 1 Corinthians 15:22, the apostle stresses the parallelism between Christ, the second Adam, and Adam himself.[37] The new Adam came to repair the damage wrought by sin and its consequences. He will destroy definitively the last enemy, death. Christ proposes to humankind a new life. In verse 45, Paul says that Christ is a life-giving spirit, *(πνεῦμα ζῳοποιοῦν)*. Not only by his resurrection, but also by his exaltation does Christ enable humankind to enter into a new creation. In verse 23, Paul approaches the issue of chronology: first Christ, then the others. This passage on eschatology, stretching to verse 28, is complemented by verses 51–54. In verse 24, the end is mentioned; but it is impossible to know at which moment it will take place. The apostle's concern is to affirm the superiority of Christ over all hostile powers, and God's everlasting reign.[38] Paul is not so much concerned with the chronological issue of the eschatological events as with the opposition of the forces of evil against those of good. Once their annihilation has been completed, Christ will have completed fulfilled/consummated? his mission, and 'he hands over the kingdom to God the Father' (verse 24).[39] The hostile powers have already been challenged through the cross (Col 2:15). But the Christian is still involved in an ongoing conflict (Eph 6:12).

Christ's reign will last till all his enemies have been vanquished (verse 25). When Paul was writing this, he was referring to Jesus' sovereignty on over the whole creation. In Christ's reign, we should see the period following the resurrection, lasting till what Paul calls the end *(τὸ τέλος)*. In Psalm 110:1, God himself places the enemies under Christ's feet. Paul does not quote this Psalm word-for-word in 1 Corinthians 15:25b: he adds all the enemies. But, concurrently, he modifies slightly Psalm 110:1; he also modifies the subject of the verb. While God was the subject in Psalm

---

36. Pierre Prigent, *L'Apocalypse de Saint Jean* (Lausanne, Paris: Delachaux et Niestlé, 1981), 18.
37. Cf Romans 5 and 7; 1 Corinthians 15:20–24.
38. Donald Guthrie, *New Testament Theology*, 86.
39. Lucien Cerfaux, *Le Christ dans la théologie de Saint Paul* (Paris: Cerf, 1951), 42–3. 'This last act, in the end of time, corresponds with what was, at the beginning, the creation by Christ and for Christ; just as the Son was before creation, so he is after the end of all things: after summing up in himself all that had been created by him and for him, he is henceforward near the Father as the sum of all things.'

110:1, in the sense that it was he who put the enemies under the Lord's feet, in 1 Corinthians 15:25b, it is Jesus himself who 'has put all his enemies under his feet'. In verse 27, God submits the world to the Son. Death, which did not belong to God's original plan for humankind, will be destroyed at last (verse 26). While death is the destruction of life, Christ' life is the absolute and definitive destruction of death.

God and Jesus in the Saving Act

In 1 Corinthians 25:27a, Paul quotes freely Psalm 8:6. For the apostle, nothing of what takes place in the plan of salvation happens outside the Father's authority. It is Him who placed everything under the feet of his Son[40]. Even death was subject to him[41]. But it remains that it will be Christ himself, and he alone, who will bring about this change, this final victory on the last enemy. Christ remains the absolute master as long as his mission is fulfilled only in part. God is really the subject of the verb 'subjugate' (ὑπέταξεν). God placed everything under the authority of the Son.

In verse 27b, the subject of 'says' (εἴπῃ) seems to be God. Paul's sentence is a complex, but important one. Christophe Senft notes that:

> The evidence it proclaims is not that of a correct catechism, but that of the meaning of the historico-eschatological process launched by God when he raised Christ from the dead: 'raised from the dead through the glory of the Father' (Rom 6:4), he is, when exercising his kingship (verse 25), the representative of God, on behalf of whom and for whom he challenges and vanquishes the powers which have marred creation and are leading it to death.[42]

In verses 27 and 28, the apostle uses the word 'everything' ([τὰ] πάντα) six times. Paul emphasises the goal he is aiming at by the two twice using the word *everything* at the end of his a sentence. This goal had already been defined in verse 20 when he introduced into his reasoning the image

---

40. Jean Héring, *La première épître de Saint Paul aux Corinthiens* (Neuchâtel, Paris: Delachaux et Niestlé, 1949), 141.
41. Cf 1 Corinthians 15:54. FW Grosheide, *Commentary on the First Epistle to the Corinthians* (Grand Rapids, MI: Eerdmans, 1983), 368.
42. Christophe Senft, *La première épître de Saint-Paul aux Corinthiens* (Neuchâtel, Paris: Delachaux et Niestlé, 1979), 200.

of the first fruits. This verse is difficult to understand, because on the one hand because it deals with issues which transcend the human mind and, on the other hand, because it approaches a universal issue. As a mediator, Jesus fulfills a mission between man and God, a mission which has as its finality to eradicate for humankind all the obstacles standing on the way to salvation for humankind. This mission is the mission of the one sent by the Father. Once this mission has been completed, Jesus gives back the restored universe between the hands of God the Father. The difficulty of understanding this passage resides in the trinitarian dimension of the saving act. We should humbly acknowledge that man's finiteness does not enable him to understand fully the mystery of the Trinity. The fact that we do not fully understand this mystery, however, cannot possibly should not lead us to negate the Trinity.

Conclusion

Christ's redeeming act and the revelation of his person to the world are written in time: they are therefore temporary actions. These two Christ-centric revelations do not exclude neither his pre-incarnation nor his glorification. To mention the temporality of Christ's mission does not suppress his eternity. His mission on earth was limited in time and, once this mission had been completed, Jesus resumed his place by the Father (John 17:5). This mission had a double aspect: first, the personal and physical presence of the historical Jesus and, second, the spiritual presence of the Holy Spirit sent by Jesus himself as the Comforter. The redemptive act was indeed completed at the cross, but it continues till its total realisation in the parousia. Here, the mission of the Holy Spirit is essential. The end of Christ's mission is realised in the eschatological resurrection, the resurrection being the divine demonstration of God's omnipotence and ability to dominate the enemy. This demonstration had already been given when God raised Jesus from the dead. This is why Paul called Jesus the firstfruits.

In 1 Corinthians 15:28, Paul specifies: 'When he has done this, then the Son himself will be made subject to him who put everything under him, so that God may be all in all.' Senft proposes that the translation of the last part of verse 28 be 'God all in everything' instead of 'all in all'. This translation fits better the context where all hostile powers will be definitively subject to God. The subjection of the Son to the Father—an active submission, emphasised by the middle mode of the verb to submit—is totally different from the submission of the hostile powers to God. Héring proposes to translate ἵνα ᾖ ὁ θεὸς [τὰ] πάντα ἐν πᾶσιν by the words *'so that God may be totally present in the universe'*.[43] Fernando Canale writes:

> When the task of redemption entrusted to Christ is achieved, the delegation of the Father to the Son as the counterpart to the Son's total subordination to the Father will end. As interrelated aspects of the intratrinitarian life, the delegation of the Father to the Son and the subordination of the Son to the Father do not constitute the trinitarian nature of God but rather assume it.[44]

Christ's submission to God is the expression of the trinitarian unity and of the perfect match between God's will and Jesus' will for the salvation of humankind.

---

43. Jean Héring, *Saint Paul aux Corinthiens*, 138. See his development on page 141. For Héring, it means 'a pan-entheism, that is. the affirmation of the total and visible thought of God's kingdom'.
44. Fernando L Canale, 'Doctrine of God', in *Handbook of Seventh-day Adventist Theology*, edited by Raoul Dederen (Hagerstown, MD: Review and Herald, 2000), 128.

The Firstborn in Colossians 1:15

Ekkehardt Mueller

'He is the image of the invisible God, the firstborn of all creation' Colossians 1:15 [NRSV]

Introduction

Colossians 1:15 is part of one of the elaborate christological hymns in the New Testament.[1] CR Holladay states: 'If Christ is the theological centerpiece of Colossians, the magnificent Christ hymn in 1:15–20 is the defining flower of the whole arrangement. Perhaps most striking is the boldness of its christological claims. Roles or status previously reserved for God are now asserted to Christ.'[2]

However, the interpretation of this verse and especially the term 'firstborn' has been quite controversial during church history. In the early trinitarian and christological controversies Arianism taught that Jesus Christ, the Son of God, is not God in the full sense but a created being, though the highest created being who in turn was the creator of the rest of creation.[3] However, there was a time when supposedly the Son did not exist. Arius based his argument partially on the term 'first-born' as found in Colossians 1:15. MJ Erickson notes:

> The Arians did not formulate their view only upon an a priori philosophical or theological principle. Rather, they based it upon a rather extensive collection of biblical references

---

1. Arthur G Patzia, *Ephesians, Colossians, Philemon*, New International Biblical Commentary (Peabody, MA: Hendrickson, 1990), 27, notes: 'Scholars are virtually unanimous in their opinion that verses 15–20 constitute a hymn.'
2. Carl R Holladay, *A Critical Introduction to the New Testament: Interpreting the Message and Meaning of Jesus Christ* (Nashville, TN: Abingdon, 2005), 400.
3. Such a position is today held, for example, by Jehovah's Witnesses.

... For example, the references to Jesus as the 'first-born' of creation are assumed by the Arians to have a temporal significance.[4]

Arius was opposed by Athansasius,[5] and the subordinationist exegesis of Colossians 1:15 was rejected by Dionysius, the bishop of Rome, who understood Jesus as begotten but not made.[6] The debate is still alive in some circles of Christianity.[7]

In this chapter we will take a look at Colossians 1:15 in its literary setting and will study particularly the term 'first-born' (πρωτότοκος).

Contextual Analysis

1. The Colossian heresy

By means of his letter addressed to them, Paul undoubtedly tried to help church members in Colossae face the heresy with which they were struggling. We do not know the precise nature of that heresy but can try to reconstruct it by looking at Paul's refutation. Obviously, this false teaching was detracting from the person and status of Christ. The Letter to the Colossians portrays Jesus in highest terms showing his preeminence. The heresy must have downplayed the importance of Jesus. This may have been due to a form of Proto-Gnosticism which developed more fully in the second century AD.

In Colossians 2:8 Paul warns against 'philosophy and empty deception' which may point to Hellenistic elements. Angel worship is found in Col 2:18, and 'the elements of the world' occur in Colossians 2:8, 20. These elements of the world can be understood as elementary spirits, namely 'the

---

4. Millard J Erickson, *Christian Theology*, second edition (Grand Rapids, MI: Baker, 1998), 713–714. Gerald O'Collins, *Christology: A Biblical, Historical, and Systematic Study of Jesus* (Oxford: Oxford University Press, 1995), 160, states: 'In Col. 1:15 they [the Arians] read the "image" and "first-born" language ... as meaning, respectively, that the Son was an inferior copy as contrasted with the original (God) and that he was a created being.'
5. Cf Marianne Meye Thompson, *Colossians and Philemon*, The Two Horizons New Testament Commentary (Grand Rapids, MI: Eerdmans, 2005), 32.
6. Cf O'Collins, *Christology*, 160.
7. Holladay, *A Critical Introduction*, 40, suggests: 'Had these images been read as poetry rather than literal theological assertions, the church might have been spared some controversy.' We are not sure, if this assertion is correct. The person of Jesus as described in the NT begs the question whether or not he is human-divine. On the other hand, Holladay seems to be opposed to Arianism (401).

powerful spirit-world', or elementary teaching which 'would presumably describe a purely materialistic doctrine concerned only with this world'.[8]

Furthermore, extreme forms of asceticism associated with mystical experiences may have accompanied that heresy (Col 2:16),[9] and finally, the heresy may have contained Jewish elements such as circumcision (Col 2:11; 3:11) and references to feasts, new moons, and a or the Sabbath (Col 2:16). The 'human tradition' of Colossians 2:8 may also be a Jewish element. Therefore, it seems best to understand this heresy as a mixture of Jewish and pagan ideas. Such types of syncretism were attractive to many people at that time including some church members.[10]

How to help the church? Paul's struggle for the Christians in Colossae is recognisable right from the beginning of his letter when he talks about truth (Col 1:5,6), about Epaphras' faithful teaching (1:7), and his own desire that the Colossian Christians may be filled with and grow in the knowledge of God (1:9,10). The solution to the problem with heresy is found in Jesus. 'A firm grounding in Christology, then, and in its practical implications for the daily life of believers was the best defence against the illusory attractiveness of the Colossian heresy.'[11] Therefore the christological hymn as well as other statements about Jesus (for example, Col 1:26-28; 3:2-3, 6-15,19; 3:1,11, 23-24: 4:3) throughout the epistle are of great importance.[12]

The christological hymn in Colossians 1:15-20 portrays Jesus' all encompassing greatness as creator, redeemer, and sustainer of the entire cosmos so that 'indeed you continue in the faith firmly established and steadfast, and not moved away from the hope of the gospel that you have heard, which was proclaimed in all creation under heaven, and of which

---

8. Donald Guthrie, *New Testament Introduction* (Downers Grove, IL: InterVarsity, 1970), 548.
9. FF Bruce, *The Epistles to the Colossians, to Philemon, and to the Ephesians*, International Commentary on the New Testament (Grand Rapids, MI: Eerdmans, 1984), 26, holds: 'The Colossian heresy evidently encouraged the claim that the fulness of God could be appreciated only by mystical experiences for which ascetic preparation was necessary. Paul's answer to such a claim is that the fulness of God is embodied in Christ, so that those who are united to him by faith have direct access to him to that fulness and have no need to submit to ascetic rigor . . .'
10. For a discussion of the heresy, see, DA Carson, DJ Moo, L Morris, *An Introduction to the New Testament* (Grand Rapids, MI: Zondervan, 1992), 335-7; Guthrie, *New Testament Introduction*, 546-51; and *The Seventh-day Adventist Bible Commentary*, edited by Francis D Nichol, et al (Washington DC: Review and Herald, 1980), 7:184.
11. Bruce, *The Epistles*, 28.
12. Cf Patzia, *Ephesians*, 29.

I, Paul, was made a minister' (Col 1:23).[13] Again in Colossians 2 adherence to heresy is contrasted with life in Jesus. Having received Jesus (Col 2:6), being rooted in him (2:7), having been made complete in him (2:10), having been circumcised in him with a spiritual circumcision (2:11), having been buried with Him in baptism and raised with him from the dead (2:12), having been made alive with Him, and having experienced forgiveness (2:13) is to rule out all involvement with heresy.

2. Thanksgiving, prayer, and the christological hymn

After a short opening salutation (Col 1:1-2) Paul engages in thanksgiving and—beginning with verse 9—in a prayer for the church in Colossae (1:3-14) stressing in a remarkable way the present reality of the church members' salvation (1:12-14). Then follows the hymn praising the importance and magnificence of Jesus (1:15-20).

In Greek verses 9-20 consist of one long sentence which makes it somewhat difficult to tell where the prayer ends.[14] Since a poetic section begins with verse 15 and since Paul's prayer for the Colossian Christians to be filled with knowledge, wisdom, and understanding in order to live worthy of the Lord is followed by four present participles describing the actions and the experience of the believers–bearing fruit (1:10), increasing in knowledge (1:10), being strengthened (1:11), and giving thanks (1:12)—we assume that the prayer reaches up to verse 14.

> We have not ceased to pray and ask . . . (1:9)
> that you may be filled with knowledge . . .
>   to live worthy of the Lord . . . (1:10)
>   bearing fruit (1:10),
>   increasing in knowledge (1:10),
>   being strengthened (1:11),
>   giving thanks to the Father (1:12)
>   who has qualified you to share in the inheritance . . .
>   (1:12)

---

13. Thompson, *Colossians and Philemon*, 28, says about the hymn that 'it contains a number of affirmations about Christ that lay the theological foundation for challenging the Colossian heresy. Specifically, the passage asserts the complete adequacy of God's revelation and salvation in Christ in order to show the futility of trying to gain deeper understanding of or relationship to God through any other means.'
14. Cf Charles H Talbert, *Ephesians and Colossians*, Paideia Commentary on the New Testament (Grand Rapids, MI: Baker Academic, 2007).

> who has rescued and transferred us to the kingdom of
> his Son . . . (1:13)
>> in whom we have redemption,
>> The forgiveness of sins (1:14)

The hymn is clearly linked to and grows out of this section on intercessory prayer. For instance, the mention of God the Father is followed by a participle in the dative and a relative pronoun in the nominative. The mention of the Son is followed by a prepositional phrase in the dative and a relative pronoun in the nominative.

> . . . just as there is movement from 'you' to 'us,' where the latter included Gentile and Jew together, so also there is movement from the role of the Father to that of the Son. Thus vv 12–13 are all about what the Father has done . . . With the mention of the Son at the end of v 13, the focus then shifts altogether to what the Son has done (v 14) and finally to who the Son is in relation to the whole created order (vv 15–16).[15]

Verses 21–23 are also related to the hymn, because they apply reconciliation achieved by Jesus to the church members in Colossae.

3. The hymn itself

A syntactical diagram of Colossians 1:15–20 seems to indicate that the section consists of three parts, a central piece and two other parts that correspond with each other.

---

15. Gordon D Fee, *Pauline Christology: An Exegetical-Theological Study* (Peabody, MA: Hendrickson, 2007), 294.

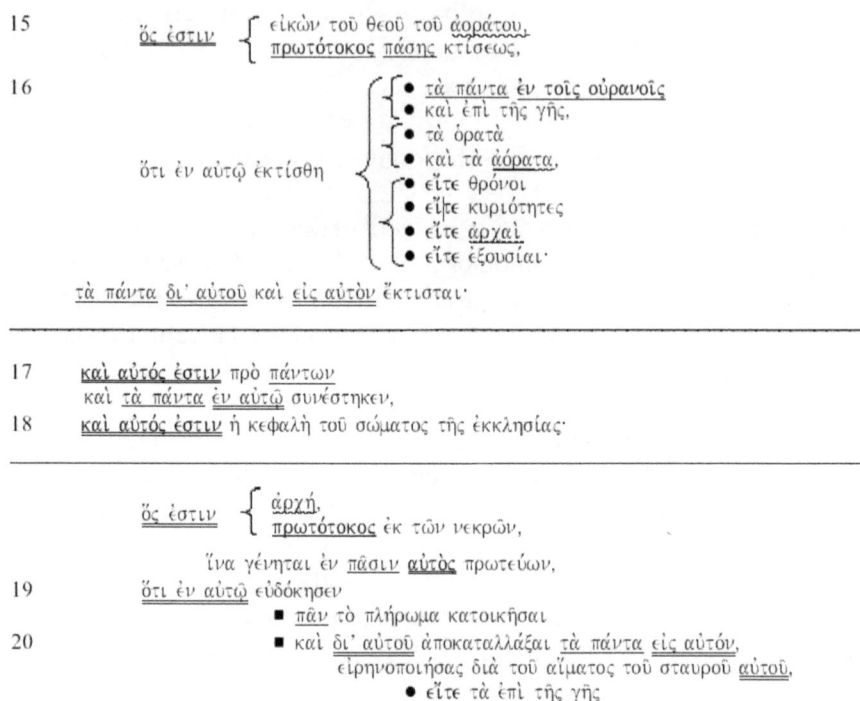

From this digram the following outline is derived:

A   **He is** { the image of the invisible God,
                 the **firstborn** of all creation.
        For in Him all things were created . . .
        <u>*all things*</u> have been created *<u>through Him</u>* and for Him.

B   <u>And He is</u> before all things,
       C   and in Him all things hold together.
B'   <u>And He is</u> the head of the body, the church;

A'   **He is** { the beginning
                  the **firstborn** from the dead . . .
       For in Him it was His Father's good pleasure for all the fullness to dwell,
and *<u>through Him</u>* to reconcile *<u>all things</u>* to Himself . . .

This hymn has an interesting structure, which may even be a chiastic structure. The first and the last part seem to correspond:

1. The opening phrase *ho estin* in verse 15 is repeated in the beginning of the third part (verse 18b). Both times it refers to Jesus and introduces his supreme status and quality.
2. The term *prōtotokos* follows the opening phrase in verses 15 and the same phrase in verse 18a.
3. As in verse 15 Jesus is characterised in a twofold way—he is the image of God and the firstborn—so he is in verse 18b being the beginning and the firstborn. These two pairs of two seem to be parallel.
4. Verse 16 begins with the phrase *hoti en autç*. Verse 19 uses the same phrase right at its beginning.
5. *Ta panta en tois ouranois kai epi tēs gēs* occurs in verse 16 and in a slightly modified and inverted form in verse 20, namely *eite ta epi tēs gēs eite ta en tois ouranois* pointing to the cosmic and universal dimension of Jesus' activity as creator and redeemer.
6. *Di' autou* and *eis auton* is found at the end of verse 16. All things have been created through Jesus and for him. The same phrases reoccur in verse 20 now relating to reconciliation.[16] Actually, in both parts the same prepositional phrases occur in the same order: *en autō, di' autou, eis auton*.
7. The term *pas* is found three times in verses 15-16 and again three times in verses 18b-20. *Ta panta* is employed in verses 16 (twice) and 20. It stresses the all-inclusiveness of Christ's work.

---

16. Cf James DG Dunn, *The Epistles to the Colossians and to Philemon*, The 16 New International Greek Commentary (Grand Rapids, MI: Eerdmans, 1996), 104. Due to textual ambiguity there is, however, some discussion whether the phrase *eis auton* in verse twenty refers to God the Father or Jesus Christ. The majority view is that it refers to God the Father. See, Patzia, *Ephesians*, 34; NT Wright, *Colossians and Philemon*, Tyndale New Testament Commentaries, revised edition (Grand Rapids, MI: Eerdmans, 1991), 76; Margaret Y MacDonald, *Colossians and Ephesians*, Sacra Pagina (Collegeville: The Liturgical Press, 2000), 64. However, Fee, Pauline *Christology*, 309-313, shows convincingly that *eis auton* in verse twenty refers also to the Son. Among others, he argues that otherwise the personal pronoun must be converted into a reflexive which 'was not once done in the long history of the textual tradition' (310) and that the flow of personal pronouns in verse 20 (*di' autou, eis auton, autou, di' autou*) would be destroyed by introducing God the Father and having to revert back to Christ.

The middle section, consisting of verses 17 and 18, is not disconnected from the other two parts. On the contrary, it shares with them the prepositional phrase *en autō*. It also shares with them the auxiliary verb *estin* in the phrase 'he is'. And it shares with the other sections the term *pas* and even its neuter plural form including the definite article, namely *ta panta*.

Part 1 All things (*ta panta*, twice) were created through him and for/to him.
Part 2 All things (*ta panta*) hold together in him.
Part 3 All things (*ta panta*) are reconciled through him to him.[17]
This central part, also called part 2, consists of three lines which point to three aspects of Jesus' nature and work:

(1) He was preexistent, being before all things.
(2) He is the sustainer of all things.
(3) He is the head of the body, the church.

While preexistence refers back to creation, that is, to the first part of the hymn, because as the creator of all things Jesus must have been preexistent, headship of the church points forward to reconciliation through his death on the cross being mentioned in the third part with its implications being described in verses 21–23. Those who are reconciled form the church whose head Jesus is.[18] On the other hand, reconciliation through

---

17. Fee, 312, notes, '... we should probably understand the τα παντα of this strophe to be identical with the τα παντα of the first strophe, so that the 'all things' of both strophes refer to the whole creation ...'
18. The concept of the church as a body is found also in other 18 Pauline letters, for example, 1 Corinthians 12:12; Romans 12:4–5. Peter T O'Brien, *Colossians, Philemon*, Word Biblical Commentary 44 (Waco, TX: Word Books, 1982), 49, observes: 'In Colossians (and Ephesians) there is an advance in the line of thought so that the relationship which the church, as the body of Christ, bears to Christ as head of the body is treated.' Patzia, *Ephesians*, 32, adds: 'Only in Colossians and Ephesians is Christ designated as *head* over *the church*. The reason for this surely lies in Paul's intention to proclaim the lordship of Christ over all things.' Thompson, 32–33, states: 'The church is the body of which Christ, rather than any other lord or deity, is the head; in him the church has its origins, and hence it also finds its identity and unity in Christ ... The church is a body drawn from every people and social class (3:11), because the head of the church is one whose work is universal and cosmic in its scope, not only in redemption, but already in creation.' Holladay, *A Critical Introduction*, 402, suggests: 'At this point [verse 18] the hymn shifts from creation to new creation. Christ as "the head of the body, the church" moves well beyond earlier Pauline conceptions of the local congregation as the "body of Christ" (cf 1 Cor 12:12, 27; also 10:16–17; Rom 12:5). In view is the universal church

the shedding of his blood requires his incarnation,[19] and his being the first-born from the dead requires his resurrection. Jesus is the head of the church because of his incarnation, death on the cross, and resurrection.[20]

This christological hymn contains many aspects of and deep insights into the life and ministry of Jesus. No wonder that G Fee declares: 'A higher Christology does not exist in the NT.'[21] Jesus is the creator of the cosmos. He is its sustainer[22] and 'the cosmic glue that holds everything together'.[23] He is the reconciler and redeemer who brings about a new creation. These aspects of Jesus' work cannot be separated from each other.[24]

4. The hymn's relations to other writings and the letter as a whole

The hymn's Old Testament background has been widely discussed. The creation account and Adam, Israel and David as firstborn, and biblical as well as extra-biblical wisdom tradition as possible backgrounds have been proposed.[25] Gordon Fee, going back to Colossians 1:12–15, points out various echoes in this passage of Israel's story listing creation, Abraham, the exodus, the giving of the law, the Davidic kingship, the Babylonian exile, and the restoration afterwards. He mentions that Jesus as the Son of God's love (Col 1:13) echoes the LXX of 2 Samuel 7:14,18 pointing to the Davidic character of his sonship as well as his relationship with the Father which will be in focus throughout the hymn.[26] '. . . the parts of the sentence that form our vv 13b and 14a anticipate the two strophes of the "hymn": (1) God's beloved Son as kingly Lord ends up as the primary concern of vv 15–17; (2) God's beloved Son as Redeemer is then the focus of vv 18–20.'[27]

---

and Christ's "headship" . . .'
19. Fee, *Pauline Christology*, 313.
20. Cf Holladay, *A Critical Introduction*, 402.
21. Fee, *Pauline Christology*, 303.
22. 'The world is not part of God nor is God part of the world, but neither does the world exist independently of the sustaining power of God', writes Thompson, *Colossians and Philemon*, 30.
23. Holladay, *A Critical Introduction*, 402.
24. Thompson, *Colossians and Philemon*, 28, notes: 'In its structure, it sets creation and redemption parallel to each other. Each has its focal point in Christ, who is the firstborn, agent, and goal of both creation and new creation.'
25. Cf Bruce, *The Epistles to the Colossians*, 58–60, 62; Dunn, *The Epistles*, 87–90; Fee, *Pauline Christology*, 295, 299–301; 521; O'Brien, *Colossians, Philemon*, 43–44; Petr Pokorný, *Der Brief des Paulus an die Epheser*, Theologischer Handkommentar zum Neuen Testament 5 (Berlin: Evangelische Verlagsanstalt, 1992), 62–4.
26. Fee, *Pauline Christology*, 295–298.
27. *Ibid*, 298.

The christological hymn contains various echoes to other New Testament texts such as Romans 8:29, where the 'image' and the 'firstborn' of Colossians 1:15 occur together; Romans 11:26 and 1 Corinthians 8:6 where prepositional phrases are used in a manner similar to Colossians 1:16, 19, 20; Hebrews 1:2–3 and John 1:1–3 where Jesus is also described as creator and as the radiance of God's glory (cf Col 1:15–16); and Revelation 3:14 where Jesus is identified as the beginning (cf Col 1:18).[28]

On the other hand, many terms and concepts found in the hymn occur again in the rest of the letter to the Colossians so that Fee wonders if 'the "hymn" serves as a kind of prelude (or overture) to the whole letter'.[29] For instance, the term 'image' occurs in Colossians 1:15 and 3:10; the terms 'creation' and 'creating' are found in Colossians 1:15–16 and 1:23; 3:19; the phrases 'through him' and 'for him' in Colossians 1:16,20 and 2:9,15; 3:17; the 'head', and its 'body', the 'church' in Colossians 1:18 and 1:24; 2:10, 19; 3:15; 4:15–16, 'the fullness dwelling' in him in Col 1:19 and 2:9, and the 'cross' in Colossians 1:20 and 2:14. Thus the hymn indeed introduces themes which will be discussed again later. On the other hand, Old Testamant background, New Testament background, and later references to the same concept in the Letter to the Colossians may shed light on certain terms being mentioned in the hymn.

Textual Analysis

1. 'Who is'

Verse 15 begins with a relative pronoun followed by the auxiliary verb 'to be'. Its antecedent has to be found in verses 13 or 14.[30] As already mentioned it is God's beloved Son. The hymn is thus closely related to Paul's prayer. In addition, the Son is closely linked to the Father who is said to have rescued us (*ruomai*, Col 1:13) while the Son has set us free/delivered us/redeemed us (*apolutrōsis*, Col 1:14). Thus, Father and Son are involved in the process of salvation.

Furthermore, the Father has 'transferred us to the kingdom of his beloved Son' (Col 1:13). The kingdom is Christ's. The only other text in Co-

---

28. Cf Dunn, *The Epistles*, 97; Fee, *Pauline Christology*, 298, 302; Talbert, *Ephesians and Colossians*,192.
29. Fee, *Pauline Christology*, 299.
30. Fee, *ibid*, 297, notes: 'What is especially significant for the rest of the narrative is that 30 "the Son of his love" is the antecedent to all the subsequent pronouns through v 22 . . .'.

lossians talking about the kingdom attributes it to God (Col 4:11). Clearly, the kingdom belongs to the Father and the Son. Although Jesus talked about his Father's kingdom (Matt 6:10,33; 26:29) or the kingdom of God (John 3:3,5), he would also refer to it as his kingdom (Matt 16:28; John 18:36).

Therefore the phrase 'who is' which is oftentimes translated in verse 15 as 'he is' brings along a context pointing to the unity between Father and Son, who share the same concerns, actions, and privileges and thereby point to the divinity of Christ. '. . . the Son who redeems through his own blood is the ultimate expression of God's love for us . . .'[31]

2. 'The image of the invisible God'

The term *eikōn* can be translated as 'likeness', 'image', 'appearance' or 'form'. The term is used only once in Colossians to refer to Jesus as he relates to God the Father. According to Colossians 3:10 the believer is to be 'renewed to a true knowledge according to the image of the One who created him'.[32] The same usage is found elsewhere in the Pauline writings.[33]

MM Thompson points out that an image is something visible, while God is invisible.[34] This sounds almost like a paradox. On the other hand, 'How then can God be known, if he is invisible?', asks Dunn and points to the 'image' as bridging 'the otherwise unbridgeable gulf'.[35] '. . . to say that Christ is the *image* of God means that, in some way, the unseen or invisible God becomes visible, moves into our sphere of sense perception, in the life of this human being.'[36] A Patzia explains:

> By image, Paul does not mean mere resemblance or similarity, because the Greek word used is *eikōn*. This communi-

---

31. *Ibid*, 142.
32. Cf O'Brien, *Colossians, Philemon*, 43.
33. Repeatedly we hear about believers to be transformed into the image of Jesus or the Lord (Rom 8:29; 1 Cor 15:49; 2 Cor 3:18). Only twice is Jesus declared to be the image of God (Col 1:15; 2 Cor 4:4). According to 2 Corinthians 4:4 Jesus is the image and glory of God the Father. However, the concept of an image is not only used in a positive way. An image can also be negative. Frequently, negative images are associated with idolatry (for example, Isa 40:19–20; Dan 3, Rev 13).
34. Thompson, *Colossians, Philemon*, 28. The invisibility of God is confirmed in other thirty-four places such as Romans 1:20; 1 Timothy 1:17; Hebrews 11:27.
35. Dunn, *The Epistles*, 87–8.
36. Thompson, *Colossians, Philemon*, 28.

cates the idea that Christ participates in and with the nature of God, not merely copying, but visibly manifesting and perfectly revealing God in human form (in 2 Cor 4:4 Paul talks about 'the glory of Christ, who is the image of God').[37]

The major Old Testament background for the image of God is most probably Genesis 1:26-27.[38] In verse 27 the phrase 'image of God' is used. Originally, humankind was created in the image of God, but humanity failed in truly representing God. However, Jesus is God's true representative. Through him God can indeed be known. Yet Jesus surpassed Adam and Eve by far in that he became also the one into whose image believers are now being transformed in a kind of new creation. By becoming like Jesus they become in some way like God. 'In other words, "Christ is not only *eikōn tou theou*, as was Adam, but also king over creation in a way vastly different from the first man"'.[39]

3. The firstborn of all creation

a. The Old Testament background

In the LXX, the term *prōtotokos* (firstborn) occurs about 130 times. With a few exceptions this adjective is a translation of the Hebrew *bekôr/bekîrâh*.[40] Two related terms are *prōtokeuō* and *prōtotokeia*.

The verb *prōtokeuō* means 'to grant the right of a first-born' and is used in Deuteronomy 21:16 only. It is interesting that in a polygamous relationship it was not allowed to make the son of the loved wife firstborn, if his half brother and son of the unloved wife was older than him. Such a command indicates that such a practice must have existed and may—under different circumstance—have been legal and acceptable. It also shows that

---

37. Patzia, *Ephesians*, 30. Bruce, *The Epistles*, 57-58, supports this suggestion: 'To say that Christ is the image of God is to say that in him the nature and being of God have been perfectly revealed–that in him the invisible has become visible.' He points among others to the Johannine literature and texts such as John 1:18 and 14:9. In the latter Jesus claims: 'He who has seen me has seen the Father.' Wright, *Colossians and Philemon*, 70, goes so far as to say: 'From all eternity Jesus had, in his very nature, been the "image of God", reflecting perfectly the character and life of the Father. It was thus appropriate for him to be the image of God as man . . .'
38. Cf Pokorný, *Der Brief*, 62-3.
39. Thompson, *Colossians and Philemon*, 29.
40. On the other hand, *bkôr* is always translated 40 *e* with the Greek term *prōtotokos*.

the issue of actually being born first was not as important as the transferral of a specific dignity and status was.

The noun *prōtotokeia*, birthright is found seven times in the Old Testament and once in the New Testament.[41] The majority of the texts focuses on the Isaac-Esau story. They indicate that the birthright could be taken away from the firstborn or voluntarily given to the younger brother. Reuben was Jacob's firstborn; 'but because he defiled his father's bed, his birthright was given to the sons of Joseph . . .' (1Chron 5:1). Again the status was more important than the time of the birth.

We now turn to the adjective *prōtotokos* which is more important to us. Typically, the term *prōtotokos* in the Old Testament is used in the literal sense. There were first-born among humans which at least sometimes included females.[42] The first-born belonged to God but were replaced by the tribe of Levi.[43] There were firstborn of the animals[44] which were included in some of the regulations concerning the firstborn of humans.[45] The human firstborn enjoyed the birthright (Gen 43:37) and a double portion of the inheritance (Deut 21:16–17). According to 2 Chronicle 21:3 the firstborn son of the king received the kingdom while various gifts were given to the other sons. The chiefs of the tribes of Israel were the firstborn (1Chron 5:12).

However, the term was also used in a different ways:

(1) Israel as God's people (Exod 4:22) was called 'my son, my firstborn'. Israel was neither directly and in a literal sense born by God nor was Israel the first of all peoples. According to 2 Samuel 19:44 the ten tribes contrasting themselves with the tribe of Judah claimed to be the firstborn and have a better claim to David. God declared to be 'a father to Israel, and Ephraim is my firstborn' (Jer 38:9).

---

41. Genesis 25:31–34; 27:36; Deuteronomy 21:17; 1Chronicles 5:1; and Hebrews 12:16.
42. Genesis 10:15; 22:21; 25:13, 25; 27:19, 32; 35:23; 36:15; 38:6, 7; 41:51; 43:33; 46:8; 48:18; 49:3; Exodus 6:14; 11:5 (twice); 12:29 (twice); 13:13, 15 (twice); 22:29 (LXX 22:28); 34:20; Numbers 1:20; 2, 12, 13, 40, 41, 45, 46, 50; 8:16, 18; 18:15; 26:5; 33:4; Deuteronomy 21:15, 16, 17; Josuha 6:26 (twice); 17:1 (twice); Judges 8:20; 1 Samuel 8:2; 14:49 (daughter); 2 Samuel 3:2; 13:21; 1 Kings 16:34; 2 Kings 3:27; 1 Chronicle 1:29; 2:3, 13, 25 (twice), 27, 42, 50; 3:1, 15; 4:4; 5:1 (twice), 3, 12 ; 6:13 (some translations 6:28, LXX 6:13); 8:1, 30, 38, 39; Psalm 78:51 (LXX 77:51); 89:28 (LXX 88:28); 105:36 (LXX 104:36); 136:10 (LXX 135:10); Micah 6:7; Zecharia 12:10.
43. Numbers 3:12, 41, 45; 8:16, 18.
44. Genesis 4:4; Exodus 11:5; 12:29; 13:15; 34:19 (twice),20; Leviticus 27:26; Numbers 3:41; 18:15, 17 (thrice); Deuteronomy 12:6,17; 15:19 (thrice); 33:17; Nehemiah 10:37.
45. Exodus 11:5; 12:12, 29; 13:2, 13, 15; Number 3:13; 8:17..

(2) A number of times the second born was put in the place of the firstborn and received his position so that a reversal took place. In these cases, the time element was no longer important. Ephraim, the younger brother of Manasseh, was raised to the rank and position of the firstborn (Gen 48:18–20; Deut 33:17; Jer 38:9). Although Shimri was not the firstborn, his father made him first (1Chron 26:10).

(3) Very enlightening is Psalm 89 (Ps 88 in the LXX). This Psalm describes God's loving-kindness and faithfulness. He had made a covenant with David promising that his throne would endure. David is mentioned in verse 3 and again in verses 20, 35, 49. In verse 27 an incomplete parallelism is found:

I also shall   make him [David]   firstborn,
                          the highest of the kings of the earth.

David who was the eighth child of his parents (1 Sam 16:10–11) would be made the firstborn. What this means is expressed in the second half of the verse: David as the firstborn would be the highest of the kings. The covenant with David was finally fulfilled in the Messiah, the antitypical firstborn and the King of kings. Psalm 89:27 does not stress the issues of being born or being the first chronologically, but emphasises the special honor, greatness, and authority of the firstborn.[46]

(4) Zechariah 12:10 is a Messianic prophecy which was understood as such by John in his Gospel (John 19:37). The Messiah, who would be pierced, is compared to a firstborn.[47] The context seems to suggest that Yahweh is speaking about himself, first in the first person singular and then in the third person singular. Here the issue of being born as well as the time element are irrelevant.

---

46. W Michaelis, 'πρωτότοκος', in *Theological Dictionary of the New Testament*, volume 6, edited by G Friedrich (Grand Rapids, MI: Eerdmans, 1982), 874, suggests that in Psalm 89 adoption is implied.
47. Francis D Nichol, editor, *The Seventh-day Adventist Bible Commentary*, 7 volumes (Hagerstown, MD: Review and Herald, 2002), 4:1113, states: 'Looking upon the "pierced" Messiah . . . perceiving as never before the marvellous love of God in the gift of His Son, men would deeply mourn over their past defects of character . . . John notes that this scripture was fulfilled when one of the Roman soldiers pierced the side of Jesus (John 19:37).'

C Spicq provides a helpful description. He suggests that in the Old Testament the term *prōtotokos* is used primarily in the literal sense but admits that it is also employed figuratively.

> There are religious connotations, because the firstborn is consecrated to Yahweh; a qualitative connotation, because . . . it is the best or the most excellent . . .; an affective connotation, because it is the best-loved; an honorific connotation, since the firstborn, through the birthright, shares in the father's authority and is given much property. All of these nuances appear in figurative uses of the term . . .[48]

b. The New Testament usage

In the New Testament *prōtotokos* occurs eight times.[49] Apart from Hebrew 11:28 and 12:23 the term always refers to Jesus Christ or, stated differently, all places in which *prōtotokos* appears in the singular talk about Jesus: Jesus was the firstborn of Mary (Luke 2:7), but he is also the firstborn among many brothers (Rom 8:29), the firstborn of all creation (Col 1:15), the firstborn from/of the dead (Col 1:18; Rev 1:5), and the firstborn whom the angels worship (Heb 1:6).

As in the Old Testament the New Testament uses the term literally or figuratively.[50] Michaelis holds that Luke 2:7 'is the only instance in the New Testament where . . . *prōtotokos* refers unequivocally to the process of birth, and this in the natural sense'.[51] Spicq, however, considers all New Testament references to *prōtotokos* apart from Hebrew 11:28 as figurative pointing to 'honor, dignity, or preeminence'.[52] In Hebrew 11:28 the situation of the last of the Egyptian plagues is reiterated, while in Hebrew 12:23 the 'church of the first-born' may describe the true members of the invisible church.[53] The last text must be understood figuratively, because 'obvi-

---

48. Ceslas Spicq, *Theological Lexicon of the New Testament*, 3 volumes (Peabody, MA: Hendrickson, 1994), 210–11. Cf KH Bartels, '*prōtotokos*', in *Theologisches Begriffslexikon zum Neuen Testament 1. Abraham- Israel*, edited by Lothar Coenen, Erich Beyreuther, and Hans Bietenhard (Wuppertal: Theologischer Verlag R. Brockhaus, 1977), 280.
49. Luke 2:7; Romans 8:29; Colossians 1:15,18; Hebrews 1:6; 11:28; 12:23; Revelation 1:5.
50. Bartels, '*prōtotokos*', 281, distinguishes between *prōtotokos* 'im wörtlichen Sinn' and *prōtotokos* 'in übertragenem Sinn als Würdeprädikat Jesu'.
51. Michaelis, '*prōtotokos*', 876.
52. Cf Spicq, *Theological Lexicon*, 211–12.
53. Cf Nichol editor, *The Seventh-day Adventist Bible Commentary*, 7:487; Bartels, '*prōtotokos*', 282.

ously the church does not consist only of literally firstborn human beings. The expression "firstborn" emphasises their preeminent status among the "sons of God".[54]

c. Figurative or literal?

As established above, the term *prōtotokos* as used in the Old Testament and New Testament points in any case to the special rank and dignity of the firstborn. The term 'first-born' by itself can be understood literally, namely as the first being born to respective parents. However, since being the first or being born is not always stressed, it is not necessarily important to the understanding of this term in a certain context. In addition the issue of being created does not seem to belong to the semantic range of the term.[55] So Jesus was either born in ages past by the Father or he was coeternal with the Father and the title 'first-born' points only to his specific rank, dignity, and position. Therefore the question is: Should 'first-born' in Colossians 1:15 been understood literally or figuratively?

Among scholars there is widespread agreement that the firstborn of Colossians 1:15 should be understood figuratively. W Grudem suggests: '... Colossians 1:15 means that Christ has the privileges of authority and rule, the privileges belonging to the 'first-born,' but with respect to the whole creation'.[56] MJ Erickson states: '... the expression "first-born" does not primarily mean first in time, but first in rank or preeminent. This is indicated, for example, by the context of Colossians 1:15, for the following verse notes that Jesus was the means of origination of all created beings.'[57] W Elwell calls *prōtotokos* a 'messianic title'.[58] For the following reasons we would opt for a figurative understanding of *prōtotokos* in Colossians1:15.

(1) *The Old Testament background of prōtotokos*. We have already discussed the Old Testament usage of the term *prōtotokos*. Although Colos-

---

54. Woodrow Whidden, Jerry Moon, and John W Reeve, *The Trinity: Understanding God's Love, His Plan of Salvation, and Christian Relationships* (Hagerstown, MD: Review and Herald, 2002), 99.
55. Cf *ibid*, 98.
56. Wayne Grudem, *Systematic Theology: An Introduction to Biblical Doctrine* (Grand Rapids, MI: Zondervan, 1994), 243–244.
57. Erickson, *Christian Theology*, 714. Pokorný, *Der Brief*, 63, holds: 'Sein Vorrang als des Erstgeborenen besteht nicht nur in seiner zeitlichen Priorität. Der Erstgeborene ist hier ein Ehrenprädikat (vgl Hebr 1,6), das vor allem die Rechte des Erstgeborenen ausdrückt (vgl Gen 27, bes V 29).'
58. Walter A Elwell editor, *Evangelical Dictionary of Theology* (Grand Rapids, MI: Baker, 1984), 416.

sians 1:15 is not a quotation from the Old Testament, most likely it is an echo of Psalm 89:27. Not only is the term *prōtotokos* used in both cases, also the idea of superiority and being the most exalted ruler is found in Psalm 89:27 and Colossians 1:15–20. While according to the context of Psalm 89:27 David calls God 'my Father' (Ps 89:26), who has anointed him (Ps 89:20), and while God is portrayed as 'the rock of salvation' (Ps 89:26), Colossians 1:2 talks about 'God, the Father of our Lord Jesus Christ', and Colossians 1:12–13 states that the Father has 'rescued us'. Thus this theme is picked up in Colossians 1. A parallel text in the New Testament is Revelation 1:5 in which Jesus is described as 'the first-born of the dead, and the ruler of the kings of the earth'. It is generally acknowledged that in this case we have an allusion to Psalm 89:27.[59] Psalm 89:27 indicates that the time element related to the firstborn as well as the issue of being born is not relevant. What matters is the parallelism of Psalm 89:27 which equates the act of being made firstborn with the positioning of the Davidic ruler as the most exalted king. This applies also to Colossians 1:15. C Talbert states: 'The term *prōtotokos* (firstborn) can be used to convey priority in times or priority in status (cf Ps 89.27, where it expresses the unique status of the king). The latter fits this context.'[60] P O'Brien, notes: 'The title "first-born", used of Christ here and in verse 18, echoes the wording of Psalm 89:27, where God says of the Davidic king: "I also will make him my firstborn, the highest of the kings of the earth." But as many have noted this title belongs to Jesus Christ not only as the Messiah of David's line, but also as the Wisdom of God . . .'[61] NT Wright goes even further and talks about Psalm 89:27 as referring 'to the coming Davidic Messiah' which may be debatable.[62] In any case, following the Old Testament lead 'first-born' should be understood in terms of priority and not of birth.

(2) *The use of prōtotokos in the New Testament.* It has been stated above that most of the New Testament references to 'first-born' must be understood figuratively. Luke 2:7 is the only text referring to Jesus where a literal

---

59. Cf Nestle-Aland, *Novum Testamentum Graece*, twenty-seventh edition (Stuttgart: Deutsche Bibelgesellschaft, 1995), 632.
60. Talbert, *Ephesians and Colossians*, 187. Thompson, *Colossians and Philemon*, 32, mentions Psalm 89 stating that 'the designation of *firstborn* has as much to do with priority, status, and rank as it does with birth order, and that is the sense here, where Christ's supremacy as *firstborn* connotes his sovereignty over all powers and authorities.'
61. O'Brien, *Colossians and Philemon*, 44. Bruce, *The Epistles*, 59, comes to the same conclusion.
62. Wright, *Colossians and Philemon*, 71.

understanding may be implied. Mary gave birth to her firstborn son. This would not militate against a figurative understanding of 'first-born' in the other places, because in Luke 2:7 the context is—contrary to the other texts—Jesus' actual birth by Mary. But even this is discussed. It is held that Luke lets Mary call Jesus 'first-born' in order to point to his Messianic role.[63]

(3) *The use of prōtotokos in Colossians.* Probably the most crucial question is, How is the term 'first-born' understood in the Letter to the Colossians itself? The term occurs twice in this epistle, namely in Colossians 1:16 and 1:18. This is the same immediate context. As shown above *prōtotokos* appears in the corresponding places of a chiasm which means that both occurrences are parallel. 'The first-born of all creation' is 'the first-born from the dead'.[64] When it comes to the second usage, it is obvious that a reference to birth is not intended. Jesus was raised from the dead but not born from the dead. The issue is not birth but supremacy. The first-born of the dead may remind of the resurrection order as described in 1 Corinthians 15:20–24. Jesus' resurrection as the 'first fruits' allows for the general future resurrection.[65] On the other hand, Jesus as the firstborn may also remind us that all resurrections whether past–those in the Old Testament and those during Jesus life on earth[66]—present or future were and are dependent on Jesus and his resurrection.

(4) *The image of God.* Jesus as the image of God is the visible representation of the invisible God. Since the term supports Christ's divinity and is used together with *prōtotokos*, it shapes the meaning of 'first-born'. The firstborn in Colossians 1:15 must be part of the deity. Colossians 3:10 talks about the Christian's new self being renewed in the image of his or her creator. A Patzia notes: 'This new self is God's doing! . . . In the light of Paul's christological teaching in the epistle, one may have expected him to refer to a renewal in Christ's image . . .'[67] NT Wright states: 'At last, in Christ,

---

63. Spicq, *Theological Lexicon*, 211, writes: 'All of these nuances appear in figurative uses of the term . . . and Luke probably had them in mind when he wrote concerning Mary, "She gave birth to her firstborn" . . . He chose this word because of these connotations, and perhaps also to signal that this Davidic firstborn might be a claimant to messiaship.'
64. Cf O'Collins, *Christology*, 35. In addition, as mentioned above, another element is added to each of the two occurrences: 'The image of God'—"the first-born of creation", "the beginning"—"the firstborn from the dead." The two double titles correspond with each other.
65. Cf Pokorný, *Der Brief*, 70; Bruce, *The Epistles*, 71; O'Brien, *Colossians*, 51.
66. Cf Whidden, *The Trinity*, 99.
67. Patzia, *Ephesians*, 76. Cf Dunn, *The Epistles*, 222.

human beings can be what God intended them to be. This passage looks back to 1:15–20; the intention of creation is fulfilled in redemption, and, conversely, redemption is understood as new creation.'[68] Jesus as divine creator and redeemer is the image of God. According to his image humans who are committing their lives to him are shaped.

(5) *The creator of all things.* Jesus as creator has created all things (Col 1:16). The term 'all' is stressed throughout the christological hymn in Col 1:15-20 and occurs eight times, three of the eight occurrences being connected to creation: Verse 16 begins and ends with the statement that all things were created by him and through him.[69] The list of created realities in verse 16 is all inclusive and presents a cosmic picture: heaven and earth, the visible and the invisible, and all the rulers and authorities. This leaves no room for Jesus to be a created being.[70] Since all things are created by him, he cannot be created, or he must have created himself. But the latter option does not work, because it would require a conscious part of him to exist prior to his self-creation, which in turn would not be a real creation. 'He [Jesus Christ] is not simply part of the created world itself.'[71] 'He [the Son] is not a creature, not even the first creature; he is creator. That places him on God's side of the line ontologically: creator not created.'[72] On the other hand, since Jesus has created all powers and authorities, he surpasses them as the firstborn of all creation. 'No power structures are . . . independent of Christ . . .'[73] Elsewhere in the New Testament the creator is also clearly portrayed as being God (John 1:1–3).

(6) *The sustainer.* The centre of the hymn depicts Jesus as the sustainer of 'all things' (Col1:17). The term *ta panta* used twice in connection with

---

68. Wright, *Colossians and Philemon*, 138–139.
69. Pokorný, *Der Brief*, 64, talks about a chiastic structure of verse 16. O'Brien, *Colossians*, 45, points out that 'in the first clause the aorist tense is employed to draw attention to the historical act, while the second reference uses the perfect to focus on creation's continuing existence', Cf Wright, *Colossians and Philemon*, 73.
70. Cf Bruce, *The Epistles*, 59.
71. Wright, *Colossians and Philemon*, 71.
72. Talbert, *Ephesians and Colossians*, 193. Fee, *Pauline Christology*, 504, writes: 'So intent is Paul in placing Christ as supreme, and thus above "the powers," that he elaborates the Son's role in creation in two ways: first, by using two of the three prepositions that in Rom 11:36 he had used of God the Father . . .; and second, by twice using the all-embracing ἐν αὐτῷ (*in him*) regarding the Son's role both in creation itself and in its currently being sustained. Christ the Son is thus both the Creator and the sphere in which all created things have their existence.' Cf, Thompson, *Colossians and Philemon*, 31.
73. Wright, *Colossians and Philemon*, 73.

Christ's creation activity links the previous verse to verse 17. The term 'all things' that were created by Jesus are now sustained by him who was before all things and who is the head of his church. The verb 'to hold together' is used in the perfect tense underlining Jesus' continuous sustaining activity of all things. 'Apart from his *continuous* sustaining activity . . . all would disintegrate.'[74] 'No creature is autonomous.'[75] Being the sustainer again places Jesus on the divine side.

(7) *The beginning*. Jesus is the beginning (Col 1:18). *Archē* can mean 'beginning' (Luke 1:2), 'beginner'/'origin'/'first cause' (Rev 21:6), 'ruler'/'authority' (Luke 12:11), 'rule' (1 Cor 15:24), 'domain'/'realm' (Jude 1:6), 'principle' (Heb 5:12), and 'corner' (Acts 10:11). In order to determine the right meaning the context must be consulted. The most important shades of meaning are 'beginning' and 'ruler'. The term occurs four times in Colossians. According to Colossians 1:16 Jesus has created all rulers (*archai*). According to Colossians 1:18, he is the beginning (*archē*.), the ruler that has supremacy over all other rulers. Therefore, the term points to Christ's primacy and sheds light on *prōtotokos* found in the immediate context.[76] This is confirmed by the other two texts dealing with *archē*. in this letter. According to Colossians 2:10 Jesus 'is the head over all rule (*archēs*) and authority'. Colossians 2:15 teaches 'that God has, in Christ, "stripped" the rulers (*archas*) and authorities and held them up to contempt.'[77] Consequently, Jesus is the supreme ruler. According to Revelations 21:6; 22:13 both, God the Father and Jesus, are the beginning (*archē*) and the end.

(8) *The one who has first place in everything*. The second part of Colossians 1:18 is interesting, because it explains by the somewhat related term *prōteuō* how *prōtotokos* should be understood.[78] The firstborn is the one who 'will come to have first place in everything'. That means he will have supremacy. Again the term 'all' occurs. Jesus who has created all things and sustains all things will have supremacy in all things. NT Wright suggests that 'this part of the poem refers particularly to Christ's rule over the final great enemies of humankind, sin and death . . . That which he has by right he became in fact'.[79] In a similar way the idea of headship should

---

74. O'Brien, *Colossians, Phileomon*, 47.
75. Wright, *Colossians and Philemon*, 73.
76. Cf O'Brien, *Colossians, Philemon*, 50.
77. Wright, *Colossians and Philemon*, 115.
78. O'Brien, *Colossians, Philemon*, 51, notes: 'The words "be the first" (*prōteuō*) resume the double reference to "first-born" (*prōtotokos*, vv 15 and 18), as well as the phrase "he is before all things . . ."'
79. Wright, *Colossians and Philemon*, 74, 75.

be understood. The term *kephalē* occurs in Colossians 1:18; 2:10, 19. The concept that Jesus is the head of the body, the church (Col 1:18; 2:19) is widened in Colossians 2:10. Jesus is the head over all rule and authority. He is also seated at God's right hand (Col 3:1).

(9) *All the fullness.* Colossians 1:19 ascribes fullness to Jesus Christ. 'For it was the Father's good pleasure for all the fullness to dwell in Him.' What that means is further developed in Colossians 2:9: 'For in him [Jesus] all the fullness of Deity dwells in bodily form.' '... the word translated "Godhead" is the Greek *theotēs*, which literally means the very essence of divinity ... And this very essence of divine nature dwells "bodily" in the incarnate Christ, the "first-born"!'[80] NT Wright commenting on Colossians 1:19 states: 'The full divinity of the man Jesus is stated without any implication that there are two Gods. It is the one God, in all his fullness, who dwells in him.'[81]

(10) *The reconciler.* Reconciliation of all things through Jesus and to Jesus is stressed in Colossians 1:20 and applied to the Colossian Christians in verse 22. Ephesians 2:16 employs the same term *apokatalassō* to describe the reconciliation brought about by Jesus which unites Gentiles and Jews that believe in Jesus in 'one body'. In Romans 5:10 and 2 Corinthians 5:18–20 the same term, however without prefix *ana*, *katalassō*, describes the reconciliation of humanity with God. The Father's saving activity mentioned in Colossians 1:13 and the Son's saving activity, although described with different terms, refer to the same reality. The *ta panta* and the sphere of reconciliation encompassing *epi tēs gēs* and *en tois ouranois* reflect precisely creation in verse 16.[82] The same phrases occur in verses 15 and 20 with the exception that heaven and earth are reversed. Jesus the Creator God is Jesus the Saviour God. 'The Colossian vision sets forth the incarnate Son in whom the fullness of God dwells bodily, who effects a universal reconciliation, and who exercises a universal reign . . .'[83]

---

80. Whidden, *The Trinity*, 100.
81. Wright, *Colossians and Philemon*, 75–6. Cf Fee, *Pauline Christology*, 308–9; Patzia, *Ephesians*, 32.
82. Patzia, *Ephesians*, 33, notes: 'In other words. It is not just the church (humanity) that has been reconciled; the reconciliation wrought by Christ extends to the entire cosmic order ... every part of the universe is included in the reconciling work of Christ.' Talbert, *Ephesians and Colossians*, 196, asks the question, if reconciliation means 'ultimate reconciliation of all people and all hostile powers as well'. He answers this question by saying: 'All things may be reconciled, but in Pauline thought the powers are reconciled through subjugation (1 Cor 15:24–28; Phil 3:21; Col 2:15).'
83. Talbert, *Ephesians and Colossians*, 197.

Conclusion

Paul counters the Colossian heresy with an exalted Christology. Jesus surpasses all powers and rulers, philosophies and esoteric ideas, even the angels, because he himself is God. As the firstborn he is neither created nor is he born, but his supremacy is affirmed. '. . . those spiritual powers which received such prominence in that heresy must have been created by him'. They 'owe their very existence to the Christians' Saviour', writes FF Bruce.[84] And MM Thompson adds:

> First, he [Paul] dispels the notion that there is viable access to God through other cult figures, deities, spirits, or angels, whoever and whatever they are; indeed, Christ is supreme over all of them because all were created through him. . . Second, by stressing Christ's supremacy over all visible and invisible powers, Paul reiterates the sufficiency of God's revelation and redemption in Christ . . . the cross, not the powers, determine the shape of Christian existence.[85]

---

84. Bruce, *The Epistles*, 63.
85. Thompson, *Colossians and Philemon*, 35.

PART 2
Historical and Theological Studies

Trinity: Toward a (Somewhat) Postmodern Perspective
Ray CW Roennfeldt

Introduction

During the latter part of the twentieth century Christian theologians have shown great interest in the doctrine of the Trinity and that interest continues to intensify. Previously, many theologians and pastors saw the doctrine as having 'no apparent pastoral value' and as something that church people 'wouldn't properly understand anyway'.[1] Immanuel Kant had stated (almost triumphantly) that 'The doctrine of the Trinity, taken literally, has no practical relevance at all, even if we think we understand it; and it is even more clearly irrelevant if we realise that it transcends all our concepts'.[2] Karl Rahner lamented that 'Despite their orthodox confession of the Trinity, Christians are, in their practical life, almost mere "monotheists"'.[3] It has now, however, become almost impossible to keep abreast of the major works and articles that are flowing from all quarters of Christian theology—mainline and evangelical Protestant, Roman Catholic, and Eastern Orthodox—on the subject.[4]

---

1. Joseph A Bracken, *What are They Saying about the Trinity?* (New York: Paulist Press, 1979), 3.
2. Immanuel Kant, *The Conflict of the Faculties*, translated by Mary J Gregor (New York: Abaris Books, 1979), 65.
3. Karl Rahner, *The Trinity*, translated by Joseph Donceel (New York: Herder and Herder, 1970), 10.
4. To name just a few of the most important works is to risk accusations of bias or incompleteness.. Nevertheless, the following books appear to be some of the most important: Leonardo Boff, *Trinity and Society*, translated by Paul Burns (Maryknoll, NY: Orbis, 1988); David S Cunningham, *These Three are One: The Practice of Trinitarian* Theology (Oxford: Blackwell, 1998); Brian Edgar, *The Message of the Trinity: Life in God* (Leicester, UK: Inter Varsity Press, 2004); Colin Gunton, *The Promise of Trinitarian Theology*, second edition (Edinburgh: T&T Clark, 1997); Colin Gunton, *The One, the Three and the Many: God, Creation and the Culture of Modernity* (Cambridge: Cambridge University Press, 1993); Catherine Mowry LaCugna, *God for Us: The Trinity and Christian*

The change in the last thirty years or so has been so marked that the doctrine of the Trinity has once again 'captured the attention of theologians more than any other doctrine'. The Trinity dogma which caused theological storms in the fourth and fifth centuries is again on the agenda. And, it is no longer thought of as 'obtuse, secondary and impractical'. Instead, it is being spoken of as 'foundational to the Christian faith because it articulates what is most distinctive in the biblical revelation of God—he is triune'.[5]

Why the increased and increasing interest in the subject? Very likely a number of factors have combined to produce the change: the demise of modernity's optimism in regard to the possibility of obtaining absolute truth in favour of postmodernism's more pragmatic approach to truth; the rise of Pentecostalism with its emphasis on the work of the Holy Spirit; and the increasing knowledge of and interest in Eastern Orthodox theology. Whatever the reasons, we now have the opportunity, as Millard Erickson suggests, to 'enunciate the doctrine in a way that will be ... appropriate for our age'.[6] This chapter attempts to contribute in a small way to an age-appropriate definition or re-definition of the Trinity.[7]

Life (San Francisco, CA: Harper/Collins, 1991); Jürgen Moltmann, *The Trinity and the Kingdom: The Doctrine of God*, translated by Margaret Kohl (New York: Harper and Row, 1981); Roger E Olson and Christopher A Hall, *The Trinity* (Grand Rapids, MI: Eerdmans, 2002); Ted Peters, *GOD as Trinity: Relationality and Temporality in Divine Life* (Louisville, KY: Westminster/John Knox, 1993); Karl Rahner, *The Trinity*, translated by Joseph Donceel (New York: Herder and Herder, 1970); Christoph Schwöbel, editor, *Trinitarian Theology Today: Essays on Divine Being and Act* (Edinburgh: T&T Clark, 1995); Thomas F Torrance, *The Christian Doctrine of God, One Being Three Persons* (Edinburgh: T&T Clark, 1995); and John D Zizioulas, *Being as Communion: Studies in Personhood and the Church* (Crestwood, NY: St. Vladimir's Seminary Press, 1985).

5. Kevin Giles, 'The Doctrine of the Trinity and Subordinationism', in *Evangelical Review of Theology* 28 (2004): 270.
6. Millard J Erickson, *Christian Theology*, second edition (Grand Rapids, MI: Baker, 1985), 348.
7. A further motivation for me is the fact that the doctrine of the Trinity has always been on the 'backburner' of theological reflection in my own community. First, it appears certain that the majority of the pioneers of the Seventh-day Adventist movement were non-trinitarians. Second, while the Adventist Church has grown away from this perspective, there have (in recent times) been some quite strident, laity-led calls for Adventist Christians to return to their non-trinitarian, Arian, or semi-Arian roots. Third, it seems to me that while Adventist theologians have not entirely ignored the doctrine of the Trinity, it has not had the attention which has been expended on soteriology and eschatology. Fernando Canale makes this final point in his 'Doctrine of God', in the *Handbook of Seventh-day Adventist Theology*, edited by Raoul Dederen (Hagerstown,

In the past, the doctrine of the Trinity has often been addressed from the perspective of answering questions such as 'What does the Bible teach in regard to the Father, Son, and Holy Spirit?' Now, the focus is instead on questions such as 'What specific impact does the doctrine of the Trinity have on the Christian life?'[8] And, 'What benefits might accrue for other areas of Christian theological reflection from an increased emphasis on trinitarianism?'[9]

The approach taken here includes an overview of the postmodern approach which asks for pragmatic truth, a discussion of the systematic connections between the doctrine of the Trinity and other theological themes, and an examination of the doctrine's potential impact on the Christian life.

The Postmodern Challenge

I had originally titled this chapter 'The Trinity: So What?' I was certainly not wishing to be trivial, arrogant, or irreverent. Rather, my intention was to highlight the fact that discussion of the doctrine of the Trinity has for centuries focussed on what is true for the inner being of God without asking how this impacts on the lives of Christians other than those who are philosophical theologians.[10] In other words, trinitarian theology has generally placed its emphasis on the 'immanent Trinity' (God's inner triune being) rather than the 'economic Trinity' (God's revelation of his activities in the plan of salvation as Father, Son, and Holy Spirit).[11]

MD: Review and Herald, 2000), 150.

8. See, for instance Edgar's *The Message of the Trinity*. Note that although Edgar deals with the Trinity in the Old Testament, in the life and teaching of Jesus, and in the experience and teaching of the early church, his emphasis is on the doctrine's practicality for Christian living and community (see especially 22-23).
9. The possible nexus between the Trinity and other doctrines is illustrated in recent UK-based research which indicates that Adventist theological students displayed 'the greatest preference for the modalist model' as compared with evangelical and Pentecostal students. Mark J Cartledge, the researcher comments that 'this may have implications for other aspects of Adventist theology'. See Cartledge, 'Empirical-Theological Models of the Trinity: Exploring the Beliefs of Theology Students in the United Kingdom', in *Journal of Empirical Theology* 19 (2006): 157 (also 152).
10. Probably this direction was set in the early and middle church periods with the contributions of Origen, Tertullian, Athanasius, Augustine, and Aquinas (to name just a few). For a convenient summary see Olson and Hall, *The Trinity*, 15-66.
11. A full discussion of these terms is available in Rahner, *The Trinity*, and in Veli-Matti Kärkkäinen, *The Doctrine of God: A Global Introduction* (Grand Rapids, MI: Baker

Contemporary society is no longer satisfied with truth as information. For the doctrine of the Trinity this means that unless there is a strong practical connection between the 'oneness' and 'threeness' of the inner life of God and everyday life, it is not something that is relevant even if the inner life of God could be known by humankind.[12] Rather, if there is actually such a thing as 'truth' it is seen in terms of its functionality. That is, does it work in real life? While this approach has its weaknesses and may give way to other perspectives, it is helpful for theologians and pastors to listen carefully to the 'so what?' questions posed by Generation X-ers and Ys, Baby-boomers and -busters, and some older people as well.

In this connection it is important to notice the biblical approach to theologising. Scripture actually appears to show less than primary interest in theology *per se* or in theology as information.[13] Instead, the focus is on rather more practical matters. For instance, while some might think that the point of the details of last day events is to inform the believer in regard to what will happen and when, it seems that the biblical writers were operating with a decidedly practical mindset. In 1 Thessalonians 4:13–18 Paul provides a simple chronology of events surrounding the second advent of Jesus Christ. Notice the 'time' indicators: those who are alive and remain will not *precede* those who have fallen asleep; and *after that* (that is, the Lord's coming down from heaven) both living and dead will be caught up together to meet the Lord in the air.[14] Yet, Paul is clearly focussed on the practical rather than the theoretical. He says, 'Brothers [and sisters], we do

---

Academic, 2004), 144–45. Kevin J Vanhoozer extends the debate in his *Remythologising Christianity: Divine Action, Passion, and Authorship* (Cambridge: Cambridge University Press, 2010), 243–51.

12. Many theologians and philosophers suspect that the inner life of God cannot be known, unless God has specifically revealed such to humans. Scripture seems to support the idea that God is only known via his revelation of himself through his interactions with humans. For a brief Christian introduction to postmodern epistemology see Stanley J Grenz, *A Primer on Postmodernism* (Grand Rapids, MI: Eerdmans, 1996), 165–67. For Grenz's discussion of the postmodern turn to pragmatic 'truth', see 151–58. A range of Christian perspectives on postmodernism is to be found in *Christianity and the Postmodern Turn: Six Views*, edited by Myron B Penner (Grand Rapids, MI: Brazos, 2005).

13. This conclusion is borne out by the fact that theologising has long been recognised as a 'secondary' task. See, for example, Millard Erickson's discussion of the 'process of doing theology' in his *Christian Theology*, 70–83; also Fritz Guy, *Thinking Theologically: Adventist Christianity and the Interpretation of Faith* (Berrien Springs, MI: Andrews University, 1999), 3–23.

14. Notice also 1 Thessalonians 5:1.

not want you to be ignorant about those who fall asleep, or to grieve like the rest of men, who have no hope' and 'Therefore encourage each other with these words' (1 Thess 4:13 and 18).

Jesus' approach to the Sabbath may also illustrate the same point. While there are certainly many connections with Sabbath themes from the Old Testament, his whole approach—especially in regard to his seven Sabbath miracles and his associated sayings—could be summed up in the practical concept that 'The Sabbath was made for [the benefit of] man, not man for the Sabbath. So the Son of Man is Lord even of the Sabbath' (Mark 2:27–28).

Now to come closer to our topic: the doctrine of the Trinity. Paul's discussion of what might be construed as a deep theological reflection on Jesus Christ's incarnation with strong trinitarian themes in Philippians chapter two is really a hymn to Christ in the context of Paul's appeal to the Philippian believers to put aside 'selfish ambition or vain conceit' for an 'attitude . . . the same as that of Christ Jesus: Who, being in very nature God, did not consider equality with God something to be grasped' (Phil 2:4–6). To put it in the postmodern idiom, Paul appears to be very intent on answering vital 'so what?' questions, rather than merely emphasising a theory of the 'kenosis'.[15]

So, where does this leave us in regard to the doctrine of the Trinity? Is the Trinity dogma primarily about the inner life of the Godhead, or does it say something that believers cannot live without? We will attempt to answer this question from two separate directions: (a) the connections between the doctrine of the Trinity and some other major theological motifs, and (b) the connections between the doctrine and Christian life and community.

The Doctrine of the Trinity within a Theological System

To approach the doctrine of the Trinity from within a theological system is (it seems to me) particularly appropriate. Millard Erickson claims that 'Formulating a position on the Trinity is a genuine exercise in *systematic* theology'. Because 'the Trinity is not explicitly taught in Scripture' we must 'put together complementary themes, draw inferences from biblical

---

15. Paul's overall approach in many of his Epistles is illustrative of the movement between 'theory' and practicality. For instance, Romans 1–11 deals with soteriology while Romans 12–16 deals with living as saved people. The Epistle to the Galatians appears to follow the same format.

teachings, and decide on a particular type of conceptual vehicle to express our understanding'.[16] All of those processes are involved in constructing a systematic theology.

Many systematics texts approach the doctrine of the Trinity through an examination of the biblical data (the oneness and threeness of God), historical constructions, orthodox formulations, and the search for anthropomorphic analogies.[17] Here, important as it is, I want to take that aspect of the process as given and ask how the doctrine of the Trinity stands as the basis of and is interlinked with what is usually considered the primary biblical and Christian idea—salvation. Ted Peters hints at this when he says of the Trinity that 'It reports the gospel. It echoes the offer of grace. It invites us into the divine life of love.'[18] So, how (for instance) are trinitarian perspectives implicit in soteriology, the key teaching of Christianity? Does a non-trinitarian view corrode the doctrine of salvation by grace through faith in Jesus Christ?

What Comes First; Soteriology or Christology?

For the early Arians, it appears that their doctrine of salvation produced their Christology. At least, this is the thesis of Robert C Gregg and Dennis E Groh.[19] These authors argue that 'early Arianism is most intelligible when viewed as a scheme of salvation. Soteriological concerns dominate the [ancient] texts and inform every major aspect of the controversy'.[20] For the Arians 'Christ was a 'creature' or the 'work' of God the Creator who had been promoted to the rank of divine son and redeemer . . .'[21] Why did they take this line? Or, as Gregg and Groh succinctly put it: 'What gains were secured by the advocacy of *this* Christology?' The answer for the Arians was that 'what is predicated of the redeemer must be predicated of the redeemed'. 'Christ gains and holds his son-ship in the same way as other creatures' and that is by 'adoption'.[22] As Jesus was adopted as a Son by the

---

16. Erickson, *Christian Theology*, 347–48 (emphasis, Erickson).
17. See, for instance, *ibid*, 348–57.
18. Peters, *GOD as Trinity*, 26.
19. Robert C Gregg and Dennis E Groh, *Early Arianism: A View of Salvation* (Philadelphia, PA: Fortress, 1981).
20. *Ibid*, x.
21. *Ibid*, 1. Gregg and Groh cite Alexamder of Alexandria and Athanasius in the regard (see fn 8, 30).
22. *Ibid*, 50–51.

Father because of his obedience, so believers too are adopted as sons of God. Gregg and Groh sum up the Arian campaign to equate humans with the Son in the following: 'Christ's limitations, they declared, are exactly ours (willing, choosing, striving, suffering); and likewise Christ's benefits and glories are exactly ours. The Arians proclaim no demotion of the Son but a promotion of believers to the full and equal status as sons . . .'[23]

In Arianism, then, we have a clear illustration of soteriology and anti-trinitatian Christology inextricably intertwined.

What might a more orthodox soteriology and Christology look like? Matthew's Gospel almost immediately puts the two ideas together. In the angel's declaration to Joseph, he is told that Mary would 'give birth to a son, and you are to give him the name Jesus, because he will save his people from their sins' (Matt 1:21). This is followed immediately with Matthew's observation that 'All this took place to fulfil what the Lord had said through the prophet: "The virgin will be with child and will give birth to a son, and they will call him Immanuel"—which means, "God with us"'.[24]

John's Gospel begins with an affirmation regarding who Jesus was—he is the Word who is God (John 1:1)—but one cannot proceed too far into the Gospel without noticing matters distinctly soteriological: 'to all who received him, to those who believed in his name, he gave the right to become the children of God' (John 1:12); 'No one has ever seen God, but God the One and Only, who is at the Father's side, has made him known' (verse 18); 'Look, the Lamb of God, who takes away the sin of the world' (verse 29); 'For God so loved the world that he gave his one and only Son, that whoever believes in him shall not perish but have eternal life' (John 3:16); and 'I am the way and the truth and the life. No one comes to the Father except through me. If you really knew me, you would know my Father as well. From now on, you do know him and have seen him' (John 14:6–7). Such affirmations indicate that the earliest Christians encountered God so personally in Jesus Christ that 'the only way they could adequately express their experience was to speak of Jesus as the personal presence of God himself'.[25] Paul seems to sum up this perspective in his

---

23. *Ibid*, 70. The dustcover of Gregg and Groh's work puts it this way: 'The heart of early Arian theology rests not in the doctrine of God but in a scheme of salvation in which the redeemer brought and modeled the salvation into which all creatures were to grow. The Christology, soteriology, and cosmology of Arius and his circle grew out of their conviction that what scripture said about the redeemer had to be predicated also of the redeemed.'
24. Matthew 1:23; cf Isaiah 7:14, 8:8–10.
25. Richard Rice, *The Reign of God: An Introduction to Christian Theology from a Seventh-*

affirmation that 'God was reconciling the world to himself in Christ, not counting men's sins against them' (2 Cor 5:19).

Jesus stated his mission in terms of an inauguration of the 'kingdom of God' (Mark 1:14–15; Matt 5 – 7), his miracles are the signs of the kingdom, Jesus is both the representative and agent of that kingdom, and it is in his death and resurrection that God is active for the salvation of humankind. In fact, it is in the cross (paradoxically) where God comes closest to us and it is there that Christians find the central foundation of our knowledge of the Trinity.[26]

Just like Arian Christology, orthodox Christology also arises out of soteriology. However, while it includes the metaphor of adoption in its telling of the story of salvation,[27] this is not the only model or even the dominant one. Rather, a wide variety of metaphors are used including salvation, redemption, justification, reconciliation, and forgiveness. The focus of these terms in not on the Christian believer being adopted or becoming 'sons of God' through the process of obeying as a son would obey his father, but something that is far more radical—a gift! For instance, the Epistle to the Hebrews indicates that Jesus was made like his brothers in every way so 'that he might become an atonement for the sins of the people' (Heb 1:17–18); and that 'Although he was a son, he learned obedience from what he suffered' and 'became the source of eternal salvation' (Heb 4:8–9.). While living for God like Jesus did is an outgrowth of a relationship with, it is not the root of salvation. Instead it is based in a gift.[28]

However, trinitarians who affirm the co-equality of Father, Son, and Holy Spirit, do not have everything their own way. There are some texts of Scripture that do suggest that the Son is subordinate to the Father. Such passages include Jesus' confessions that 'the Father is greater than I' (John 14:28); and 'My food ... is to do the will of him who sent me' (John 4:34). Paul's comments that 'the head of every man is Christ, and the head of the woman is man, and the head of Christ is God' (1 Cor 11:3) and 'When he has done this, then the Son himself will be made subject to him, so that God may be all in all' (1 Cor 15:28) have to be included in the difficult category. Kevin Giles offers the suggestion that Jesus is speaking as the

---

day *Adventist Perspective*, second edition (Berrien Springs, MI: Andrews University Press, 1997), 166.
26. Jürgen Moltmann, *The Trinity and the Kingdom*, translated by Margaret Kohl (Minneapolis, MN: Fortress, 1993), 160.
27. See Ephesians 1:5 and 2:12.
28. The same formula is found in Ephesians 2:8–10.

incarnate Son and that 'the one sent has the same authority as the one who sends'.[29] In regard to 1 Corinthians 11:3, Giles argues that headship does not necessarily equate to a relationship of subordination/authority in that Paul goes on to offer rules for both men and women who lead in prayer and prophecy.[30] Of course, 1 Corinthians 15:28 is the most difficult and Giles suggests that 'What Paul . . . seems to be suggesting is that the rule that God the Father gave to God the Son at the resurrection is freely handed back to the Father by the Son at the end'.[31]

At very least we have to conclude that our beliefs impact on our capacity for relationships. Deficiencies in soteriology will more than likely lead to a faulty Christology which will in turn more than likely lead to weaknesses in relationship with Christ and his body. This conclusion has been borne out in some of the most recent and creative work done on the doctrine of the Trinity. Giles puts it this way: 'Because virtually all theologians agree that the doctrine of the Trinity should inform human relationships correctly, enunciating the historically developed doctrine of the Trinity is of great practical consequence.'[32] It is to this aspect that we now turn.

The Trinity and Social Relationships

An increasing emphasis on a social concept of the Trinity is due, at least in part, to the contemporary tendency to do theology from below. While this approach has resulted in the erosion of divine transcendence in nineteenth and twentieth century theological liberalism, it is important to consider that God is both transcendent and immanent.[33] Keeping both these aspects of God's nature and interaction with humans in balance is necessary in order to avoid the twin dangers of turning God into merely a philosophical construct or making God so 'human' that he is no longer worthy of worship.

The doctrine of the Trinity is a reminder that God is beyond our comprehension and is worthy of worship. Our worship of God is not only

---

29. Kevin Giles, 'The Doctrine of the Trinity and Subordination', 283.
30. *Ibid*, 283–84.
31. *Ibid*, 284.
32. *Ibid*, 283. Giles' views are developed more completely in his *Jesus and the Father: Modern Evangelicals Reinvent the Doctrine of the Trinity* (Grand Rapids, MI: Zondervan, 2006).
33. An excellent discussion of the interplay between divine transcendence and immanence from an historical perspective is Stanley J Grenz and Roger E Olson, *20th Century Theology: God and the World in a Transitional Age* (Downers Grove, IL: IVP, 1992).

based in what he has done,[34] but also in who he is in himself. The Trinity tells us that there is an otherness about God that should result in a rejection of human arrogance and a certain modesty or carefulness when speaking about God.

The idea of the divine mystery of the Trinity has enormous implications for individual and corporate Christian life. Worship—the most characteristic activity of Christians—is only possible when God is mysteriously beyond us. To worship what is completely accessible to human rationality is to create an idol 'god' in our own image. Yet, paradoxically, while remaining a mystery, through the Holy Spirit God is personally present with us. The consequence of this divine distance and closeness is to make every act of the Christian life an act of worship. Paul concludes his discussion of idol feasts, the Lord's supper, and Christian freedom with the instruction: 'So whether you eat or drink or whatever you do, do it all for the glory of God' (1 Cor 10:31).[35]

The social conception of the Trinity is also important in delineating the nature of the Christian community: the church. There can be no doubt that the church is a trinitarian community. The three most significant biblical models of the church mean that the church is at one and the same time 'the people of God', the 'body of Christ', and 'the temple of the Holy Spirit'. Each of these models emphasises something unique about the church. It is especially chosen by God, it remains the focus of Christ's present activity as its members are united in him, and it is empowered and unified by the Holy Spirit.[36] The implications for the church community are sharpened considerably when the social interactions of the Trinity are seen as a pattern for human relationships.

Jesus certainly hinted at this when he prayed that all believers would be brought to 'complete unity' as he and the Father are one (John 17:22–23). However, some of the social trinitarians have argued that the church has not taken the kind of unity exhibited in the Trinity to its full conclusions. Catherine LaCugna, for instance, maintains that support for any kind of subordinationism—including that implicit in patriarchalism and heirarchicalism—is eliminated by a trinitarian approach ecclesiology and the-

---

34. For example, Revelation 14:6–7.
35. See also 1 Corinthians 6:18–20.
36. The classic work on models of the church remains Avery Dulles, *Models of the Church*, expanded edition (New York: Doubleday: Image Books, 2002). A brief summary of the significance of the three most significant biblical models is available in Erickson, *Christian Theology*, 1044-51.

ology proper.³⁷ The flow-on effect of this view may be immense for the Christian community. It means that both unity and diversity are valued; it means that Christian ministry may return to its service-oriented roots rather than placing greater value on certain types of ministry over other roles; and it implies that God does not favour one gender over another in either salvation or in ministry.

Social trinitarianism has also stimulated a variety of reflections in various areas of church and social life. Neil Pembroke argues that the recent turn towards the pragmatic in Trinity studies has implications for pastoral care relationships. He remarks that 'just as the divine communion exists in and through polyphony [a multiplicity of voices or sounds], so too pastoral relationships require the capacity to sound polyphonic notes'. Pembroke's conclusion is that 'in the pastoral ministry we need the virtuosity to hold together toughness and tenderness, woundedness and health, wisdom and folly, and nearness and distance'.³⁸ And, Robert Vosloo, writing out of the South African context, finds the most recent reflections on the Trinity helpful in the construction of a 'Christian ethic of hospitality' which 'serves as a challenge against the isolation from the other and otherness, as well as the loss of particularity through our openness'. For Vosloo, such a conception of the Trinity 'holds the potential to emphasise the need for an openness towards otherness without forfeiting identity (contra liberalism), as well as to emphasise identity in such as way that we do not need to kill others to safeguard our identity (contra nationalism)'.³⁹

Conclusion

It is clear that many of the more recent reflections on the doctrine of the Trinity are beginning to provide answers to the postmodern 'so what?' questions. Ironically, perhaps, we may find that what ancient Scripture reveals about the relationship between Father, Son, and Holy Spirit could well be helpful in providing a pattern of what human relationships in church and community might be. After all, as Karl Barth maintains 'on

---

37. For example, LaCugna, *God for Us*, 400.
38. Neil Francis Pembroke, 'Trinity, Polyphony and Pastoral Relationships', in *Journal of Pastoral Care and Counselling* 58 (2004): 361.
39. Robert Vosloo, 'Identity, Otherness and the Triune God: Theological Groundwork for a Christian Ethic of Hospitality', in *Journal of Theology for Southern Africa*, 119 (July 2004): 89.

trinitarian grounds, it is as Godlike to be humble as to be exalted'.[40] Insights as this have the potential to change how the church might evaluate and respond to those who are marginalised socially and theologically; how it might model gender and ethnic relationships; and how it does ministry both within its own community and in the world.

While the postmodern agenda cannot be permitted to imprison the biblical metanarrative, the questions it raises may provide fresh starting points for further fruitful theological reflection on the doctrine of the Trinity, the most central of Christian concepts.

---

40. As cited in Gunton, *The Promise of Trinitarian Theology*, xxvi.

The Trinitarian Basis of Christian Community
Richard Rice

Few developments in Christian history has had greater theological significance than the development of the doctrine of the Trinity, for nothing is more fundamental to any version of Christian faith than its understanding of God.[1] A trinitarian understanding of God has important implications for the entire range of Christian beliefs, but its connection to the doctrine of the church is particularly significant. In fact, the Trinity and the church are intimately connected. It was the experience of God within the community of faith that gave rise to the trinitarian understanding of God. And a trinitarian understanding of God illuminates the origin and the nature of the church. It also has important implications for the practical life of the Christian community.

The Trinity and the Origin of the Church

According to an ancient formula, all of God is involved in the activity of each member of the Trinity.[2] And it is evident that God works through

---

1. The doctrine of the Trinity has attracted so much attention in recent decades that it looks to some less like a renaissance than a bandwagon. 'Once threatened by its relative scarcity in modern theology', Stanley J Grenz writes, 'the doctrine of the Trinity now seems more likely to be obscured by an overabundance of theologians clustered around it' (*The Social God and the Relational Self: A Trinitarian Theology of the Imago Dei* [Louisville, KY: Westminster John Knox, 2001], 24.) This is a striking contrast to the role that the Trinity played in liberal theology, which is to say, hardly any. Friedrich Schleiermacher postpones a discussion of the Trinity until the very last section of *The Christian Faith*. And although Paul Tillich employs a trinitarian motif in the central sections of his *Systematic Theology*—'Being and God', 'Existence and the Christ', 'Life and the Spirit'—and makes some interesting comments about its historical significance—Volume 2 contains a short chapter on 'The Trinitarian Symbols'—the doctrine does not make a notable contribution to his theology.
2. It would take a paper at least as long as this one to sort through the various pronominal

both the Son and the Spirit to bring the church into existence. In the words of a familiar hymn, the church has one foundation, Jesus Christ the Lord. And as Martin Luther asserted, 'It is the proper work of the Holy Spirit, to make the church'.[3] This joint activity is sometimes described as 'two divine missions'—the sending of the Son and the sending of the Spirit. And these two missions are closely related.[4]

The Spirit's role in the events of the early church is well known. The book of Acts begins with the promise of the Spirit's coming (1:5, 8). Soon after, Pentecost empowered the early believers, enabling them to speak in other tongues and 'proclaim the word of God with boldness' (1:32). Time and again Acts describes Christians as being 'filled with the Holy Spirit' (2:4, 7:55, 31:52). The Holy Spirit directs Christians to travel and preach, the Holy Spirit fell on Gentile believers, the Holy Spirit convinced the leaders of the church what sort of obligations Gentiles should assume when they joined the Christian community. The sheer number of references suggests that the central character in the book is actually the Holy Spirit, rather than the apostles and the others who followed Jesus.

Although we think of the Holy Spirit as descending on Jesus' followers after his earthly ministry was over, the Spirit's activity in the early church was really a continuation of the Spirit's activity in Jesus' life. Indeed, the overall purpose of Luke and Acts (or Luke-Acts, if we think of them as parts of a single work) may well be to show that the work of the Holy Spirit in the lives of early Christians is really an extension of the Holy Spirit's work within the life of Jesus himself.

The Holy Spirit was a factor in Jesus' life from beginning to end. The activity of the Holy Spirit surrounded Jesus' birth. In the early chapters of Luke we read that John the Baptist (1:15), Elizabeth (Lk 1:41), Zechariah (1:67) were all filled with the Holy Spirit. The Holy Spirit gave Simeon

---

candidates for divine reference, noting their respective pro's and con's. I am bowing to convention in using the masculine, not because I believe that God is male rather than female, but because the alternatives all seem to create as many problems as they solve. I employ the appellations, Father, Son, Spirit, however, not as a matter of convention, but in the attempt to remain faithful to the name of God that is central to Christian revelation.

3. Quoted in Robert W Jenson, *Systematic Theology* (Oxford: Oxford University Press, 1997–1999), 2:197.
4. In the words of Karl Rahner, 'The two missions may be understood as interconnected moments of the one self-communication of God to the world' (in *Encyclopedia of Theology: The Concise Sacramentum Mundi,* edited by Karl Rahner [New York: Seabury, 1975], 1760).

special insight and prompted him to go into the temple at the right moment (2:25–26).[5] And of course, in the middle of all these was the greatest manifestation of all—the miraculous birth of Jesus. 'And the angel said to her, 'the Holy Spirit will come upon you, and the power of the Most High will overshadow you; therefore the child to be born will be called holy, the Son of God.'" Luke 1:35.[6] Jesus would be full of the Holy Spirit from his birth, just as John the Baptist was filled with the Holy Spirit while in his mother's womb (Lk 1:15; cf Judgs 13:3–5; 16:17. Isa 44:2).

According to Acts 10:38 God anointed Jesus of Nazareth with the Holy Spirit and with power. The Spirit descended on Jesus at his baptism and remained for his entire earthly life. Jesus was 'full of the Holy Spirit,' and the Spirit led him into the wilderness, to be tempted (Lk 4:1–2; Matt 4:1). In his synagogue sermon at Nazareth (Lk 4), Jesus announced, 'The Spirit of the Lord is upon me . . .'[7] Later on, Jesus 'rejoiced in the Holy Spirit,' following the mission of the seventy-two (Lk 10:21).[8] The Holy Spirit was also active in Jesus' death and resurrection. According to Hebrews 9:14, Christ offered himself to God 'through the eternal Spirit.'[9] According to Romans 1:4 Jesus was declared to be Son of God with power according to the spirit of holiness by resurrection from the dead.

On the day of his resurrection, Jesus *breathed* on his followers and said 'receive the Holy Spirit' (Jn 20:22). The same power at work during his earthly life continues in the life of the community he founded, and through the Spirit Christ maintains his presence in the world. Accordingly, Christ's followers live by the power of the Holy Spirit. Paul puts it this way: 'The Spirit of him who raised Jesus from the dead is living in you, he who raised Christ from the dead will also give life to your mortal bodies through his Spirit, who lives in you.' (Rom 8:11). Through the Holy Spirit, therefore, believers live the resurrection life now, not just in the future. The Holy Spirit gives them a new dynamic for living, a new inner power, a new life, the life of the resurrection (2 Cor 5:17).

Moreover, the Holy Spirit binds Christ's followers to him with ties that can never be broken. He lives in them ('Christ in you'); they live in him ('the life I now live I live by Christ'), and because of its connection to

---

5. Gerald F Hawthorne, *The Presence and the Power: The Significance of the Holy Spirit in the Life and Ministry of Jesus*, (Dallas, TX: Word, 1991), 54.
6. Hawthorne, 65.
7. *Ibid*, 133.
8. *Ibid*, 148.
9. *Ibid*, 183-84.

Christ's ministry in the world the Holy Spirit receives a new identity. It is now the 'spirit of Christ.' We can see these interconnecting ideas at work in the following passage: 'But you are not in the flesh; you are in the Spirit, since the Spirit of God dwells in you. Anyone who does not have the Spirit of Christ does not belong to him. But if Christ is in you, though the body is dead because of sin, the Spirit is life because of righteousness' (Rom 8:9-10). As one biblical scholar puts it, 'abiding in Christ . . . is also abiding in the Spirit, or the abiding of Christ in us is also the abiding of the Spirit.'[10]

The close connections among God the Father, the Son and the Spirit are evident in other passages, too. According to both Paul and John, the sending of the Spirit parallels the sending of the Son. And in John, sending the Spirit is attributed to both the Father and the Son.

> But when the fullness of time had come, God *sent* his Son, born of a woman, born under the law, in order to redeem those who were under the law, so that we might receive adoption as children. And because you are children, God has *sent* the Spirit of his Son into our hearts, crying, 'Abba! Father!' So you are no longer a slave but a child, and if a child then also an heir, through God (Gal 4:4-7).
>
> But the Advocate, the Holy Spirit, whom the *Father* will send in my name, will teach you everything, and remind you of all that I have said to you. John 14:26. (Cf 'When the Advocate comes, whom *I* will send to you from the Father, the Spirit of truth who comes from the Father, he will testify on my behalf.' John 15:26).

The designations of those who send, 'God,' 'the Father,' and 'Christ,' and of the ones who are sent, the 'Son' and 'the Spirit,' indicate that all of God—Father, Son and Spirit—is involved in salvation history. The community created by the Holy Spirit as the continuation of Christ's mission to the world thus owes its existence to the salvific activity of the triune God.

Salvation and the Life of God

The close association of Father, Son and Spirit in the plan of salvation tells us something important about God's own life. Early Christians arrived at

---

10. Eduard Schweizer, *pneuma, pneumatikos,* in *Theological Dictionary of the New Testament,* editedy by Gerhard Friedrich, translated by Geoffrey W Bromiley (Grand Rapids, MI: Eerdmans, 1969), 6:433.

this insight as they worked out their understanding of Christ's divinity. Behind the question, Is Jesus Christ divine?, lay a more basic question: Is salvation God's own work, or did God send a subordinate to carry it out? In upholding Christ's full divinity, the early church affirmed that salvation is God's very own work, not that of a secondary or subordinate being.[11] In other words, God loves us so much that God himself entered human history in the person of the Son in order to effect our reconciliation.

If this is true, then there must be an intimate connection between God's saving activity and God's inner life. As Jesus declared to the disciples, 'He who has seen me has seen the Father' (Jn 14:8-9). In other words, God revealed himself in Jesus as he really is. The plan of salvation manifests something that has always been true of God. Love is the central characteristic of God's own being. God has always existed as Father, Son and Spirit, as an everlasting community of love.

The conviction that God's revelation in Jesus Christ was a genuine *self-revelation* pervades recent discussions of the Trinity. Karl Rahner puts it this way: 'the "economic" Trinity is the immanent Trinity, and the 'immanent Trinity is the "economic" Trinity.'[12] According to Karl Barth, 'God 'is amongst us in humility, our God, God for us, as that which He is in Himself, in the most inward depth of His Godhead ... In the condescension in which He gives Himself to us in Jesus Christ He exists and speaks and acts as the One He was from all eternity and will be to all eternity.'[13]

And the list goes on. For Eberhard Jungel, the incarnation is 'not a second thing next to the eternal God but rather the event of the deity of God.'[14] For Wolfhart Pannenberg, God's actions in salvation history reveal that God's inner reality consists of 'concrete life relations.'[15] And for Jurgen Moltmann, 'As God appears in history as the sending Father and the sent Son, so he must earlier have been in himself ... The relations between the

---

11. See my article, 'Trinity, Temporality, and Open Theism,' in *Philosophia: Philosophical Quarterly of Israel*, special issue on 'Models of God,' 35:3-4.
12. Karl Rahner, *The Trinity*, translated by Joseph Donceel (New York: Herder and Herder, 1970), 22.
13. Karl Barth, *Church Dogmatics*, translated by Geoffrey Bromily and Thomas Torrance (Edinburgh T&T Clark, 1956), IV/1:193.
14. *God as the Mystery of the World: On the Foundation of the Theology of the Crucified One in the Dispute between Theism and Atheism*, translated by Darrell L Guder (Grand Rapids, MI: Eerdmans, 1983), 372.
15. Wolfhart Pannenberg, *Systematic Theology*, translated by Geoffrey W Bromiley (Grand Rapids, MI: Eerdmans, 1991), 1:335, 323.

discernible and visible history of Jesus and the God whom he called 'my Father' correspond to the relation of the Son to the Father in eternity.'[16]

If the events of salvation history have their counterpart in God's own life, then the Christian community owes its identity, as well as its origin, to its unique relation to the triune God. God's activity as Father, Son and Spirit not only brings the church into existence, the love that characterises God's eternal existence imparts to the church its essential character.

The Trinity and the Nature of the Church

The conviction that the founding events of the church, the missions of the Son and the Spirit, are manifestations of God's own life leads to dramatic insights into the nature of the church. The close connection between the Christian community and the life of God becomes apparent in the 'farewell discourses' of the fourth Gospel and in 1 John.

The various statements about love in these documents seem to follow a 'fugal' pattern. They keep moving among the following themes, connecting them in more and more complex relations: the love that church members have for each other; their love for God and God's love for them; and the love that unites God himself, namely, the love between the Father and the Son.

First of all, the distinctive quality of life within the Christian community is that of love. 'By this everyone will know that you are my disciples, if you have love for one another' (John 13:35). Love is the essential feature that sets Jesus' followers apart from other human groups. Consequently; those who think they are part of the community and don't love each other are deceiving themselves. '[A]ll who do not do what is right are not from God, nor are those who do not love their brothers and sisters.' 1 John 3:10. On the positive side, 'We know that we have passed from death to life because we love one another' (1 John 3:14).

Second, it is not love per se, or just any sort of affection that identifies Jesus' followers. It is the specific love that Jesus has for them that sets the standard for their love to one another. 'Just as I have loved you, you also should love one another' (John 13.34).[17] 'This is my commandment, that you love one another as I have loved you. No one has greater love than

---

16. Jürgen Moltmann, *The Church in the Power of the Spirit*, translated by Margaret Kohl (New York: Harper & Row, 1977), 54.
17. Compare Paul's exhortation: 'Therefore be imitators of God, as beloved children, and live in love, as Christ loved us and gave himself up for us' (Eph 5:1–2).

this, to lay down one's life for one's friends' (15:12–13). Jesus' followers should be prepared to love one another to the end, just as he 'loved them to the end (John 13:1).

Third, Jesus' love for the disciples expresses the Father's own love for them. '[F]or the Father himself loves you, because you have loved me and have believed that I came from God' (John 16:27). The Father's love flows through the Son into the Christian community.

Indeed, Jesus' statements about his relation to the Father and his relation to his followers indicate that Jesus wants his followers to enjoy the same relation to God that he enjoys. Just as the Father comes to the disciples in the person of Jesus, therefore, Jesus brings the disciples to the Father. 'Those who love me will be loved by my Father, and I will love them and reveal myself to them' (John 14:21). 'Those who love me will keep my word, and my Father will love them, and we will come to them and make our home with them' (John 14:23).

The idea that Jesus' followers enjoy a relation to God very similar to his own appears in a number of passages. 'When we cry, "Abba! Father!"' wrote Paul, 'it is that very Spirit bearing witness with our spirit that we are children of God, and if children, then heirs, heirs of God and joint heirs with Christ' (Rom 8:15–17). In the opening words of the Lord's Prayer, 'our Father,' Jesus invites his followers to adopt his own form of address to God, and Jesus instructed Mary to 'Go to my brothers and say to them, "I am ascending to my Father and your Father, to my God and your God"' (John 20:17). It is thus by virtue of their relation to Jesus that his followers enjoy a close relationship to God.

Fourth, the love that Jesus has for his followers reflects the love that he and the Father have for each other. For his followers present and future, Jesus prayed, 'I ask not only on behalf of these, but also on behalf of those who will believe in me through their word, that they may all be one. As you, Father, are in me and I am in you, may they also be in us . . . The glory that you have given me I have given them, so that they may be one, as we are one, I in them and you in me, that they may become completely one, so that the world may know that you have sent me and have loved them even as you have loved me' (John 17:20–23). The author of 1 John brings together fellowship with one another and fellowship with God this way: 'that you also may have fellowship with us; and truly our fellowship is with the Father and with his Son Jesus Christ' (1 John 1:3). The divine love that creates Christian community thus manifests and extends the love that constitutes God's own life.

This line of thought leads to a dramatic conclusion. The central dynamic of the Christian community not only resembles the essential dynamic of God's own life; its members actually share in that life. The love that flows between Father and Son flows through the church. The idea that the church participates in God's life flows naturally from Jesus' parting words to his disciples. In the life and ministry of Jesus, and its continuation in the community he founded, we truly encounter 'God with us.'

For many who share this conviction, the essential link between Christian community and the life of God lies in the work of the Holy Spirit. For one thing, it is the Holy Spirit that makes the church a true community. As Robert Jenson says, 'the church exists as a community and not as a mere collective of pious individuals,' because the Spirit unites the head with the body of Christ.[18]

It is also the Spirit that gives the church its distinctive identity. Every community that is not just an aggregate has a 'spirit' of some sort—we speak of 'team spirit' and 'school spirit,' for example. But in the case of the church, this corporate spirit comes, not from the people who belong to it, but from the Spirit that creates it. To quote Jenson again, it is the church's 'founding miracle' that her communal spirit is 'identically the Spirit that the personal God is and has.'[19]

Finally, as many interpreters see it, the Spirit's role in the church bears a close resemblance to the Spirit's role within the Trinity. The Spirit creates community within God's own life. As Jungel describes it, 'the Father loves the Son, the Son returns this love, and the Holy Spirit is the love itself between them. So, the Spirit who proceeds from the Father and the Son constitutes the unity of the divine being as that event which is love itself.'[20]

Such descriptions of the relations within God suggest ways for us to envision the church's role in the divine life. Through the Spirit, as Stanley Grenz describes it, those who are 'in Christ' come to share the eternal relationship that the Son enjoys with the Father. Because participants in this new community are co-heirs with Christ, the Father bestows on them what he eternally lavishes on the Son. And because they are 'in Christ' by the Spirit, they participate in the Son's act of eternal response to the Father.[21]

---

18. Jenson, 2:182.
19. *Ibid*, 181.
20. Jungel, 374.
21. Grenz, 326.

To summarise, the church owes its existence to God's salvific activity and derives its essential character from God's own identity. Through the sending of the Son and the Spirit God enters the world in order to create a community that reflects and extends the love that constitutes God's own reality. The central dynamic of Christian community thus corresponds to the essential dynamic of God's own life. And participating in the Christian community is nothing less than a participation in God's own life. The Holy Spirit makes us one, the Holy Spirit makes God one, and the Holy Spirit makes us one with God.[22]

Practical Implications of a Trinitarian Ecclesiology

'So what?' questions are always important for theology, and in the case of the Trinity they are more important than usual. It is tempting to dismiss reflections on the Trinity as speculative intrusions into the nature of God, even though the church's earliest trinitarian thinkers anchored their understanding of God firmly in the history of salvation. What practical difference does a trinitarian ecclesiology make? Why is it so important to ground the church in God's own life?

First, of all, it emphasises the importance of the church to God. If God's acts in salvation history express God's true nature, then God has always been relational, from all eternity an everlasting community of love. It means that God creates out of love, he embraces the created world within the divine life, and from the moment of its existence, God made his relation to the world the center of his concern, not unlike the way parents place a beloved child at the center of their home. God values the world he loves so much that he even takes his identity from his relation to it. (God is the God of Abraham, Isaac, and Jacob, the Father of our Lord Jesus Christ.) Moreover, God's commitment to creation is permanent. He risks his own contentment—if not his own life—for its welfare. All this means that God places immense value on the church. It is that aspect of creation

---

22. Theologians sometimes debate the organisation of the Apostle's Creed. Does it comprise three articles or four? Does belief in the 'holy catholic church' elaborate or add to belief in the Holy Spirit? Our reflections suggest the former. The church is the creation of the Holy Spirit, and the creation of the church is the Spirit's most important work. To appreciate the importance of Christian community, we must recognise its basis within and its intimate connection to the dynamic reality of God's own life.

that attracts his particular attention. As Ellen White says, the church is the object of God's 'supreme regard.'[23]

If this is so, then salvation involves participating in the fellowship that defines God's own life, and one does this by participating in the community that God's love established. The experience of salvation is therefore social as well as individual. It has a public as well as a private dimension. It changes our relations to others as well as to God. This exposes the fundamental inadequacy of all individualistic interpretations of Christian faith. Salvation is not merely, or even primarily, a matter between an individual and God. It involves relationships with other people. It seeks social, not merely personal transformation.

This also means that the purpose of the church is to reflect and project the care and concern for others that God shows, that God is. To the extent that the church, the Christian community, embodies the love that radiates within the life of God, it provides the world the clearest manifestation of God's nature and character, *and* the clearest evidence of God's reality, evidence that is stronger than philosophical arguments could ever be.

If this is true, then the cultivation of true community, the development of caring relationships among people in the church, is the most important work of the church's ministry. Church growth is not merely, or even primarily, a matter of increasing size. It is a matter of developing among the church's members relationships of mutual care and concern, encouraging the manifestation of qualities embodied in Jesus' life. As the members of the church exhibit these qualities, their display of Christ's character will naturally attract new participants.

These reflections also suggest that corporate worship is the central act of the church's life. The gathering of the community to remember God's acts of self-giving love, to recommit its members to embody that love in all their relationships, is emblematic of the church's entire existence. It celebrates, crystallises, realises everything the church involves.

An appreciation for the trinitarian basis of Christian community thus helps us avoid inadequate and misleading concepts of the church. The church is not an organisation preoccupied with expanding its membership and its budget. The church is not a collection of individuals who assent to the same set of beliefs. The church is not a group of people who gather to meet their emotional needs. The church is not a meeting of intellectuals who enjoy tossing around ideas. The church is not a multilevel marketing

---

23. Ellen G. White, *The Acts of the Apostles* (Mountain View, CA: Pacific Press, 1911), 12.

program, social club, recovery group, or academic seminar. The church is a fellowship created by the Holy Spirit, a community which extends the mission of Christ in this world, drawing its members into a circle of love that is both characteristic of and constitutive of God's own life.

Alexandrian School and the Trinitarian Problem

Darius Jankiewicz

Among the ancient schools of theology, Alexandria holds special prominence. The school began about 185 AD with the exclusive purpose of instructing converts from paganism to Christianity. Very quickly, and under the leadership of its principal theologians, Clement and Origen, it evolved into a major theological think-tank of ancient Christianity. As such, the school played an important role in influencing the development of many Christian doctrines, including the doctrine of the Trinity. One of the important characteristics of the school was its positive approach towards Greek philosophy. While many early Christian thinkers attempted to utilise the wisdom of ancient Greeks in their theological thinking, it was the Alexandrian school that excelled in this enterprise. Its chief thinkers saw in pagan Greek philosophy an ally and an excellent tool that could aid in explaining some of the intricacies of the Christian faith and, at the same time, make Christianity reasonable to the pagan mind. Let us begin with a brief overview of the developments up to the rise of the Alexandrian thinking.

Pre-Alexandrian Solutions

The New Testament leaves its readers with a somewhat ambiguous picture regarding the doctrine of the Trinity and the divinity of Jesus Christ. On the one hand, it is evident that the New Testament has no argument with the monotheistic tradition of the Old Testament (See, for example, Acts 17:22–31 and 1 Cor 8:4). On the other hand, it is also evident that a monotheistic *status quo* of the Old Testament is challenged. While, from the outset, the Christian believers saw themselves as the continuators of the Jewish monotheistic tradition, they also presented themselves as believing in Jesus Christ, whom they described as having the characteristics that in the Old Testament had been exclusively reserved for the deity. Moreover, the Holy Spirit also receives more attention and is presented in a different way from that found in the Old Testament. It is not surprising, therefore, to find early post-apostolic Christians grappling with the new vision of the divine. While all recognised the special status of Christ (and the Holy Spirit), they nevertheless struggled to explain how this harmonised with the monotheistic conception of God. Thus at one side of the spectrum there were those who tended to speak of Christ as an elevated human being, the Messiah, but not God. The other extreme was populated by those who yearned to protect the unity of God and tended to identify Christ with God.[1] The remainder of the early Christians found themselves somewhere between these two extremes.

Two things can be said of these early, pre-Nicaean efforts to explain the relationship between God, Christ, and the Holy Spirit. First, they all placed a strong emphasis on the unity of God, and, second, they invariably placed Christ and the Holy Spirit in some form of a subordinate relationship to the supreme God of the Old Testament. Despite this, significant strides towards the understanding of the Trinity were made during the second century by thinkers such as Justin Martyr, Irenaeus, and Tertullian. The Alexandrian school of theology fits well within this tradition of trinitarian thinking.

Clement of Alexandria (ca 155–215 AD)

Apart from a few biographical details, very little is known of Titus Flavius Clemens, otherwise known as Clement of Alexandria. It appears that he received a good education, was a pagan convert to Christianity, became the head of the Alexandrian school of theology upon the death of its founder, Pantaenus, and was the teacher of Origen.[2] Three extant works are attributed to him: the *Protreptikos* (*Exhortation to the Heathen*), in which he urges pagans to convert to Christianity; the *Paidagogos*, the purpose of which was to teach Christians the fundamentals of Christian conduct; and the *Stromateis* (*Miscellanies*), a collection of loosely organised notes dealing with various theological issues.[3] Clement left behind

---

1. Both of these views, already considered as heresies during the early Christian centuries, are still present within modern Christianity.
2. Kenneth S Latourette, *A History of Christianity* (New York: Harper and Brothers, 1953), 146–7; cf Henry Chadwick, *The Church in Ancient Society: From Galilee to Gregory the Great* (Oxford: Oxford University Press, 2001), 124–5.
3. Williston Walker, *A History of the Christian Church* (New York: Charles Scribner's

no systematic theology, a task later accomplished by his most illustrious student, Origen.[4] He held strong beliefs that Greek philosophy, and especially Middle Platonism,[5] was closely related to Christian theology and saw Christianity as the final development of Greek philosophical ideals. God, he argued, gave philosophy to the Greeks in much the same way he provided the Hebrews with the Law of Moses.[6] He thus felt no restraints in using pagan Greek philosophy to explain the intricacies of the Christian faith. 'All truth', he wrote, 'is God's truth wherever it may be found'.[7]

Clement's teachings on God and the Trinity began with his affirmation of the absolute transcendence of God, an idea clearly echoing the main characteristic of the Supreme Mind, or 'The One', of Middle Platonism.[8] As such, God was completely beyond the power of human comprehension and thus needed a mediator, the *Logos*. This *Logos* was the source of all knowledge available to humanity and, most especially, of the knowledge of God. It was the *Logos* who 'gave philosophy to Greeks', prepared the way for Christianity, and became *paidagogos*, or instructor, for the followers of the latter.[9]

Clement spoke very highly of the *Logos*, whom he identified with the biblical Son of God. He described the Son as the 'wisdom of God', 'the energy of the Father', the 'cause of all good things', 'the first efficient cause of motion', and the first 'administrator of the universe, who by the will of the Father directs the salvation of all'.[10] Despite using exalted language in

---

Sons, 1970), 73; Latourette, *A History*, 147.
4. Walker, 74.
5. Middle Platonism, sometimes referred to as pre-Neoplatonism, was an improvement on Platonic 'good' and postulated the existence of the divine mind that could, at a stretch, be reminiscent of a Christian God. The Platonic 'ideas', or 'forms', thus existed in the mind of God. Middle-Platonism was the form of Greek philosophy used and adapted by the Alexandrian theologians. For a concise description of Middle Platonism, see Everett Ferguson, *Backgrounds of Early Christianity* (Grand Rapids, MI: Eerdmans, 1993), 364–6.
6. Clement, *Stromateis* 7.2.5, in *Ante-Nicene Christian Library*, edited by Alexander Roberts (Edinburgh: T&T Clark, 1872), 410; cf Alister McGrath, *Historical Theology* (Oxford: Blackwell Publishing, 1998), 89.
7. Roger E Olson and Adam C English, *Pocket History of Theology* (Downers Grove, IL: InterVarsity, 2005), 20.
8. Francis Osborne, *Clement of Alexandria* (Cambridge: Cambridge University Press, 2005), 113–4; cf. Ferguson, 365.
9. Clement *Stromateis* 7.2.5 (Roberts, 411); cf. Justo Gonzalez, *A History of Christian Thought: From the Beginnings to the Council of Chalcedon* (Nashville, TN: Abingdon, 1970), 191–3.
10. Clement, *Stromateis* 7.2.5–10 (Roberts, 411–412).

speaking of the Son, endowing Him with pre-existence and even bestowing upon Him the title 'God', Clement hesitated to ascribe to Him the supreme, underived divinity that would make the *Logos* equal with God. Nowhere in his writings is such identification made in clear terms.[11] Instead, his language almost rules out such a possibility and suggests a form of subordination.[12]

A careful exegesis of Clement's writings by the scholar of antiquity, Alvan Lamson, prompted him to conclude that 'none of the Platonising Fathers before Origen have acknowledged the inferiority of the Son in more explicit terms than Clement'.[13] Louis Berkhof concurs when he concludes that, though Clement came close to the recognition of Christ's full divinity, he nevertheless could not escape the clutches of subordinationism. While he spoke of the *Logos*' eternity, he 'defines the phrase in such a way as to teach not merely an economic but an essential subordination of the Son to the Father'.[14] Thus it is not surprising to find Clement speaking of Christ as *theos deuteros* (second God).[15] Indeed, the Middle Platonic monistic understanding of the deity as simple and undivided would preclude any complexity in the nature of God while, at the same time, welcoming the existence of inferior intermediaries such as the *Logos*.

How did the *Logos* become Christ, according to Clement? At one point in the past, the *Logos* separated (emanated) from the Father[16] and became incarnated in the human form of Jesus Christ, the Son of God. Clement described this process in terms closely resembling the bringing forth of the World Soul from the Supreme Mind of the Middle Platonic philosophy.[17] The life of Christ, as the incarnated *Logos*, represented the ideal of

---

11. Alvan Lamson, *The Church of the First Three Centuries* (New York: Hurd and Houghton, 1877), 123–5.
12. Thus we find in Clement such statements as: 'For the Son is the power of God, as being the Father's most ancient Word before the production of all things'; 'But the nature of the Son, which is nearest to Him who is alone the Almighty One, is the most perfect, and most holy . . .' Clement, *Stromateis* 7.2 (Roberts, 409–413).
13. Lamson, 124.
14. Louis Berkhof, *The History of Christian Doctrines* (London: The Banner of Truth Trust, 1937), 72; cf Chadwick, *The Church in Ancient Society*, 128.
15. Berkhof, *The History of Christian Doctrines*, 72.
16. Lamson suggests that, in Clement's belief system, rather than pre-existing throughout all eternity as a distinct 'being', the *Logos* existed in the form of 'wisdom' in the mind of God and potentially as a being. In this way, Clement could boldly ascribe eternity to Christ. *Idem*, 124.
17. Richard Tarnas, *The Passion of the Western Mind* (New York: Ballantine Books, 1991), 102–3.

perfect union with God in this life.[18] Thus Clement wrote of the Son: 'Now, O you, my children, our Instructor is like his Father God, whose Son He is, sinless, blameless, and with a soul devoid of passion; God in the form of man, stainless, the minister of his Father's will, the Word who is God, who is in the Father, who is at the Father's right hand, and with the form of God is God.'[19] From this it is clear that rather than focusing on Christ's accomplishments as the Saviour who on the cross paid the price for the sins of humanity, Clement was more interested in the 'philosophical' qualities of the incarnated *Logos,* such as sinlessness or passionlessness.

Unfortunately, such *hellenising* exerted a heavy price on his soteriology and took Clement on a path foreign to that of the New Testament writers. The main reason for the incarnation of the *Logos* became the mediation of divine knowledge to humanity. The attainment of this knowledge equaled human salvation. Thus Clement's understanding of salvation had little to do with Christ's sacrifice on the cross but followed the well-established trajectory of thought present in the various strands of Greek philosophy, where special knowledge led to 'salvation' which enabled humans to become 'God-like', devoid of passion, anger, and worldly desires.

While Clement opposed pagan Gnosticism and considered Christianity as the highest philosophy, he nevertheless equated Christian faith with a certain kind of *gnosis* about God. Through this *gnosis,* a believer was to be acquainted with God's ways of thinking and, like the pagan philosopher, could rise to become God-like by turning away from carnal desires and becoming free from passion and anger.[20] Such state he named a 'condition of blessedness' which could only be achieved by following the example of Christ.[21] This, Clement believed, was the highest accomplishment of the Apostles.[22] Clement thus promoted 'divinisation', or becoming God-like, as the mode of salvation. In this process, Christ was the medium as well as the 'teacher' through whom God 'cures the unnatural passions of the soul by means of exhortations'.[23]

Clement also wrote about the Holy Spirit who completed his divine triad. He described the Spirit as the 'light' which emanated from the *Logos*

---

18. Chadwick, *The Church in Ancient Society,* 128.
19. Clement, *Paidagogos* 1.13 (*ANF* 2:209-210).
20. Olson, *The Story of Christian Theology* (Downers Grove, IL: InterVarsity, 1999), 88.
21. *Ibid.*
22. Clement, *Stromateis* 6.9.1 (Roberts, 344).
23. Clement, *Stromateis* 1.20.1, in *Clement of Alexandria: Stromateis Book One to Three,* translated by John Ferguson (Washington, DC: The Catholic University of America Press, 1991), 96–7; cf Clement, *Paidagogos* 1.13 (*ANF* 2:210).

and whose work was to enlighten the mind of humanity. The Spirit was 'the power of the Word, which pervades creation and attracts individuals to God'.[24] The language in which Clement described the Spirit, however, leaves the readers in the dark as to the Spirit's exact nature or relationship to the Father and the Son.[25]

Clement thus presents one of the earliest, ante-Nicaean images of the Trinity and is considered by historians as one of the church fathers who propelled Christianity towards the trinitarian definitions of the fourth century. He nevertheless left unansweredquestions as to the exact nature of the *Logos* and the Holy Spirit, and their relationship to God. In summary, it may be stated that, in his views on the Trinity, while unquestionably clothed in Christian terminology, Clement borrowed heavily from the model of the divine found in the prevailing philosophy of the age in which he lived.[26] While Clement's subordinationistic views were more tacit than pronounced, his most eminent student, Origen, took the former's theology and developed it into a systematic vision of the philosophical Trinity.

Origen of Alexandria (ca 185 – 254 AD)

Recognised for his brilliancy, Origen was chosen by Clement to take over the leadership of the catechetical school in Alexandria, a position he held until at least 231 AD. Unlike Clement, Origen was born into a Christian family and, from an early age, was exposed to the teachings of the Bible and the early church fathers. As a student, and later the head of the catechetical school, he distinguished himself by careful scholarship and a successful writing career. With regards to the scope of his work, Origen is often compared to Augustine, and it is estimated that he produced over six thousand scrolls containing various theological discourses. Known as the systematic theologian of the Alexandrian school, he surpassed Clement in constructing a theological system in which he sought to harmonise the emerging Neoplatonism with Christianity. Unlike many other church fathers, and notwithstanding his extraordinary contributions to theology, Origen was never canonised as a saint, as posterity was unable to decide

---

24. Clement, quoted in William G Rusch, *The Trinitarian Controversy* (Philadelphia, PA: Fortress, 1980), 12.
25. Latourette, *A History of Christianity*, 148.
26. Rusch, *The Trinitarian Controversy*, 12; cf Tarnas, *The Passion of the Western Mind*, 103.

whether to perceive him as orthodox or heretic.[27] His theological legacy is thus ambiguous. On the one hand, his work led many pagan thinkers to begin to take Christianity seriously. On the other hand, his syncretistic approach to theology created confusion and much heartache to future generations of theologians.[28] His greatest works on theology are *Contra Celsum* and *De Principiis*. Despite his fame, he lived a simple, ascetic life.[29]

The entire trinitarian theology of Origen is governed by three *a priori* principles that he considered as self-evident teachings of the New Testament: first, that there is one God who is the Father of Jesus Christ; second, that Jesus Christ was born of the Father before all creatures; and, third, that 'the Holy Spirit was associated in honour and dignity with the Father and the Son'.[30] Origen's theology of the Trinity thus also began with the person of God and his nature. Like Clement, he tended to describe God in monistic terms. God the Father, he insisted, was 'altogether *Monad*, and so to speak, *Henad*'. In philosophical language, both of these terms referred to an indivisible, hence ultimately simple and unknowable entity, the latter even more strongly conveying these qualities.

God was thus incomprehensible, transcendent, perfect in every way, without body, parts or passion, the Absolute One nothing of whom could possibly be known.[31] No other form of existence could ever assume its place. For this, Origen found support in Jesus' statement that the Father is 'the only true God' (John 17:3). Thus Jesus' Father alone was ingenerate, having no explanation for his existence.[32] Those who attempted to explain God in terms of complexity thus endangered his absolute unity and eternal existence. Origen explained: 'But God, who is the beginning of all things, is not to be regarded as a composite [complex] being, lest perchance there should be found to exist elements prior to the beginning itself, out of which everything is composed, whatever that be which is

---

27. While many theologians of the early church were deeply influenced by Origen, and his views were considered influential for formulation of trinitarian doctrines in the fourth century, he was condemned as a heretic during the Second Council of Constantinople in 553.
28. Olson, *The Story of Christian Theology*, 102.
29. Earle Cairns, *Christianity Through the Centuries* (Grand Rapids, MI: Zondervan, 1996), 109–110; cf Walker, 75.
30. Origen, *De Principiis, Introduction* 4, in *ANF* 4:240; cf Bernhard Lohse, *A Short History of Christian Doctrine* (Philadelphia, PA: Fortress, 1966), 46.
31. Origen, *De Principiis* 1.1.6 (*ANF* 4:243).
32. *Ibid*, 1.1.1 (*ANF* 4:242).

called composite.'³³ This being alone, the uncreated Creator, Sustainer of the universe, was the ultimate source of all existence.³⁴ In spite of Origen's frequent use of New Testament language, his 'God' thus had more in common with the Platonic conception of the deity than with the God of the Bible.

Since Origen conceived his God in terms of perfect goodness and power, he claimed that there must have always existed the object towards which he could exercise his goodness and power. Origen thus posited the existence of the timeless and eternal universe inhabited by spiritual beings (or souls), which existed in co-eternal relationship with him but were always subordinate.³⁵ The unity of God and the multiplicity of the universe, however, were incompatible. To bring together the absolute divine unity with the multiplicity of the spiritual beings, Origen argued for the eternal existence of a mediator, the eternal *Logos*. But where did the *Logos* come from? To explain the existence of the *Logos*, Origen turned to Neoplatonism, which explained the existence of subordinate beings in terms of generation, procession, or emanation rather than in the language of creation.

Neoplatonism taught that out of the 'Absolute One' there proceeds (emanates) the Mind (*nous*). This Mind, they insisted, was not created and thus has no beginning.³⁶ While Clement appeared to be somewhat ambivalent with regards to the concept of Middle Platonic generation, the genius of Origen lies in the fact that he embraced the idea of generation wholeheartedly and thus explained the relationship between the Father and the Son (the *Logos*).³⁷ The concept of 'eternal generation' can be made intelligible by comparing it to the process of yeast reproduction. Yeasts are unicellular organisms, which reproduce asexually through a process known as budding. When yeasts reproduce, the end result is a clone equal to and separate from the original. In the case of eternal generation, as understood by Origen, however, the primary cell would always remain primary and the secondary cell always secondary. The process of 'genera-

---

33. Peter McEnhill and GM Newlands, *Fifty Key Christian Thinkers* (Florence, KY: Routledge Publishers, 2002), 204.
34. Origen, *De Principiis* 1.1.6 (ANF 4:244).
35. *Ibid*, (ANF 4:243–244).
36. Thus Origen wrote: 'As no one can be a father without having a son, nor a master without possessing a servant, so even God cannot be called omnipotent unless there exist those over whom He may exercise His power.' Idem, *De Principiis* 1.2.10 (ANF 4:249, 250).
37. Ferguson, *Clement of Alexandria*, 368.

tion', moreover, is suspended in eternity in such a way that the secondary cell never separates from its originator.

Another useful metaphor to explain the concept of generation, and one probably closer to Origen's own thought, might be that of the will's emergence from the mind.[38] Explaining the relationship between the Father and the Son in terms of eternal generation allowed Origen to speak unabashedly of Christ as sharing co-eternal existence with the Father and thus participating in his nature.[39] Moreover, Origen also appeared to be the first Christian theologian to utilise the well-known trinitarian expression *homoousios* (of the same substance), although he used this term in a somewhat different way from what is found in the Nicaean creed. Thus we can see in Origen a strong tendency to underline the full divinity of Christ.

Despite such forceful emphasis on Christ's 'full' divinity, however, all of Origen's trinitarian theology was nevertheless marked by an unrelenting tendency towards subordinationism.[40] This is understandable, considering the fact that he was a strong opponent of a heresy known as Modalistic Monarchianism, which, in the name of the unity of God, identified Christ with the Father.[41] To counter this, Origen was forced to find terminology that would point to the distinctions between the three beings within the Godhead. To accomplish it, he introduced another complicated Neoplatonic term: *hypostasis*, which carried strong connotations of distinct personalities.[42] While the Father was considered by Origen to be the absolute God, and thus a special or unique category of *hypostasis*, the *Logos* could not possibly fulfil such a function and, in the end, had to be subordinated to the Father. It is not surprising, therefore, to find Origen in agreement with Clement and referring to Christ as the *theos deuteros* (second God).[43]

Origen's subordinationism was most clearly asserted in his *Commentary on John*, where he argued against those who tended to exalt the Son excessively. 'This is why we say the Savior and the Holy Spirit transcend all created beings, not by comparison, but by their exceeding pre-eminence. The Father exceeds the Savior as much (or even more) as the Savior him-

---

38. Origen, *De Principiis* 1.2.6 (*ANF* 4:248).
39. *Ibid.*
40. James Orr, *The Progress of Dogma* (Grand Rapids, MI: Eerdmans, 1960), 84.
41. See, for example, Origen *Against Celsus* 5.39 (*ANF* 4:561).
42. Gonzalez, *A History of Christian Thought*, 219.
43. Alister McGrath, *Christian Theology* (Oxford: Blackwell, 2007), 251.

self . . . exceed[s] the rest.'[44] Thus it can be stated, in agreement with William Rusch, that in Origen we find the Son whose 'deity is derived from the fountainhead, the Father . . . In spite of the fact that the Word is one with the Father, he stands on a lower level in the hierarchy.'[45]

But what of the Holy Spirit? Here Origen went beyond Neoplatonism. While discussing the nature of the Father and the Son and their relationship, he utilised the subtleties of Greek philosophical language. In his discourse on the Holy Spirit, however, he tended to rely primarily on the testimony of the Scriptures.[46] As with the Father and the Son, he described the Holy Spirit in *hypostatic* language, thus as a being that had a separate divine personality. The scriptural evidence was so obvious to him that he wondered how anyone could ever question the existence of the third person of the Trinity. The 'authority and dignity' of the Holy Spirit was of such magnitude 'that saving baptism was not complete except by the authority of the most excellent Trinity of them all, that is, by the naming of Father, Son, and Holy Spirit'.[47]

The Spirit, he further argued in his *Commentarii in Romanos*, '. . . is always with the Father and the Son; and he always is, was, and shall be, just like the Father and the Son'.[48] Origen thus strongly affirmed the co-eternity of the Spirit. How then is the Holy Spirit related to the Father and the Son? Consistent with his subordinationist tendencies, Origen ranked the Holy Spirit below the Father and the Son. The Spirit was the highest of all beings that proceeded, or was eternally generated, from the Father and from the Son. Accordingly, he states, 'The Holy Spirit seems to have need of the Son ministering to his hypostasis, not only for it to exist, but also for it to be wise, and rational, and just, and whatever other thing we ought to understand it to be by participation in the aspects of Christ'.[49] The role of the Spirit was limited to supplying the believers with God's gifts that enabled the church to function as the body of Christ.[50]

---

44. Origen, *Against Celsus* 5.39 (ANF 4:561).
45. Origen, *Commentary on the Gospel of John* 13.151, in *Origen: Commentary on the Gospel According to John, Books 13–32*, translated by Ronald E Heine (Washington, DC: The Catholic University of America Press, 1993), 100.
46. Rusch, *The Trinitarian Controversy*, 14.
47. Origen, *De Principiis* 1.3 (ANF 4:251-254).
48. *Ibid*, 1.3.2 (ANF 4:252).
49. Origen *Commentarii in Romanos* 6.7.19, in *Origen: Commentary on the Epistle to the Romans, Books 6–10*, translated by Thomas P Scheck (Washington, DC: The Catholic University of America, 2002), 29; cf Tarmo Toom, *Classical Trinitarian Theology* (New York: T&T Clark, 2007), 68.
50. Origen, *Commentary on the Gospel of John* 2.76 (Heine, 114).

In Origen therefore we find two seemingly conflicting trends of trinitarian thinking. On the one hand, he came closer than any other contemporary church father to the orthodox trinitarian expression of Christian faith. None of the early Christian thinkers exalted Christ and the Holy Spirit as much as he did. On the other hand, his philosophical presuppositions rendered him unable, or perhaps unwilling, to shake off the strong undercurrent of subordinationism that typifies his theological thinking.

Origen's subordinationism clearly went hand in hand with his soteriology. Like the rest of his theology, Origen's soteriology is deeply marked by Greek philosophy. As mentioned above, Origen posited the co-eternal existence of the universe inhabited by spiritual beings, or souls, towards whom God needed to exercise his perfect power and goodness and whom he endowed with free will. At one point in the past, some of these beings turned away from God. To punish and reform them, God created the physical, visible world. The visible, physical universe, therefore, was created in order to accommodate these fallen beings who now had to be saved, or restored, by God.[51]

Salvation of the lost souls was the primary reason for the incarnation of the *Logos* who, through becoming a man, united himself with a soul that did not sin in the previous existence. The incarnation allowed the *Logos*, or the Son, to reveal to the fallen humanity the truth (*gnosis*) about God. While on earth, Christ was both God and man. After the resurrection and ascension, however, Christ's humanity was transformed, or absorbed, into divinity. Such transformation, Origen taught, was now available to all believers who, following Christ's example, could be 'changed into God'.[52]

Thus he wrote that from Christ, 'there began the union of the divine with the human nature, in order that the human, by communion with the divine, might rise to be divine, not in Jesus alone, but in all those who not only believe, but enter upon the life which Jesus taught'.[53] Salvation, thus, was accomplished through the process of divinisation, or *theosis*, which Origen saw as the reversal of the original fall. He described it in terms of a life-long process of cooperation with God in which the followers of Christ worked on overcoming their sinful nature. Through this process, human beings were gradually transformed in such a way that they would eventually reflect God's glory and be able to participate in his immortal nature.[54]

---

51. *Ibid.*
52. Lohse, *A Short History of Christian Doctrine*, 47.
53. Origen, *Against Celsus* 3.41 (ANF 4:480).
54. *Ibid*, 3.28 (ANF 4:475).

Just as the Son participated in the divinity of the Father, he now opened the way for the rest of humanity to follow his example.[55]

What of the New Testament teaching that salvation is to be obtained through the blood of Christ on the cross? Origen would argue that such teaching only nourished the faith of simple believers who were unable to grapple with the true reality of salvation. While Christ indeed suffered and died on the cross, the primary value of his death lay in the fact that he provided an example of perfect piety 'for the good of the human race.' Moreover, his death served as 'the first blow in the conflict which is to overthrow the power of that evil spirit the devil,' who stood in the way of humanity towards perfect sanctification.[56] Christ's sacrificial death on the cross thus only played a secondary role in Origen's soteriology.

While rejecting his soteriology and many other elements of his teachings, many Christian theologians who came after Origen acknowledged his theological genius and attempted to refine his trinitarian thinking. Some moved towards full trinitarianism and affirmed the unity and equality of Father, Son, and Holy Spirit. Others, like Arius, brought Origen's subordinationist views to their ultimate conclusions and rendered Christ as a creature. These conflicting points of view clashed during the first ecumenical council of the church of Nicaea in 325 AD.

Conclusion

The impact of the Alexandrian school of theology on ancient Christianity was of such magnitude that no theologian who came after Origen could ignore its speculations. To this day, church historians and theologians alike consider the theological synthesis of Origen as one of the greatest theological achievements of ante-Nicaean antiquity. Yet the Alexandrian school left behind a dubious legacy. On the one hand, its principal thinkers came closer than any other contemporary thinkers to defining the nature of Christ and the Holy Spirit as fully divine and co-eternal with that of the Father himself. On the other hand, their insatiable thirst for the philosophical wisdom of the age and a desire to harmonise it with a New Testament faith resulted in a creeping syncretism that threatened the core of the Christian faith. As a result of their lasting influence, even the pillars of Christian orthodoxy, namely, the trinitarian creeds of the patristic era,

---

55. Olson, *The Story of Christian Theology*, 112.
56. Origen, *Against Celsus* 3.28 (ANF 4:475).

are not free from philosophical contaminants. Encouraged by their example, Catholic thinkers began to refer to philosophy as *ancilla theologiae*, the 'handmaid of theology', thus facilitating a departure from true biblical Christianity.

It appears, however, that Christian theology's infatuation with philosophy had another, even more sinister, outcome, for it affected Christian soteriology for generations. In this context, crucial questions relating to the relationship between subordinationism and divinisation, or *theosis*, must be asked. Was it coincidental that most pre-Nicaean church fathers were subordinationists who believed in *theosis* as the mode of salvation? Or was it an integral part of their Christology, where the emphasis was on the achievements of the man-Christ who, while on earth, attained a divinised status by his own efforts? Would that be the primary reason why Christ's sacrifice on the cross is de-emphasised in Clement's and Origen's writings in favour of following the example of Christ towards perfect sanctification?

By arguing for the full divinity of Christ, the Catholicism of the fourth century rejected the soteriological implications of Alexandrian Christology. Instead, under the influence of Cyprian and likeminded theologians, the church became a salvation vending organisation, where the emphasis was on the teaching that there was no possibility of salvation outside of the church. The desire for *theosis*, or perfect sanctification, however, was never entirely extinguished, and manifested itself in the monastic movement and various self-mortification activities of medieval Catholicism.

Only with the advent of the Reformation was *theosis* dealt a mortal blow. But the reformers, such as Calvin and Luther, went too far and completely divorced any form of sanctification from their soteriology, focusing instead on the exclusive value of the cross of Christ in the process of salvation. This is understandable. When salvation is placed within a predestinarian framework, thus based entirely on God's eternal decrees, there is no place for any form of sanctification. Only with the advent of Arminian, Wesleyan, Adventist soteriology did sanctification regain its proper position: that of being the fruit of salvation.

The Holy Spirit: His Divinity and Personality
Frank M Hasel

The nature and role of the Holy Spirit has significant theological and practical implications. At stake is nothing less than the very conception of God, of meaningful worship, and how believers should live their everyday lives.

Controversy about the Holy Spirit has swirled through the worship practices of most Christian denominations. Beginning with Topeka, Kansas (1901) and Azuza Street in Los Angeles (1906 – 1913), where the classical Pentecostal Movement had its modern origin, in each of the various waves of the Charismatic Movement[1] the emphasis of the Holy Spirit is almost on every lip. Several developments show that the issue of the Holy Spirit is apparently of great significance: the miracles of healing and the new worship styles which are charismatic in appearance and which found their way into many Evangelical and Protestant churches, but also the widespread glossolalia[2] which is also prevalent in the Catholic Church and has also become a significant ecumenical factor. However, many writers address primarily the function and the work of the Holy Spirit, rather than his nature and his substance.

Yet, the correct understanding (of the function and) of the working of the Holy Spirit is considerably connected with a right understanding of his nature. Depending on how I understand the nature and the substance of the Holy Spirit, my answer to his working in my life is impacted.[3] Only

---

1. PD Hocken, 'Charismatic Movement', in *Dictionary of Pentecostal and Charismatic Movements,* edited by Stanley M Burges, and Gary B McGee (Grand Rapids, MI: Zondervan, 1993 sixth edition).
2. Gerhard F Hasel, *Speaking in Tongues: Biblical Speaking in Tongues and Contemporary Glossolalia*, Adventist Theological Society Monographs, volume 1 (Berrien Springs, MI: Adventist Theological Society, 1991).
3. Ron EM Clouzet, 'The Personhood of the Holy Spirit and Why it Matters', in *Journal of the Adventist Theological Society* 17 (2006): 11.

if I understand correctly who the Holy Spirit is, can I really appreciate and classify his work and above all meet Him in an appropriate way. The question of the divinity and personality of the Holy Spirit is so controversial for many not least because it concerns the issue of the Trinity and thereby the issue of God Himself. And eventually we touch also the issue of the right worship of God, the issue of the true worship service, and thereby also a centrepiece of our Christian identity. It is little wonder, then, that the topic of the Holy Spirit has proved so controversial in many circles. Nor is there a lack of challenges faced in forming an adequate understanding of the topic.

One of the challenges in studying the topic of the Holy Spirit and attempting to discover who he is, is that the doctrine of the Holy Spirit does not present itself with the same intensity and attention in the Bible as the statements on God the Father and God's Son Jesus Christ. Although the statements of the Apostle Paul on the Spirit are more central and characteristic than his teaching on righteousness by faith,[4] it is true that the divinity of the Father is simply assumed in the Bible, the divinity of the Son is affirmed and endorsed in many places, while the divinity of the Holy Spirit is derived from diverse scriptural texts and implied statements.[5] This fact is actually in harmony with the ministry of the Holy Spirit, since it is not his responsibility to push Himself to the fore but to glorify the Son ('he [the Spirit of Truth] shall glorify Me' John 16:14). The biblical statements on the Holy Spirit are nevertheless plain and they demonstrate the divinity of the Holy Spirit, as will be seen later.

Another challenge grows out of the observation that we can imagine a somewhat tangible God the Father because the figure of the father is known to all of us. The Son can also be conceived easily for he appeared to us in human form and he was extensively described in the Gospels. However, the Holy Spirit is somehow impalpable. One can only hardly envision him.[6] He does not fit into the known scheme. Further, the word 'spirit' is one of 'the most ambiguous words of our language'.[7] With the

---

4. So Stephen Neill and Tom Wright, *The Interpretation of the New Testament 1861–1986*, second edition (Oxford: Oxford University Press, 1988), 203.
5. Millard J Erickson, *Christian Theology* (Grand Rapids, MI: Baker, 1985), 847, 857.
6. Erickson, *Christian Theology*, 847.
7. Friso Melzer, *Das Wort in den Wörtern: Die deutsche Sprache im Dienste der Christus Nachfolge*, Ein theo-philophisches Wörterbuch (Tübingen: JCB Mohr [Paul Siebeck], 1965), 150. He says, 'In this word flows together ideas of non-Christian religions with insights of biblical revelation, also superstition and every kind of philosophical reflections use the word'. In his dictionary of the German language Grimm dealt with

word 'spirit' many people associate the Holy Spirit as something intangible, that appears bodiless and ghostly, and already therefore it is (purely subjectively) understood as something or somebody who in relation to the Father and the Son occupies somehow an inferior, subordinate role and position.

Eventually it is necessary to consider that in the issue on the Holy Spirit and the Trinity we deal with the question of God, and here we encounter a mystery. A mystery does not necessary mean nothing can be known about it. Yet, the idea of the Holy Spirit is mysterious in that we are reliant on God's revelation. Neither nature nor humanity enables us to fathom and explain this mystery. However, God has revealed and made Himself known in his Word, the Holy Scriptures, and therefore in this important question it is necessary for us note: not less than that what Scripture has told us about God, and 'not to exceed what is written' (1 Cor 4:6). Since it is a divine mystery we deal with here, we need the necessary humility and self-modesty. Humility is needed because in perceiving and understanding the Godhead we depend upon someone who goes beyond us, upon God Himself. Humility is needed because from within myself I cannot understand God correctly and that I am dependent upon God for my correct perception of God. My knowledge of God is limited—for I am a creature, and not God! In addition, I am a sinner and sin has also darkened my thinking!—and that is why I must not make my reasoning about God the standard of what, who, and how God is. Otherwise we create for us a God according to our image. If we make our reason the standard, we will admit only what is in harmony with the requirements of human reason and is comprehendible to human thinking.[8]

---

its richness of meaning on almost twelve columns and differentiated between 30 different meanings (*ibid*).

8. 'The mysteries of the Bible, so far from being an argument against it, are among the strongest evidences of its divine inspiration. If it contained no account of God but that which we could comprehend; if His greatness and majesty could be grasped by finite minds, then the Bible would not, as now, bear the unmistakable evidences of divinity.' So Ellen G White, *Education* (Mountain View, CA: Pacific Press, 1952), 170. Ellen G White agrees that in thinking about the Holy Spirit we deal with a divine mystery. Thus she writes: 'It is not essential for us to be able to define just what the Holy Spirit is . . . The nature of the Holy Spirit is a mystery. Men cannot explain it, because the Lord has not revealed it to them. Men having fanciful views may bring together passages of Scripture and put a human construction on them, but the acceptance of these views will not strengthen the church. Regarding such mysteries, which are too deep for human understanding, silence is golden.' Ellen G White, *The Acts of the Apostles* (Boise, ID: Pacific Press, 1911), 51–52.

This knowledge on the final inscrutableness of God shows that we are not God but that we remain dependent on him. And it means also that we will never know too much of God but that there will always be new things which we will learn of him and about him.[9] In other words, it will never become boring to us.

Oftentimes the question is asked why the doctrine of the Trinity should be of such a foundational significance to our knowledge about God if it is not fully developed right from the beginning of the Bible. In response it may be said: That has to do with the character of God's self-revelation. God does not disclose himself instantly as a dogmatic text book but in a living history lasting for centuries. In a long, varied succession of events of salvation he reveals something of his essence. It is a challenge for us to reflect with our mind this succession of biblical revelatory history, to fathom it in its entirety, and to develop the increasing knowledge in its context. Hereby it is necessary to remember that the knowledge of the triune God was already indicated biblically and present in the beginning at the creation but that the Trinity becomes definitely manifest not until the end of time through the incarnation of God in Jesus Christ and in the outpouring of the Holy Spirit. God's innermost nature becomes visible now as that what the triune God was already since the beginning of all time.[10]

Considering our human limitation in understanding we nevertheless need to say that we can correctly recognise the things that God has revealed about himself in his Word, even if they exceed our full cognition. With the Apostle Paul we speak, 'For we write nothing else to you than what you read and understand, and I hope you will understand until the end' (2 Cor 1:13). In a way it is similar as with the love of God: 'May be able to comprehend with all the saints what is the breadth and length and height and depth, and to know the love of Christ which surpasses knowledge, that you may be filled up to all the fullness of God' (Eph 3:18, 19). If I can stress a comparison: With God's Trinity it is as with the light of the sun. When we try to look directly into the sun, we cannot see anything because we are blinded. On the other hand, in its light everything else becomes bright.

---

9. Wayne Grudem, *Systematic Theology: An Introduction to Biblical Doctrine* (Grand Rapids, MI: Zondervan, 1994), 150.
10. Rolf Hille, 'Gottes Dreieinigkeit - Reichtum und Tiefe der Erkenntnis Gottes', in *Wer ist Gott?: Unser Glaube an den Vater, den Sohn und den Heiligen Geist,* edited by Rolf Hille (Wuppertal: R. Brockhaus, 2007), 24.

With those transitory considerations we now turn to concrete statements of the Holy Scriptures that shall help us to understand better who the Holy Spirit is from a biblical point of view.

The Holy Spirit is God

We begin our exploration of the biblical data regarding the Holy Spirit by considering the question, does the Scripture portray the Holy Spirit as a (divine) power, or do the biblical writers themselves understood the Holy Spirit as God. A related issue is whether the Bible portrays the Holy Spirit in terms of personality and if it does, what implications this might have for the nature God?

The Holy Spirit and God the Father and God the Son are distinguished from each other in the Bible so that one receives the clear impression that the Holy Spirit is a distinct divine personality. Furthermore, designations for God are used for the Holy Spirit as well in the Bible. Indeed, the Holy Spirit is *called* God.[11] Thus we read for example in Exodus 17:7, that 'the sons of Israel . . . tested the LORD', in fact, Yahweh. Psalm 95:8, 9 refers to this incident. There God admonishes the people: 'Do not harden your hearts, as at Meribah, as in the day of Massah in the wilderness; when your fathers tested Me, they tried Me, though they had seen My work.' This passage of the Psalm is quoted in Hebrews 3:7–11, and there the voice of admonition is attributed to the Holy Spirit. In other words, the God who speaks in the Psalm—Yahweh who was tested in the wilderness—is no one else but the Holy Spirit! The Holy Spirit is equal to God.

The same thing can be seen in Isaiah 6:8, 9. Here Isaiah hears the voice of the Lord asking, 'Whom shall I send . . . ?' Shortly afterwards Yahweh commissions him as his prophet: 'Go, and tell this people . . . ' (Isa 6:9). In Acts 28:25–27 Paul quotes those words as being spoken by the Holy Spirit. In Isaiah it is God who speaks. Paul says: The Holy Spirit had spoken. In other words: The Holy Spirit is equal to God.

The same discovery is made through a comparison of Jeremiah 31:33 and Hebrews 10:15–17, where the writer of Hebrews testifies that what was said by God in Jeremiah was testified to us through the Holy Spirit. Also here the Holy Spirit is utilised in a way that he is equal with God.

---

11. Hereafter I follow the explanations found in Stuart Olyott, *Drei, die eins sind: Vom Geheimnis der Dreieinigkeit* (Stuttgart: Christliches Verlagshaus, 1984), 54ff.

In 2 Samuel 23:2 it says, 'The Spirit of the LORD spoke by me, And his word was on my tongue.' In verse 3 the parallel statement is made: 'The God of Israel said . . . to me.' The conclusion that we have to draw from this parallel is: The Holy Spirit is equal to God.[12]

In Genesis 6:3 it is said concerning the people who lived prior to the flood: 'My Spirit shall not strive with man forever.' In 1 Peter 3:20 it talks about the same event: 'who once were disobedient, when the patience of God kept waiting in the days of Noah'. In the patience of God they withstood the Holy Spirit. Here we find the same indication, namely that the Holy Spirit is equal to God.

In Isaiah 63:10–14 the following statements are made in the remarkable passage about Israel and God's guidance through Moses: 'But they rebelled and grieved his Holy Spirit. . . . Where is He who put his Holy Spirit in the midst of them . . . The Spirit of the LORD gave them rest. So didst Thou lead Thy people' (verses 10, 11, and 14). However, the parallel account in the Old Testament as found in Numbers 14:11 writes: 'And the LORD said to Moses, How long will this people spurn Me?' And in Deuteronomy 32:12 we are told that 'the LORD alone guided him, and there was no foreign god with him'. God and the Holy Spirit are on par with each other here.[13]

Another biblical hint that God and the Holy Spirit were on par for the biblical writers and that those terms were interchangeable is found in 1 Corinthians 3 and 6. In chapter 3:16, 17 the Apostle Paul asks: 'Do you not know that you are a *temple of God*, and that the Spirit of God dwells in you?' Three chapters later Paul employs almost the same formulation: 'Or do you not know that your body is a *temple of the Holy Spirit* who is in you' (1 Cor 6:19). The temple of God or the temple of the Holy Spirit. Again Paul uses 'God' and the 'Holy Spirit' synonymously (cf 2 Cor 6:16, where Paul writes: 'We are the temple of the living God'). The Holy Spirit is equal to God.

In 1 Corinthians 12:11 Paul writes that it is the Holy Spirit who distributes the spiritual gift to each one individually just as he wills. In verse 28 in the chapter we are told that it is God who is doing it. The basic statement

---

12. Max Hatton, *Understanding the Trinity* (Grantham: Autumn House, 2001), 107.
13. Edward Henry Bickersteth, *The Trinity* (Grand Rapids, MI: Kregel, 1993), 138. In his book, Bickersteth gives many other parallels and examples that make plain the equality of the Holy Spirit with God.

in those verses is clear: The Holy Spirit does the same action that God is doing; the Holy Spirit is equal to God.[14]

The identification of the Holy Spirit with God becomes most clear in the statement of the Apostle Paul in Acts 5:3, 4, where he asks Ananias: 'Why has Satan filled your heart to lie to the Holy Spirit, and to keep back some of the price of the land?' (verse 3). And then he adds: 'You have not lied to men, but to God' (verse 4). In Peter's thinking 'to lie to the Holy Spirit' and 'to lie to God' is the same! The Holy Spirit is definitely equal to God.

This statement is even more significant in light of the fact that Luke, the writer of Acts, had recorded those things from the point of view of the mighty works of the Spirit (cf Luke 24:49). What happened here in the early church is an echo to what had occurred earlier to the people of Israel. Pentecost was known among the Jews as the day when on Mt. Sinai the law of God had been given, which was written with the finger of God. Interestingly enough Jesus employs the term 'Spirit of God' (Mt 12:28) for the expression 'finger of God' (Luke 11:20). Only a few days after Israel had experienced the mighty works of God at the exodus from Egypt and after God had given them his law, they made themselves the golden calf. At Pentecost in the year 31 AD the 'finger of God' came down with mighty signs and wonders upon the waiting believers of the young Christian church and God's law was written into their hearts. But similar to the Israel of old, Ananias and Sapphira decided to set their heart on the mammon rather than to follow God with an undivided heart. Therefore their destiny was the same as the destiny of the three thousand who had perished in the wilderness back then. Sometimes we ask ourselves why the two befell such a severe sentence. They had to die because they became

---

14. Hatton, *Understanding the Trinity*, 107. Also Jesus used the words 'God' and 'Holy Spirit' in a way suggesting that both are interchangeable. During his encounter with Nicodemus He talks about how it is possible to be born again (John 3:3, 5-9). This new birth happens through the Spirit (John 3:9), although Nicodemus considered it improbable. Thereby it has to do with the question of salvation. Later in his ministry when another group of disciples of Jesus asked how one could be saved, Jesus answered: 'With people this is impossible, but with God all things are possible' (Matt 19:26). For Jesus it was God who makes possible our salvation, just as it is the Holy Spirit who gives us a new birth. For the Holy Spirit is the one who has the ability to open in us the eyes concerning sin, righteousness, and judgment (John 16:8-11).

guilty before the omnipotent God of the same offense as Israel 1,500 years before.[15]

Moreover, in various places of the Bible divine attributes and features are attributed to the Holy Spirit.

- *The Holy Spirit is eternal:* In Hebrews 9:14 we find the only biblical reference to 'the eternal Spirit.' It is the same word that is used for the self-existent God.[16] In Deuteronomy 33:27 we find the only text that speaks about the 'the eternal God.' How many eternal ones do exist? We know that only God is eternal. The Holy Spirit is equal to the eternal God.
- *The Holy Spirit is omnipresent:* The Spirit is omnipresent at all times: 'Where can I go from Thy Spirit? Or where can I flee from Thy presence?' (Ps 139:7).
- *The Holy Spirit is omniscient:* Isaiah 40:13, 14; 1 Corinthians 2:10, 11 ('The Spirit searches all things, even the depths of God.'); Romans 11:34.
- *The Holy Spirit reveals the future:* It is said about Simeon: 'And it had been revealed to him by the Holy Spirit that he would not see death before he had seen the Lord's Christ' (Luke 2:26). The Holy Spirit will disclose to us 'what is to come' (John 16:13). John was moved by the Spirit on the Isle of Patmos (Rev 1:10), and he was shown things to come.
- *The Holy Spirit is holy and good:* 'You gave your good Spirit to instruct them' (Neh 9:20). 'Let your good Spirit lead me on level ground' (Ps 143:10). In the Old Testament he is explicitly called the Holy Spirit of God (Ps 51:11; Isa 63:10). In the same manner he is called the Spirit of Truth (John 14:17) and the Spirit who sanctifies (Rom 1:4).
- *The Holy Spirit is omnipotent:* The Holy Spirit can do everything he likes (1 Cor 12:11; Rom 15:19; John 3:6 [he gives the new birth]).
- *The Holy Spirit is present and active at the creation:* 'The *Spirit of God has made me,* and the breath of the Almighty gives me life' (Job 33:4; cf Isa 40:12–14; Ps 104:30; Gen 1:2); may be compared to 'O LORD, you are our Father, we are the clay, and you our potter; and all of us are the work of Your hand' (Isa 64:8; cf John 1:17; Col 1:16). Only God has the ability to create. Only someone who is God can be our Creator. The Holy Spirit is equal to God.

---

15. Clouzet, 'The Personhood of the Holy Spirit and Why it Matters', 18–9.
16. Bickersteth, *The Trinity*, 128.

- *The Holy Spirit can raise from the dead:* 'But if **the Spirit** of Him who **raised** Jesus **from the dead** dwells in you, he who raised Christ Jesus from the dead will **also give life to your mortal bodies through his Spirit** who dwells in you' (Rom 8:11); might be compared to 'For just as the Father raises the dead and gives them life, even so the Son also gives life to whom he wishes' (John 5:21); and 'Jesus said to her, I am the resurrection and the life; he who believes in me will live even if he dies' (John 11:25). Only God has the power to raise again the dead. The Holy Spirit is equal to God.
- *The Holy Spirit inspires the biblical writers:* '. . . men moved **by the Holy Spirit** spoke from God' (2 Pet 1:21); might be compared to 'All Scripture is inspired **by God** and profitable for teaching . . .' (2 Tim 3:16). Only God has the ability to inspire chosen people and to communicate them his will. The Holy Spirit is equal to God.
- *The Holy Spirit gives life:* '. . . the Spirit gives life' (2 Cor 3:6); and the Holy Spirit makes new ' . . . renewing by the Holy Spirit' (Titus 3:5); might be compared to 'For just as the Father has life in Himself, even so he gave to the Son also to have life in Himself' (John 5:26; cf Gen 2:7). Only God has life in himself and is therefore able to give life. Also the Holy Spirit gives life, creates anew. The Holy Spirit is equal to God.
- *The Holy Spirit holds divine titles:* Lord – 2 Corinthians 3:17; God – Acts 5:3, 4; Saviour – Titus 3:5; Truth – 1 John 5:6; Life – Romans 8:10.
- *The Holy Spirit is brought into connection with worship:* In Psalm 95:6-9 it says: 'Come, let us worship and bow down, let us kneel before the LORD our Maker . . . if you would hear his voice, Do not harden your hearts, as at Meribah, as in the day of Massah in the wilderness, when your fathers tested me, they tried me . . .' In Hebrews 3:7–9 this statement is attributed to the Holy Spirit. Cf Isaiah 63:10 and Acts 7:51, where it is apparent that they withstood the Holy Spirit. That is why we can draw the conclusion that the One the psalmist calls us to pray to is the same one who was tested and tempted by the Israelites. The parallel texts reveals that it was again the Holy Spirit. That means that the Holy Spirit is also included in the worship of God and that he is equal to God.

The Holy Spirit and the Great Commission

Converted people are baptised in the name of the Holy Spirit. It is interesting note the wording used by Jesus, when he commands his followers to make disciples, '... baptising them in *the name* [singular] of the Father and the Son and the Holy Spirit' (Matt 28:19). It does not say: 'baptising them in the *names* of the Father and the Son and the Holy Spirit'. In the Bible the name is always also an expression of the character of the one who bears this name. God is one in three persons. This text is biblically very well testified and there is no reason to think that this statement would not be authentic or had been added later.[17]

Other texts where all three persons of the Godhead are mentioned alongside one another include the following: 2 Corinthians 13:14 (the apostolic blessing); 1 Corinthians 14:4–6 (in the context of the gifts of the Spirit); and 1 Peter 1:1–2 (where Peter mentions the triune God together).

Now, we understand better the deeper meaning of the threefold 'Holy, Holy, Holy is the LORD of hosts' (Isa 6:3), and we comprehend why a few verses later in verse 8 it is stated: 'Then I heard the voice of the Lord, saying, "Whom shall I send, and who will go for *us*?"'

Jesus is God. Therefore it would be surprising if the person that he Himself sent in order to take his place would be something lesser than he.[18] If we look closer at chapter 14 in the Gospel of John, we read that Jesus says in verse 9 and 10 that he and the Father are one: 'He who has seen Me has seen the Father' (verse 9). The other (*allos*)[19] comforter (*parakletos*) that Jesus promised to his disciples in the same chapter (John 14:16, 17), is a comforter who from his kind and quality is equal to Jesus, on one par with Him. If Jesus is one with the Father this means that the Holy Spirit, who was sent by Jesus to take his place, is also one with the Father and is equal to God.[20] Who could mean as much to his disciples as Jesus Himself if he would not be God?

Not that we have looked at some biblical statements concerning the Godhead of the Holy Spirit, we turn now to the question if the Holy Spirit is a person or merely a divine power.

---

17. Alexander Rohleder, *Trinität und Heiliger Geist* (Gondelsheim: Eigendruck, 2006), 91–100, deals extensively with the claims of the antitrinitarians in regard to John 14 and refutes the thesis that this text would be spurious or that it was added later.
18. Olyott, *Drei, die eins sind*, 53.
19. Jesus uses here the Greek word *allos* in contrast to the term *heteros*. *Heteros* denotes the different that distinguishes itself in its kind; we have derived eg the term 'heterosexual' in order to show that two different sexes are meant by that. Although the term *allos* expresses the numerical difference, it shows at the same time that the other one is like him, is of the same kind as Jesus. Cf R Ch Trench, *Synonyma des Neuen Testaments* (Tübingen: JCB Mohr [Paul Siebeck], 1907), 226–30.
20. Clouzet, 'The Personhood of the Holy Spirit and Why it Matters', 20.

The Personality of the Holy Spirit

Here the question is posed if and how far the Spirit can be understood as a real personality. Many have the impression that the Holy Spirit would not be a person but rather an impersonal divine power. If we talk about Jesus Christ as the 'Son of God', we immediately image something personal because the Son of God came to us as a human being. The Holy Spirit, in contrast, appeared nowhere in such a obvious manner in a personal form. In addition to that the Holy Spirit is described by different, rather impersonal images: among others he is like a wind, a breath (Hebrew: *ruach*, Greek: *pneuma*; cf Genesis 2:7 and Acts 17:25; Genesis 8:1 and John 3:8; Ezekiel 37:5, 9 [the wind is not tangible, physical, personal]); water (John 7:38, 39); fire (Matt 3:11; Acts 2:3); like a dove (Matt 3:16); and a seal (Eph 1:13).

But we need to look at all texts of the Bible in order to gain a comprehensive picture of the Holy Spirit. Doing that will reveal that the Holy Spirit is spoken of in personal antecedents.

A couple of biblical examples shall illustrate that:

If we look closer at chapters 14 – 16 of the Gospel of John, it becomes clear obvious how Jesus views the Holy Spirit.[21] Jesus says:

- The Holy Spirit *guides, hears, speaks, proclaims, and glorifies* (John 16:13, 14).
- The Holy Spirit *teaches* and *reminds* you (John 14:26).
- The Holy Spirit *dwells* in you (John 14:17).
- The Holy Spirit *testifies* (John 15:24, 26).
- The Holy Spirit *convicts* (John 16:8).

If we consider Jesus' statements seriously, we need to recognise that a mere power or divine force cannot perform all those activities. The Holy Spirit has to be an independent personality.

This is also repeated in other passages in the New Testament (cf Luke 12:12; 1 Cor 2:13; Acts 5:32), and the Bible confirms the thought of a personality of the Holy Spirit in many other places where we learn that:

- The Holy Spirit *can be invoked* (Eze 37:9).
- The Holy Spirit *speaks* (Acts 8:29; 10:19, 20; 28:25; Heb 3:7).
- The Holy Spirit *calls into the ministry* (Acts 13:2).

---

21. I follow the presentation of Olyott, *Drei, die eins sind*, 50–51.

- The Holy Spirit *sends out* (Acts 13:4).
- The Holy Spirit *prohibits certain enterprises* (Acts 16:6-7).
- The Holy Spirit *intercedes* (Rom 8:16).
- The Holy Spirit *reveals* (1 Cor 2:10).
- The Holy Spirit *searches all things* (1 Cor 2:10; Rom 8:27), and *knows things* (1 Cor 2:11).
- The Holy Spirit *sanctifies* (Rom 15:16).
- The Holy Spirit *raises from the dead* (Rom 8:11) and *works miracles* (Acts 2:4; 8:39).
- The Holy Spirit *renews* (Titus 3:5).
- The Holy Spirit *seals* (Eph 4:30).
- The Holy Spirit *can be insulted* (Heb 10:29).
- The Holy Spirit *can be lied to* (Acts 5:3).
- The Holy Spirit *can be tempted* (Acts 5:9).
- The Holy Spirit *can be blasphemed* against (Matt 12:31).
- The Holy Spirit *can be resisted* (Acts 7:51).
- Especially important: The Holy Spirit *loves* (Rom 15:30; no impersonal force can love!).
- The Holy Spirit *has a will and decides of his' own volition* (1 Cor 12:11), and *has his own mind* (Rom 8:27).
- The Holy Spirit *represents the saints* (Rom 8:27).
- The Holy Spirit *can have communion with us* (2 Cor 13:14).
- The Holy Spirit *can be grieved* (Eph 4:30).
- It is possible to *sin* against the Holy Spirit (Matt 12:31, 32).

Can those things be said about an impersonal power or force?[22] All those statements would make no sense if the Holy Spirit would not be a person. Who would treat an impersonal force in such a way? The Holy Spirit must be spoken of in a personal way because God himself is present 'in person' in that which comes from God and is granted by God. There are no divine activities that are similarly simply 'factual' effects of a God who keeps a distance, so as high voltage current is still effective in long distance from the power plant that generates it. In his activities God himself is the one who works.[23]

The statement of the Apostle, 'it seemed good to the Holy Spirit and to us . . .' (Acts 15:28), would be absurd if the Spirit would only be a power

---

22. Cf Bickersteth, *The Trinity*, 127.
23. Wilfried Joest, *Dogmatik: Die Wirklichkeit Gottes*, 2 volumes, UTB für Wissenschaft Uni-Taschenbücher (Göttingen: Vandenhoeck & Ruprecht, 1984), 1:308, 309.

or an influence. How can believing people be baptised 'in the name of the Father and the Son and the Holy Spirit' (Matt 28:19) if the two first-mentioned would be persons but not the third one?

Certain statements of the Bible would make no sense if the Holy Spirit would only be a force. Could it be reported of Jesus that he 'returned ... in the power of the Spirit' (Luke 4:14) if the word 'Spirit' would just refer to a power? It is the central point of this verse that the Spirit and his power are two separate things: the Holy Spirit has power but he is no power.[24] The same is true for quite a number of other Bible verses:

- 'You know of Jesus of Nazareth, how God anointed Him with the Holy Spirit and with power ...' (Acts 10:38).
- '... that you will abound in hope by the power of the Holy Spirit' (Rom 15:13).
- 'And my message and my preaching were not in persuasive words of wisdom, but in demonstration of the Spirit and of power' (1 Cor 2:4).

In 1 John 2:1 Jesus is identified as comforter or advocate (*parakleton*). I John 14:16 Jesus promises another 'comforter' (*parakleton*) who shall take his place. He employs the same word as the one used for him in 1 John 2:1. Thereby Jesus shows clearly that the Holy Spirit is also a person like Himself and not a thing. The Holy Spirit has to be a person in the same manner as Jesus himself is a person. Similarly, it becomes obvious as well that Jesus and the Spirit differ from one another.

The Greek word for 'Spirit' (*pneuma*) is a neuter noun. The Greeks considered 'pneuma' neither male nor female but as neuter. But in John 16:8, 13, 14, etc. Jesus assigns a male pronoun to the neuter noun (*pneuma*). In other words: Jesus spoke of the Spirit as of a 'He,' where he according to the rules of grammar should have spoken of an 'It'. This point does also indicate that the Holy Spirit is a person and not a thing.[25]

When Jesus speaks of an advocate in John 15:26, whom 'I will send to you from the Father, that is the Spirit of truth who proceeds from the Father ... ' He makes unmistakenly plain that the Holy Spirit is not the Lord Jesus Christ whom Christ promises to send. It is unmistakable in the same way, that the Holy Spirit is not the Father for Christ sends him

---

24. Olyott, *Drei, die eins sind*, 52.
25. Woodrow W Whidden, Jerry Moon, and John W Reeve, *The Trinity: Understanding God's Love, His Plan of Salvation, and Christian Relationships* (Hagerstown, MD: Review and Herald, 2002), 71–72.

from the Father. Every one of them is God but every one of them is also independent.

All this leads us to the conclusion that the Holy Spirit is an independent person. He is God as the Father. He is God as the Son. Yet, he is not the Father and not the Son.

The Meaning of Personhood When Attributed to God

That the concept of the Trinity occurs in the Bible can be recognised from the above evidence. Nevertheless, as human beings we often struggle to imagine the Trinity concretely and to present it properly in a symbolic way. Attempting to do that, a variety of different words have been utilised in the course of the centuries.[26] A difficulty to understand the Trinity has to do with the term 'person'. Our word 'person' is derived from the Latin word 'persona', which was used by theologians of the Western Church (Latin writers as, for example, Tertullian). Initially it denoted the mask of an actor; later it developed the meaning of an individual character in a play and in Roman law it referred to an objectively existing individual that possessed its own substance or property.[27] Well, we need to use the word 'person' very carefully. We should certainly not use it with its original Latin meaning. The three persons of the Godhead are not like an actor who appears in three different roles or costumes in one play. We should also not use the word as in our vernacular so that we read something from our understanding into the Bible what is not meant so therein. God does not consist of three individuals, next to one another and separate from each other, which—at least theoretically—could work against each other.

When using the expression 'persons' we rather think of the personal autonomy within the divine existence, which identifies itself with the word 'I' and which talks of the others with the words 'You' and 'He', that bear simply the characteristic of a personality.

---

26. Greek writers usually used the word '*hypostasis*', which means literally so much as 'the substance, the reality, the position, the condition'. See Walter Bauer, *Griechisch-Deutsches Wörterbuch zu den Schriften des Neuen Testaments und der übrigen urchristlichen Literatur*, fifth edition (Berlin: Walter de Gruyter, 1971 fifth), 1675. Another word was '*substantia*' (substance, essence). Roman writers, however, employed the word '*persona*' what refers literally to the mask of an actor, later becoming a rather ambigious term which denoted the role that someone played in life or also his characteristics, his reputation, his dignity. Cf Richard A Muller, *Dictionary of Latin and Greek Theological Terms: Drawn Principally from Protestant Scholastic Theology* (Grand Rapids, MI: Baker, 1985), 223–7.
27. Muller, *Dictionary of Latin and Greek Theological Terms*, 223.

There is an early church symbol that illustrates this Trinity of God:[28]

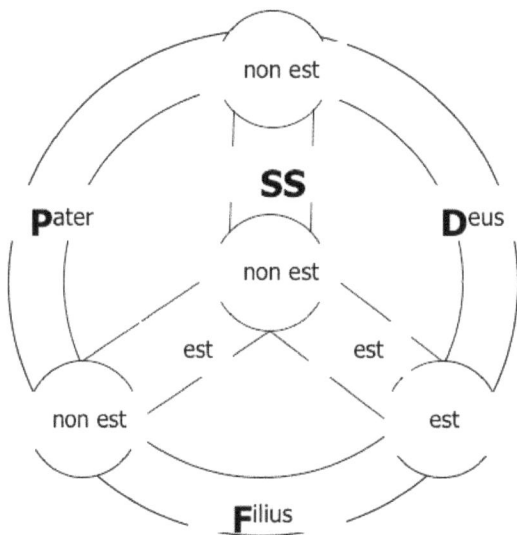

Deus (God) is = the Father (Pater); = the Son (Filius); = the Holy Spirit (Spiritus Sanctus). But the Father is not the Son, the Son is not the Holy Spirit, and the Holy Spirit is not the Father. Each one of the three divine persons possesses the same essence or substance. It is not a tri-theismus, not a belief in three gods. Every one of the three persons in God possesses the same nature and therefore also the same attributes of God. The plural of the persons is not a plural of substance or nature.[29] We do not say that three substances are one substance, or that three persons are one person, but that three persons are one substance. Thus the basics of the Trinity are summarised in the following two sentences: 'Every person of the Godhead is in himself God'; and 'Every person of the Godhead is united inseparably with the others.'

The three persons in the one God have one substance, one will. They pursue together one goal:

> In the Father God is for us.
> In the Son God is with us.

---

28. AJ Conyers, *A Basic Christian Theology* (Nashville, TN: Broadman & Holman, 1995), 42.
29. Wolfgang Trillhaas, *Dogmatik,* second revised edition (Berlin: Alfred Töpelmann, 1967), 109.

In the Holy Spirit God is in us.
The Father is the originator of salvation.
The Son is the realiser of salvation.
The Holy Spirit is the preparer of salvation.

We cannot fully grasp how three persons can only have one will and share the same substance. And that is why it must be emphasised that we do not believe that because we are able to understand or explain it fully, or because the ecclesiastical tradition did say it so, but because God has revealed it so about Himself in his Word. God is inseparably three and mysteriously one.[30]

Martin Luther expressed something similar when he wrote:

> If reason considers the doctrine of the holy Trinity to be folly, why do we ask for it? For it is not an art to sophisticate in such things. I would do it just as well as others. But thank God, I have the grace that I do not covet to dispute too much here. If I know that it is God's Word and that God has spoken so, I stop asking how it could be true and I let only the Word of God satisfy me; may it rhyme with reason as it wants. In this way should every Christian also do in all the articles of our faith that it is not much sophisticated and disputed about it if it might be possible, but to see only there and ask if it is God's Word. Is it a word that He has said, then do confide in it with certainty. He will neither lie at you nor betray you, if you do not understand it how and when.[31]

In another place Martin Luther states:

> Here God speaks. I hear that there is one God and three persons. How it is like, I do not know. I want to believe.[32]

---

30. Olyott, *Drei, die eins sind*, 66. Note that Ellen G White uses very similar language to express her view. For example, in *Evangelism* (Hagerstown, MD: Review and Herald, 2002), 615, she said, 'There are three living persons of the heavenly trio . . . the Father, the Son, and the Holy Spirit', in *Patriarchs and Prophets* (Nampa, ID: Pacific Press, 2005), 34, she said, 'Christ . . . was one with the eternal Father—one in nature, in character, in purpose', in *Testimonies for the Church*, 9 volumes (Nampa, ID: Pacific Press, 2002), 8:269, she said, 'They [Christ and the disciples] are one in purpose, in mind, in character, **but not in person**. It is thus that God and Christ are one', in *Evangelism*, 616, she said 'The Holy Spirit . . . is as much a person as God is a person'.
31. Martin Luther, *D Martin Luthers Werke*, 56 volumes (Weimar: Hermann Böhlaus Nachfolger, 1910), 41:273-4.
32. Martin Luther, *D Martin Luthers Werke*, 56 volumes. (Weimar: Hermann Böhlaus

Ellen G White manifests a similar basic attitude when she writes:

> Men of the greatest intellect cannot understand the mysteries of Jehovah as revealed in nature. Divine inspiration asks many questions which the most profound scholar cannot answer. These questions were not asked that we might answer them, but to call our attention to the deep mysteries of God and to teach us that our wisdom is limited; that in the surroundings of our daily life there are many things beyond the comprehension of finite beings. Skeptics refuse to believe in God because they cannot comprehend the infinite power by which he reveals Himself. *But God is to be acknowledged as much from what he does not reveal of Himself, as from that which is open to our limited comprehension.* Both in divine revelation and in nature, God has given mysteries to command our faith. This must be so. We may be ever searching, ever inquiring, ever learning, and yet there is an infinity beyond.[33]

Implications Concerning the Personality of the Holy Spirit

There are a number of significant implications that flow from the personality of the Holy Spirit.[34] For example, only persons can consciously choose to cooperate with one another, and we are invited to work together with the Holy Spirit, while he leads the church. But such a close connection and cooperation can only be accomplished through a trusting personal connection between two persons, who love, honour, and respect each other.

If we do not understand that the Holy Spirit is a person of the Godhead, we will treat him like a thing. If we view the Holy Spirit simply as a 'something', as a force, which lacks the characteristics of a personality, it will be easier for us to ignore him, to deafen our ears to his wooing, and to harden our hearts against his influence, for a thing or a force has no emotions, no feelings, no interest.

If the Holy Spirit is only a force, *I* then want to possess the Holy Spirit. Then *I* need to possess this force in order to work in the will of God. Yet,

---

Nachfolger, 1932), 39/II:364.
33. Ellen G White, *Ministry of Healing* (Nampa, ID: Pacific Press, 2004), 431.
34. Cf Clouzet, 'The Personhood of the Holy Spirit and Why it Matters', 28–32.

it is ultimately *I* who is standing in the centre. However, if the Holy Spirit is a divine personality then *HE* wants to possess me. Then *HE* wants me to submit to *HIM*. Then *HE* wants to do something with me, and not I with him. If the Holy Spirit is only a force that is at *my* disposal, then *I* am actually in control and *I* decide what needs to be done because *I* receive the Holy Spirit. But when I belong to *him* and *HE* can do things *with me*, this is something totally different. Only in this way God stands in the centre and not a human being.

The Holy Spirit does not just lead people to Jesus Christ; he leads them also together among themselves. That becomes more concrete for example in the worship service on Sabbath and continues in active faith-filled discipleship in the everyday life during the week. Such a fellowship renewed through the presence of the Holy Spirit is able to reconcile and to carry the weak ones. It is willing to take over responsibilities in mission, welfare work, and also in the society as well as towards God's creation.

The unpardonable sin is the sin against the Holy Spirit (Matt 12:31, 32), because he is the one who brings us into contact with God. Only through the ministry of the Holy Spirit we obtain access to the efficiency of Jesus' intercessory ministry. Without him it would be impossible to accept Christ as our saviour, redeemer, and Lord.

In the Trinity there is power. Out of his trinitarian love God works dynamically for the salvation of the world. God does not need the world in order to be fully and perfectly God but he wants it for his love's sake. The Trinity of God can be an example for us on the dealings and the cooperation in the church, where we reach in the same voluntary submission and active cooperation the mutual goal in love and thereby become like God. The love of the church members makes the triune God credible and attractive. Where this love is seen, the Holy Spirit creates—in whose power Christ was resurrected from the dead—through the Word of God again and again anew the faith in people who receive thereby the gift of new birth. Thus the church is growing to the honour of God the Father in the name of the Lord Jesus Christ.

Trinity and Tawhid in Islam—An Appraisal

Børge Schantz

The Christian doctrines of the divinity of Christ and the Trinity are the greatest obstacles for Muslims to accept. The core of the Christian faith, as it is expressed in human language, that the one and only God exist in three persons (Father, Son an Holy Spirit) in one being (substance), is completely misunderstood by many Muslims and unacceptable to all. Dialogues with and missionary approaches to Muslims will not get anywhere unless the fundamental doctrines of the incarnation of Jesus Christ, the triune nature of the Godhead, and the atonement by Jesus Christ are also accepted.

Christians admit that they are not able to fully grasp or explain the Trinity. It is a mystery that cannot be explained nor acknowledged by reason. Still it is a revelation that is not against rational thinking. It is accepted in faith as it is essential in the salvation process.

Still various Christian traditions have used much energy to explain this central Christian dogma. And although it is a mystery it is not incompatible with the principles of rational thought.

Three reasons are suggested as to why Muslims reject the deity of Christ and the Trinity. First, is its intrusion on the preserves of Allāh. In Islam it is unacceptable to name and outline the characteristics of Allāh. It is presumption to attempt to break through the transcendence of Allāh. Men should not attempt to find words for the essence of Allāh. What God is should never be a goal for human research. Acceptance of a Trinity therefore is a transgressing of these Islamic sentiments.

Second, the Trinity concept is *shirk* in the Muslim understanding. *Shirk* is the most serious and unforgiveable sin in Islam for which there is the death penalty. The word literally means 'association'. In its religious context it means holding anything or anyone equal to Allāh.[1] The Trinity

---

1. Cyril Glassé, *Concise Dictionary of Islam* (San Francisco, CA: Harper&Row, 1989),

doctrine is interpreted by Muslims to mean that Christians in the Trinity have more than one god. Such belief is *shirk*.

Third, the concept of a Trinity three in one and one in three, is a completely incomprehensible mystery for the Muslim. Christians must accept that, whatever their explanation of the Trinity, this is most difficult and problematic for Muslims.[2]

Tawhid, Allāh, Isa and Ruh in the Koran

The greatest message in Islam is the Shahadah 'There is no god except Allāh; Muhammad is the Messenger of Allāh'. This simple confession of faith is the only requirement for being a Muslim. The first part of the creed places the Muslim in the care of an almighty creator. The last part points the worshipper to a prophet and a movement that directs the road directly to Allāh and paradise.

The Tawhid defines this most important doctrine in Islam. In Arabic the word means 'to declare and acknowledge oneness'. It declares the absolute monotheism, oneness, unity and uniqueness of Allāh as creator and sustainer of the universe. The Tawhid concept is expressed in Surah 112:1–4:

> Say: He is Allāh, the One and Only; Allāh, the Eternal, Absolute; He begetteth not, nor is He begotten; And there is none like unto Him.[3]

Tawhid is expanded in Surah 59:22–24:

> Allāh is He, than Whom there is no other god;- Who knows (all things) both secret and open; He, Most Gracious, Most Merciful. Allāh is He, than Whom there is no other god;- the Sovereign, the Holy One, the Source of Peace (and Perfection), the Guardian of Faith, the Preserver of Safety, the Exalted in Might, the Irresistible, the Supreme: Glory to Allāh. (High is He) above the partners they attribute to Him. He is

---

370.
2. Niels Henrik Arendt, *Gud er stor. Om Islam og Kristendom* (Denmark, København: Forlaget Anis, 2006), 93.
3. This and subsequent Koran references are taken from, *The Meanings Of The Holy Qur'an* (Madina, Saudia Arabia: King Faud Holy Qu-ān Printing Complex).

Allāh, the Creator, the Evolver, the Bestower of Forms (or Colours). To Him belong the Most Beautiful Names: whatever is in the heavens and on earth, doth declare His Praises and Glory: and He is the Exalted in Might, the Wise.

In Islamic belief, any comparison of Allāh to human beings and their characteristics are forbidden. Only eternity can be ascribed to Allāh. Notwithstanding, it would appear that some human attributes such as lord, possessor, ownership, seeing, hearing are qualities ascribed to him. These attributes are constructed from the ninety-nine names applied to Allāh in the Koran.[4]

The *Tawhid* strongly emphasises that Allāh has no partners. Although the emphasis is on the contrast with polytheismtic atheism, wealth and political power, are also vices opposed in the *tawhid*. It is therefore clear why the cardinal belief in a Trinity upheld by most Christian traditions is fully rejected by Muslims. It is against the Oneness of Allāh, it is polytheistic and a form of idol-worship.

Allāh is the Arabic word for god and used by Muslim all over the world. The noun Allāh is pre-Islamic and used for God by Arabic speaking Christians of various traditions. In spite of Muslim claims, Allāh is not an Islamic prerogative title.

Allāh the one and only God is, however, revealed in the Koran. He is creator, sustainer, judge and ruler of the universe, as well as governor of human experiences. Allāh has guided history through his prophets (Adam, Noah, Abraham, Ishmael, Moses, Jesus and Muhammad). He particularly directs humankind as judge with rewards or punishments.

The Koran and the Hadith (reports of words and deeds of Muhammad and first Muslims) make hardly any references to Allāh's character and essence. Rather, Muslims employ the ninety-nine names of Allāh, found in various places in the Koran, as descriptions of his character. The beautiful names, however, are really not character descriptions. They have more value as portrayal of the realities of Allāh's guidance and his rule in the daily lives of Muslims.

These ninety-nine names reveal on one hand Allāh as being majestic, generous, safeguarding, and pardoning, but on the other hand as being afflicting, abasing, and avenging.

---

4. Alfred Guillaume, *Islam* (Middlesex: Penguin, 1979), 130.

These descriptions of Allāh force Islam to face some intellectual challenges. On the one hand a strict monotheism is maintained which rejects any suggestions that the transcendent Allāh is visible or human. On the other hand, the Koran speaks about Allāh in human terms. These seemingly contradictory concepts are, however, not a real problem to Muslims. They are not dealt with simply because divine will and actions are ultimately beyond human reason and is an area in which the Muslim is forbidden to enter.[5]

The general understanding of Allāh is that he is a distant and absent god, whose interest and concern for people is limited to their strict obedience to divine laws. To the Muslim, Allāh is a ruler not a father, for in Allāh power is more prominent than love. In spite of the words in the Koran and Hadiths about Allāh being 'near' (Sura 50:16) and 'most merciful' (Sura 12:92), the general impression is that Allāh's relationship to man is one of aloofness, of requiring obedience, and of minimal interference into human affairs.

It has been suggested that Allāh's mercy is confined to the fact that he called Muhammad to be his last prophet, send the Koran to him and gave clear instructions on how to get to the Muslim paradise. Furthermore, there are harsh words on the punishments of disobedience.

Isa, is the name for Jesus Christ in the Koran. He is mentioned ninety-three times where he seems to be the most appealing personality. The descriptions Jesus Christ and his prophet-hood surpass both Abraham and Noah and even Muhammad.

The Koran writes in detail that Jesus was conceived miraculously in a virgin birth (Surah 19:16–40). Christ is called an *Apostle*, however in the sense of a messenger to warn the Jews (Surah 61:6). He is called *Messiah*, not meaning redeemer, rather sinless. He is even titled the *Word*, but meaning a preacher; and *Spirit*, implying that Jesus was created like Adam by the breath of Allāh. Christ is called a *Prophet* (Surah 33:7), to be understood, however, as one in the line of Adam, Noah and Moses.[6] His prophetic call was only as a messenger to the Israel.

Some of his miracles are also listed. Among them are the cleansing of lepers, restoring of sight to the blind, and resurrecting the dead. Jesus' miraculous events extend to making a clay bird alive (Surah 3:49).

---

5. Norman L Geisler and Abdul Saleeb, *Answering Islam: The Crescent in the Light of the Cross* (Grand Rapids, MI: Baker, 1993), 16 ff.
6. Hans Heinz and Daniel Heinz, *Das Christentum begegnet dem Islam* (Zweigstelle, Switzerland: Advent-Verl, 2007), 62–63.

It is conspicuous and interesting that with the list of the more or less biblical details of the birth, life, calling, miracles of Christ there is not one single sentence that quotes any of his words, sayings, teachings or sermons. Jesus only talks of his miracles as signs that Allāh called him to be a prophet for the Jewish people.

In the Hadiths we detect a few extra reflections of the New Testament Jesus. However, references to him as a prophet and his influence are on the humanistic side. Jesus is portrayed as an ascetic person, living in absolute poverty, but dedicated to the service of men and women.[7]

In brief, the words in the Koran attribute to Jesus qualities, virtues and powers that really only belong to God. Nevertheless, the Koran makes very clear that Jesus was no more than a prophet. In Sura 4:171:

> O People of the Book! Commit no excesses in your religion: Nor say of Allāh aught but the truth. Christ Jesus the son of Mary was (no more than) an apostle of Allāh, and His Word, which He bestowed on Mary, and a spirit proceeding from Him: so believe in God and His messengers.

There is only a very small step to accepting Jesus as the son of God. Muslims, however, are not prepared to take that important step.

The important texts on the death of Jesus read as follows: in Sura 4:157:

> That they said (in boast), 'We killed Christ Jesus the son of Mary, the Messenger of Allāh.;- but they killed him not, nor crucified him, but so it was made to appear to them, and those who differ therein are full of doubts, with no (certain) knowledge, but only conjecture to follow, for of a surety they killed him not:- 158. Nay, Allāh raised him up unto Himself; and Allāh is Exalted in Power, Wise . . .

The generally accepted view by the majority of Islamic scholars is therefore that Christ was not crucified nor killed by the Jews. He was taken alive to heaven and another person was crucified in his place.

In spite of the stress on the 'humanness' of Christ, Muslims still believe that Jesus was among those closest to God, taken to heaven from where he will come again. His return will, however, be in a role like John the

---

7. Arendt, *Gud er stor*, 82, 83.

Baptist preparing the way for the coming of the Mahdi a prominent figure of Islamic eschatology.[8]

The two main reasons why Jesus in Islamic understanding is not the son of God, and part of the Trinity and saviour of the world, are: that the Tawhid, emphasises absolute monotheism. This belief has no room for Jesus as part of the divinity. And secondly, the Muslim believes that sin is not original, hereditary or inevitable. Sins confessed and repented are graciously forgiven by Allāh without a mediator. There is no need for atonement in Islam which means there is no need for Jesus Christ.[9]

Ruh, is the Arabic word for *spirit*. This word *Ruh* is used in all the possible meanings of 'spirit'. In particular it relates to the intellectual, non-individual aspects of the soul as opposed to the lower individual soul the or 'psyche' aspect. Still, from reading the Koran it is difficult to construct a consistent Islamic theology on the *Ruh*.

For example, *Ruh* is the dignity that exalts man above animals even angels.[10]

In the Koran *Ruh* is also used four times where it is translated as Holy Spirit. Some scholars suggest that the term Holy Spirit was included in the Muslim scripture in order to appeal to Christians. Indeed, the Koran alludes to the Holy Spirit as the breath or wind of Allāh, however, it is never used as part of a Trinity. The inbreathing of the spirit is used in the creation of men in Surah 15:29:

> Behold! thy Lord said to the angels: 'I am about to create man, from sounding clay from mud moulded into shape'; 'When I have fashioned him (in due proportion) and breathed into him of My spirit, fall ye down in obeisance unto him'.

The word *Ruh* is also used as a description for the archangel Gabriel as the highest ranking angel in Surah 78:38:

> The Day that the Spirit and the angels will stand forth in ranks, none shall speak except any who is permitted by Allāh Most Gracious, and He will say what is right.

---

8. Norman Anderson, *Islam in the Modern World: A Christian Perspective* (Leicester: Apollos, 1990), 12.
9. Badru D Kateregga and David W Shenk, *Islam and Christianity: A Muslim and a Christian in Dialogue* (Nairobi: Uzima, 1980), 108.
10. Glassé, *Concise Dictionary of Islam*, 338.

The archangel Gabriel is titled the Holy Spirit as he was Allāh's messenger to Muhammad. In Sura 16:102 we note:

> Say, the Holy Spirit has brought the revelation from thy Lord in Truth, in order to strengthen those who believe, and as a Guide and Glad Tidings to Muslims.

The Koran also applies the word *Ruh* to the ministry of Christ as a spirit proceeding from Allāh. In Sura 4:171 we have:

> O People of the Book! Commit no excesses in your religion: Nor say of Allāh aught but the truth. Christ Jesus the son of Mary was [no more than] an apostle of Allāh, and His Word, which He bestowed on Mary, and a spirit proceeding from Him: so believe in Allāh and His apostles.

It should be noted, however, that Muslims are prepared to misread one of the important promises of Jesus concerning the Holy Spirit is in John 14:16: 'And I will ask the Father, and he will give you another Counsellor to be with you for ever.' The Greek word for counselor is *paraklētos* of which 'Paraclete' is a transcription. It means our 'Advocate or Counsel'. In classical Greek the word *periklutos* meaning 'Praised One' is somewhat similar to Paraclete. The name Muhammad means the Praised One. Some Muslims claim that Christ in this text was in fact predicting that Muhammad would come after him., and that later Christians tampered with the Greek New Testament.[11]

Denials of the Deity of Christ and Trinity

On the Arabian Peninsula where Islam emerged and Muhammad lived 1500 years ago there were both Jews and Christians with their synagogues and churches. No doubt the first Muslims in their proclamations and attempts to win the common illiterate people in Mecca and Medina had a hard time in their attempts to explain the detailed differences between the three Abrahamic, monotheistic religions. Islam, however, is rich on rituals. They manifest and impress on the minds of worshippers visibly in

---

11. Don McCurry. *Healing the Broken Family of Abraham: New Life for Muslims* (USA, Ministries to Muslims, 2001), 267.

outward actions and gestures some of their religious beliefs. The rituals in the Tawhid especially stressed these beliefs.

Disavowal in Muslim Prayers and Rituals

Important in prayer rituals are the words that had have to be said aloud daily. The call to worship is the Shahadah, the briefest and most repeated of all religious confession. The first sentence in the ritual prayer (Salah) is a confession with mouth and belief in heart that there is no deity except Allāh and that Muhammad is the messenger of Allāh. A more correct translation of the Shahadah from Arabic is: 'I bear witness that there is no deity except God and I bear witness that Muhammad is the messenger of God.' (The Shahadah is taken from Surah 2:163: *And your Allāh is One Allāh. There is no god but He, Most Gracious, Most Merciful.* And Surah 48:29: *Muhammad is the apostle of Allāh*).

The Shahadah as a call to worship and an admonition to exclude other deities is repeated seventeen times during the five daily prayer sessions. This profesion of faith will follow the Muslim throughout his whole life. It is the first prayer a newborn baby will hear and the last that will be whispered into the ears of a dying person. And between birth and death the Shahadah is said aloud on all occasions.

Then also the phrase like *Allāhu Akbar* (God is greater) will be repeated many times during the worship. To this must be added that some Muslims during the body movements in connection with the prayers will add a minor variation by moving the right hand in a circle and point forefinger upward while the Shahadah is quoted. This custom is an extra emphasis on the oneness of Allāh.[12] The religious and psychological effect of these repeated stresses on the unification of Allāh cannot be over estimated.

A Repeated Rejection of Christ as the Son of God.

The Korannic denials of the Trinity and the deity of Jesus Christ are generally contained in the same texts so that the two concepts are intertwined. Muslims accept that Jesus was outstanding among the prophets in Islam and even superior to Muhammad himself. Nevertheless, the messages from the Koran are that Jesus was just a prophet. In Surah 5:75. it states:

---

12. Børge Schantz, *Islam in the Post 9/11 World* (Grantham: Autumn House, 2003), 57.

Christ the son of Mary was no more than an apostle; many were the apostles that passed away before him. His mother was a woman of truth. They had both to eat their [daily] food. See how Allāh doth make His signs clear to them; yet see in what ways they are deluded away from the truth!

The Koran includes many verses refuting the Christian claim that Jesus is the son of God (Surah 19:19; 10:68–69; 9:30). For example, in reference to Jesus as God's 'one and only son' (John 3:16) the Koran responds in Surah 2:116:

They say: '[Allāh] hath begotten a son': Glory be to Him.- Nay, to Him belongs all that is in the heavens and on earth: everything renders worship to Him.

The commentary to this verse explains:

It is a derogation from the glory of Allāh—in fact it is blasphemy—to say that Allāh begets a son, like a man or animal. The Christian doctrine is here emphatically repudiated. If words have any meaning, it would mean an attribution to Allāh of a material nature, and of the lower animal function of sex.[13]

Muhammad and many Muslims, probably influenced by a verbal-inspiration understanding of Scripture, seem to have interpreted the Christian concept of son-ship in a literal sense. The saying is: when there is a father and a son there must be a mother. As a consequence, at least on a folk-level, many Muslims have the idea that Christians believe the Virgin Mary to be part of the Godhead. The text is Surah 5, 116:

And behold! Allāh will say: 'O Jesus the son of Mary! Didst thou say unto men, worship me and my mother as gods in derogation of Allāh?' He will say: 'Glory to Thee! never could I say what I had no right [to say]. Had I said such a thing, thou wouldst indeed have known it. Thou knowest what is in

---

13. *The Holy Quran, English Translation and Meaning*, Commentary by Abdullah Yusuf Ali (Medinah, Saudi Arabia, 1411 H), 119.

my heart, Thou I know not what is in Thine. For Thou knowest in full all that is hidden'.

And from these literal understandings, based on a belief in verbal inspiration, it is claimed that the Trinity consist of God the Father; Jesus the Son; and Mary the Mother.

Blunt Denial of the Trinity

The Trinity is only possible when it is accepted that Jesus Christ is God. The deity of Christ and the Trinity are rejected by Muslims who claim that it is *shirk*.

> Allāh forgiveth not that partners should be set up with Him; but He forgiveth anything else, to whom He pleaseth; to set up partners with Allāh is to devise a sin Most heinous indeed.(Surah 4, 48).
> Say not 'Trinity': desist: it will be better for you: for Allāh is one Allāh. Glory be to Him: (far exalted is He) above having a son. To Him belong all things in the heavens and on earth. And enough is Allāh as a Disposer of affairs.(Surah 4, 171.)

The Korannic commentary to this text is:

> The doctrines of Trinity, equality with Allāh, and sonship, are repudiated as blasphemies. Allāh is independent of all needs and has no need of a son to manage his affairs. The Gospel of John (whoever wrote it) has put in a great deal of Alexandrian and Gnostic mysticims round the doctrine of the Word (Greek, Logos).[14]

Many other verses from the Koran could be quoted. For example, Surah 5, 17 talks about blasphemy as some say that Jesus is part of a Godhead:

---

14. Abdullah Yusuf Aziz, *The Qur'an: Text, Translation & Commentary* (Tahrike Tarsile, 2005), 676.

In blasphemy indeed are those that say that Allāh is Christ the son of Mary. Say: 'Who then hath the least power against Allāh, if His will were to destroy Christ the son of Mary, his mother, and all every—one that is on the earth?'

Reason for the Distorted Trinity Concepts in Islam

The Muslim rejection of the divinity of Christ and belief in the Trinity must be understood in the context of the intense struggles at the various church councils that took place in the fourth and fifth century BC (Nicaea, 325; Constantinople, 351, 55; Ephesus, 431; Chalcedon, 451). The Church Fathers, such as Justin Martyr, Origin, Apollinaris and others, dialogued, and even fought battles, on such topics as the nature of Christ, the Trinity and nature of man. The results of these meetings were the emergence of a reasonably sound christology that generally, with some few changes of words, would later be approved by the established Orthodox and Roman Catholic churches and, even later still, be accepted in the Protestant Reformation.[15]

At the time of Muhammad on the Arabian Peninsula there were Jews as well as Greek Orthodox and Roman Catholic Christians with clergy and monks attached to churches and monasteries and working as missionaries. There were also hermits and other dissenters that vehemently disagreed with the outcome of the church councils. These heretics were for that reason persecuted in Europe and Turkey and fled to the deserts in Egypt, Syria and also the Arabian Peninsula. Here they lived as hermits or formed various communities and sects with strange, even extreme and contradictory views on the Trinity, Virgin Mary, the nature of Christ and the atonement. They all, both traditional church people and heretics, promoted their opposing views.

No doubt their listeners, being Muslims or belonging to the traditional Bedouin religions, were confused by the ambiguous view points emanating from these different 'missionaries' who each claimed to believe in the same Christ.

On Muhammad's journeys with the caravans that brought him to Syria and Yemen, he had to stay overnight in oases where he met and had ample opportunities to communicate on spiritual things with the monks

---

15. Albert Henry Newman, *A Manual of Church History,* volume 1 (Philadelphia, PA: American Baptist Publication Society), 318f. 16; Glassé, *Concise Dictionary of Islam,* 231–232.

and hermits both orthodox and heretical.[16] It can be detected that the Korannic concept of the Trinity, Jesus Christ and Virgin Mary was not only influenced exclusively by orthodox Christianity. The apocryphal and heretical legends perhaps had an even greater influence on what became the Islamic understanding of Christian theology.[17]

The biblical material in the Koran can also be traced to the controversies between the Monophysites and Nestorians in the post-Chalcedon years, as well as to the teachings of the heretical Gospels. Muhammad, being illiterate, was completely dependent upon the biblical and extra-biblical sources that he had heard from priests with diverging ideas.[18]

To add to this confused state, it must be added that the Bible was not at that time translated into Arabic. Furthermore, most people on the Arabian Peninsula, Muhammad included, were illiterate. It must be understood that for these people their knowledge and understanding of biblical themes came second-hand and through the verbal traditions of the various disagreeing orthodox Christians as well as those heretical dissenters present in Arabia at that time.

Trinity Explained in a Muslim Context

As previously mentioned, humanly speaking the Trinity is considered to be beyond the grasp of human reason. Many sincere believers both Christians and Muslims have found it to be confusing, contrary to normal reason, and unlike anything in their experience. Christians generally assert that 'God is one, and God is three. Since there is nothing like this in creation, we cannot understand it, but have to accept it'.

In the 1400 years of history of world missions, various Christian churches have published books and written articles in their many attempts to explain the Trinity to non-Christians. Arguments and illustrations of all kinds have been developed. Endeavours both ingenious and simple have been made to find analogies and examples that will help people grasp the mystery. Some of these analogies have suggested a tri-theism rather than a Trinity. The Trinity is not a chain with three links, neither is it an actor playing three different parts in a play etc. Great care should be taken therefore in constructing and identifying and applying illustra-

---

16. Anderson, *Islam in the Modern World*, 5, 65.
17. William St Clair Tisdall, *The Original Sources of the Qur'an* (London: SPCK, 1905), 55–211.
18. McCurry, *Healing the Broken Family of Abraham*, 48.

tions lest inaccurate ideas about the Trinity are conveyed to non-Christian audiences.

The Eternal Koran

In dialogue with Muslims the best ways to illustrate the plurality in deity is to focus on the fact that the Koran, as the eternal and uncreated word, coexisted with Allāh. Educated and orthodox Muslims believe that the Koran is an expression of Allāh's mind and imperishable as Allāh himself. On that point there is in Islamic theology a plurality in unity. The Koran, as the speech of Allāh in the Arabic language, has no beginning and has always existed side by side with Allāh.[19]

The Koran is also an expression and revelation of divine will. If it should be compared with anything in Christianity, it must be with Jesus Christ.

In other words in Christianity the *Word of God became flesh*. As expressed in John 1: 1, 14: 'In the beginning was the Word, and the Word was with God, and the Word was God. . . . The Word became flesh and made his dwelling among us. We have seen his glory, the glory of the One and Only, who came from the Father, full of grace and truth.'[20]

Likewise in Islam the **Word of Allāh became book**. In Sura 10, 37. it states:

> This Qur'an is not such as can be produced by other than Allāh. On the contrary it is a confirmation of (revelations) that went before it, and a fuller explanation of the Book—wherein there is no doubt—from the Lord of the worlds.

By claiming that the word of Allāh was uncreated and co-existed with Allāh the Muslims are themselves facing the *Shirk* problem of blasphemy. They really have two gods, something that is other than God, but at the same time united with God. In this way therefore the polytheism accusations against the Christian also apply to themselves.

Full obedience to the Koran, the Word of Allāh, is a condition for entrance into the Muslim Paradise. A belief in the Word of God, Jesus

---

19. Geisler and Saleeb, *Answering Islam*, 269.
20. Scripture references are taken from, *The Holy Bible: New International Version* (International Bible Society, 1984).

Christ, is a requirement for salvation for the Christian. In this way the Koran, a book, has in Islam the same place that Christ, the Son of God, has in the Trinity.

The Ninety-nine Names of Allāh

Attributed to the transcendent character of Allāh there was a need for cataloguing divine qualities that could be understood by people. To meet that need the ninety-nine beautiful names of Allāh were chosen. In Surah 17, 110. we read:

> Say: 'Call upon Allāh, or call upon Rahman: by whatever name ye call upon Him, (it is well): for to Him belong the Most Beautiful Names. (Surah 17, 110)
>
> Allāh is He, than Whom there is no other god;- Who knows (all things) both secret and open; He, Most Gracious, Most Merciful. Allāh is He, than Whom there is no other god;- the Sovereign, the Holy One, the Source of Peace (and Perfection), the Guardian of Faith, the Preserver of Safety, the Exalted in Might, the Irresistible, the Supreme: Glory to Allāh. (High is He) above the partners they attribute to Him. He is Allāh, the Creator, the Evolver, the Bestower of Forms (or Colours). To Him belong the Most Beautiful Names: whatever is in the heavens and on earth, doth declare His Praises and Glory: and He is the Exalted in Might, the Wise. (Surah 59, 22 – 24.)

Encouraged by these texts and others in Koran, where there are more than 500 names for Allāh, ninety-nine have been selected as the most beautiful to characterise Allāh. The ninety-nine chosen names can be divided into to two categories: (1). those connected with Allāh's beauty and loving-kindness; and (2). those connected with Allāh's wrath and majesty.[21]

As we have seen the list has names that underline Allāh as being the Merciful, the Compassionate, the Judge, the Majesty, the Sovereign, and the Pardoner. On the negative side, he is also portrayed as the One who leads Astray, the Avenger, the Humbler, the Afflicter and the Abaser. Absent among the ninety-nine beautiful names are three names so important for the Christians: Father, Spirit and Love.

---

21. Parshall, 28, 29.

Muhammad is reported to have said in a famous *Hadith*:

> Verily, there are ninety-nine names of God, one hundred minus one. He who enumerates [and believes in them and the one god behind] them would get into Paradise (Sahih Muslim, volume 4, No 1410).

These ninety-nine names of Allāh therefore have an elevated redeeming quality in Islam to the extend that quoting them is sufficient to secure a place in Paradise.

In the beautiful names Allāh is expressed as being holy, merciful, forgiving, protecting, omniscient, healing, majestic and almighty. These are also characteristics that Christians apply to the Trinity. The argument could then be put that the Trinity is a description of three different modes or roles God uses in dealing with humankind. It is the way men and women perceive and experience God. The Father, God is the creator and provider. The Son, Jesus Christ, is the saviour and portrays God as a human and still fully God. Holy Spirit manifests God by his actions on Earth and within the lives of Christians.

Some Christian understanding of the concepts and functions of the Trinity are somewhat similar to the ninety-nine beautiful names of Allāh in Islam. One Muslim has even asked why only three names for God. He is much greater.

These arguments are by some used to claim that the two religions are virtually worshipping the same God (Allāh). No doubt, there are important parallels as some of the ninety-nine names reveal. These similarities can be excellent points for initial conversations with and witness to Muslims.[22] While Muslims call it tritheism when Christians believe in the Trinity, but their own devoted application of the ninety-nine beautiful names to Allāh could also be said to be worshipping ninety-nine gods.

Sin, Salvation and the Trinity

Perhaps the best way to accept, believe in, and understand the important role of the Trinity in a person's life lies in a person's understanding of sin and salvation and a sincere need for a Saviour.

---

22. Schantz, *Islam in the Post 9/11 World,* 148.

Sin in Islam

Muslims agree with Christians that Adam and Eve disobeyed God and had to leave the Garden of Eden. However, Islam teaches that there is no original sin. No change took place in Adam's nature as a result of this act. Adam, and with him all his descendants, suffered no permanent ill effect due to the Fall. Allāh forgave Adam and he was reinstated. Human beings are by nature not sinful. Rather they are weak, ignorant and forgetful. Sins and transgressions are forgetfulness and abuse of the free will Allāh gave man.

Islam recognises three categories of sin. Some are mere shortcomings, human limitations or negligence. The consequence is sanction rather than punishment. Others are more serious and incur punishment. Amongst these are disobedience to parents, murder of a Muslim, adultery, and slandering a virtuous Muslim. The unpardonable sin is '*shirk*,' the crime of setting anything alongside Allāh as, for instance, asserting the Incarnation and the Trinity.[23]

Allāh is not hurt by human actions. In his majestic aloofness Allāh cannot be troubled by human transgressions. He will forgive and then expect that the performing of additional Islamic rituals and some extra good deeds will bring balance on the scales. In such a belief system there is no need for a saviour.

All Surahs, except the first in the Koran, begin with the words: *In the name of Allāh the most Gracious, Most Merciful*. The mercy Allāh is showing is really the simple fact that he gave men the Koran as a warning on bad deeds and a guide to the good works that are necessary for salvation. In other words a Muslim is saved by works. Muslim access to the Islamic paradise is obtained by obedience to the rules and good works in agreement with the teachings in Islam. A Muslim who errs is not in need of a saviour, but rather, what is needed is Korannic instructions. As one of God's prophets, Muhammad was sent to guide, instruct and warn people.

Sin in Christianity

By contrast, the Christian believes that sin is rebellion against God and saddens the Creator. It is transgression of his commandments and only through Jesus Christ who died for humankind is there any hope of salvation. Another essential element of Christian belief is that through the Spirit we are born again and our minds are renewed.

---

23. Børge Schantz, *Your Muslim Neighbour and You* (Stanborough Park, England: Stanborough, 1993), 12-13.

It is expressed in the Fundamental Beliefs of Seventh-day Adventist in these words:

> In infinite love and mercy God made Christ, who knew no sin, to be sin for us, so that in Him we might be made the righteousness of God. Led by the Holy Spirit we sense our need, acknowledge our sinfulness, repent of our transgressions, and exercise faith in Jesus as Lord and Christ, as Substitute and Example. This faith which receives salvation comes through the divine power of the Word and is the gift of God's grace. Through Christ we are justified, adopted as God's sons and daughters, and delivered from the lordship of sin. Through the Spirit we are born again and sanctified; the Spirit renews our minds, writes God's law of love in our hearts, and we are given the power to live a holy life. Abiding in Him we become partakers of the divine nature and have the assurance of salvation now and in the judgment.[24]

These opposing concepts of sin in Islam and Christianity are probably the greatest obstacle for a Muslim to accept Christianity.

The best and perhaps only way to overcome Islamic hindrance for accepting the Trinity is to let the Trinity work through the Christian witnesses and convince about sin and point to the Trinity as the only means of forgiveness and overcoming.

> The eternal heavenly dignitaries—God, and Christ, and the Holy Spirit—arming them [the disciples] with more than mortal energy . . . would advance with them to the work and convince the world of sin.[25]

The Need of the Sinner and the Trinity

In the process of salvation for humankind the Trinity is involved.

God The Father: the Father is Creator of heaven and earth. Still he concerns Himself mercifully in the affairs of men; he hears and answers

---

24. *Seventh-day Adventist Church Manual* (Hagerstown, MD: Review and Herald, 2000), 12.
25. Ellen G White, *Evangelism* (Washington, DC: Review and Herald, 1946), 616.

prayer; and he saves from sin, its power over our life, and from spiritual death.

Jesus Christ: Christ is God manifest in the flesh. He led a sinless life, performed miracles, died on the cross for the sins of humankind. His death on the cross was substitutionary and representative and sufficient to make amends for the guilt of all men. He was raised from the dead bodily and ascended to the right hand of the Father where he now carries on a ministry as Advocate and Intercessor for the saints

The Holy Spirit: is also deity and is eternally 'proceeding' from the Father and the Son in the service for all humankind. The Holy Spirit was God's agent in the revelation and the inspiration of his Word, and it is the Holy Spirit who performs the work of salvation in the heart of the individual believer, and he then indwells believers and bestows spiritual gifts upon them

When any person in need of peace of mind and assurance of salvation is convinced by the Holy Spirit, and recognises that salvation is not accomplished by rituals or good deeds, the only hope is the saving grace of the Trinity.

God's preparedness to pardon and give a new life through the Godhead is the best and most efficient way to introduce the Trinity positively the Muslim. Such a life-giving experience will probably not make a person able to explain the mystery in the Godhead. However, there will be a convincing witness on the power and influence of a loving God. By the salvation experience the Trinity will be accepted, understood and appreciated.

The Trinity cannot be explained. It has to be experienced. When the Muslim sees him/herself as a helpless sinner in need of salvation, the saving activities of the Trinity will enlighten and fill the sinner in such a way that the Godhead will become a reality grasped and vitally believed.

PART 3
Studies in Seventh-day Adventist History and Theology

The Influence of Restorationism on Early Seventh-day Adventism and the Emergence of a Trinitarian Perspective

Kai Arasola

That anti-trinitarianism was widely spread in early Seventh-day Adventism has been well documented since Erwin Gane's ground-breaking research on the topic more than four decades ago.[1] Russell Holt, LeRoy Edwin Froom, Merlin Burt, Jerry Moon, have developed further and substantiated Erwin Gane's conclusions.[2] It is now understood that not only Joseph Bates, James White, and Uriah Smith, represent Adventist anti-trinitarian sentiments, but that virtually all key Adventist pioneers including John N Andrews, Daniel Bourdeau, Dudley M Canright, Hiram Edson, DW Hull, John N Loughborough, Ellet J Waggoner, Joseph H Waggoner, and SB Whitney, held views varying from mildly Arian (Christ not eternal but born at a point of time) to a full rejection of trinitarianism. The one notable exception was Ellen G White, and even her orthodoxy during the pre-1888 phase of Adventism has been questioned at times.[3]

The exploration undertaken in this chapter will progress in three parts. The first part discusses restorationism as one possible reason for this rejec-

---

1. For example, Erwin Gane, 'The Arian or Anti-Trinitarian Views Presented in Seventh-day Adventist Literature and the Ellen G White Answer, 1963'. MA Thesis, Andrews University. Jerry Moon, 'Early Adventists Struggle with the Truth about Trinity'. Retrieved April 26, 2008, from http://www.sdanet.org/atissue/trinity/Trinity%20Review%20art.htm#N_12_ .
2. For example, Jerry Moon, 'The Adventist Trinity Debate, Part 1: Historical Overview', *Andrews University Seminary Studies* 41 (2003): 113-29.
3. Jerry Moon observes that Ellen G White's statements from the 1850's and early 1860's are ambiguous. According to Moon's research her earliest clearly trinitarian statements are from 1869. Jerry Moon, 'The Adventist Trinity Debate, Part 2: The Role of Ellen G White', in *Andrews University Seminary Studies* 41 (2003): 275-92. Note also, Allen Stump, '1844 and the Sanctuary', Retrieved February 18, 2009, from http://www.smyrna.org/op/2007/op07_10%20main.htm.

tion of the Trinity. The restorationist movement was an important feature in the intellectual and theological climate of nineteenth century America. Both Millerism and early Adventism, were closely tied to it. This is followed by examples of the fruit that restorationist thinking bore in early Adventism as reflected in the views Adventist pioneers had on trinitarian creeds and on the development of the doctrine.

The purpose of this chapter is not to provide a full systematic analysis of the issue, but to give examples and stimulate discussion or debate on this important topic and to provide insight into the formative years of Sabbatarian Adventism.

Theological Restorationism and Anti-Trinitarianism

The America of the pioneers of the Seventh-day Adventist movement may be characterised as a time of reformatory idealism. For example, Timothy L Smith's assessment of the restorationist culture of Ante-Bellum America was that 'Men of seemingly sober judgment expressed repeatedly their confidence that Christians could remake society in the United States according to a pattern fashioned in heaven'. In partial fulfilment of this dream, the restorationist movement contributed to the rise of several churches including Seventh-day Adventism.[4] While Smith's description limits the reforms to restructuring the social order, banishing poverty, eliminating the curse of drunkenness, elevating womanhood, freeing the slaves or providing equal opportunities for education, the movement also extended into the theological and religious sphere. Winthrop S Hudson observes that this 'reforming idealism' was so integral to the American religious ferment of the early nineteenth century that it did not leave theology untouched.[5]

Restorationism, sometimes called Christian primitivism, is a descriptive title for any Christian movement which seeks to restore the original form and ideals of Christianity. In the context of North America, the term is applied in particular to a widespread indigenous American phenomenon that started towards the end of the eighteenth century with the Second Great Awakening and it culminated in the rise of a wide range of

---

4. Timothy L Smith, 'Social Reform: Some Reflections on Causation and Consequence', in *The Rise of Adventism*, edited by Edwin S Gaustad (New York: Harper & Row, 1975), 18.
5. Winthrop S Hudson, 'A Time of Religious Ferment', in Gaustad, *The Rise of Adventism*, 6f.

revivals and churches. The so called Christian Churches or Connexionists are usually considered prime examples of restorationism. Connexionism grew into thousands of independent churches and had by the 1850s up to half a million supporters.⁶ It also had, however, a powerful effect on established mainline churches and contributed to the theology and rise of Unitarianism, Millerism, Adventism, and Latter-day Saints, the Watchtower Society, and, a little later, the Pentecostals.⁷

Interestingly, many supporters of the Christian Connexion endorsed Millerism.⁸ This is no surprise, however, because William Miller's teachings, though Baptist, reflect restorationist ideals. For example, his Rules of Interpretation⁹ are a good example of a typical restorationist do-it-yourself approach to the Scriptures and his hermeneutic shows a deep distrust in established church-endorsed views.¹⁰

The restorationist movement's implicit but unstated ambition was to do to Protestantism what the Reformation had done to Catholicism. Restorationists were distrustful of church organisations and creeds. While, in general, they did not go for clear-cut doctrinal definitions, they had over the early part of the nineteenth century increasingly turned against

---

6. David Millard, 'History of the Christians or the Christian Connexion', in *History of All the Religious Denominations in the United States,* edited by John Vinebrenner (Harrisburg, PA, 1848), 164–170.
7. *Restorationism,* Retrieved October 10 2008, from Wikipedia: http://en.wikipedia.org/wiki/Restorationism.
8. See, for example, George R Knight, *A Search for Identity: The Development of Seventh-day Adventist Beliefs* (Hagerstown, MD: Review and Herald, 2000), 30–37.
9. William Miller, 'Rules of Interpretation', *Midnight Cry,* November 17 1842; *Views of the Prophecies and Prophetic Chronology* (Boston: Joshua V. Himes, 1842), 20–24. Miller's rules have been republished several times, frequently in later edited versions. Apollos Hale, *Second Advent Manual* (Boston, 1843), 103–106; Sylvester Bliss, *Memoirs of William Miller* (Boston: Joshua V. Himes, 1853), 70–72; P Gerard Damsteegt, *Foundations of the Seventh-day Adventist Message and Mission* (Grand Rapids, MI: Eerdmans, 1977), 299–300; John FC Harrison, *The Second Coming* (London: 1979), 200f; Wayne R Judd, 'William Miller: Disappointed Prophet', in *The Disappointed: Millerism and Millenarianism in the Nineteenth Century,* edited by Ronald L Numbers and Jonathan L Butler (Knoxville, TN: University of Tennessee Press, 1987), 20–21; Kai Arasola, *The End of Historicism,* ThD Dissertation (Sigtuna, Sweden: Datem Publishing, 1990), 50–53.
10. See, for example, Arasola, *The End of Historicism,* 53–59.

trinitarianism¹¹ especially in the north-eastern states.¹² Joshua V Himes, a Christian Church minister, became William Miller's key associate, publisher, travel organiser and congress manager. Also, his role in Millerism may have been an added attraction that led Connexionists into Millerite ranks.¹³ Furthermore, significantly for the topic, two founding fathers of Sabbatarian Adventism, Joseph Bates and James White were both Connexionists.¹⁴ Joseph Bates had joined his wife's New Bedford Christian Church in 1827¹⁵ and James White was baptised in his parents' Palmyra Christian Church at the age of fifteen or sixteen.¹⁶

While secondary to the topic, it is interesting to note that Adventist historians frequently suggest that the rejection of Millerism in 1842 by established churches contributed to the anti-creedal and anti-organisational spirit of early Sabbatarian Adventism.¹⁷ It is, however, equally logical to conclude that these views also stem from the credophobic and organisa-

---

11. David Millard, 'History of the Christians or the Christian Connexion', in *History of All the Religious Denominations in the United States,* edited by John Winebrenner (J Winebrenner, 1848), 164–170. Interestingly, this thought pattern can still be seen in the work of some scholars. E.g. Adolf Harnack implies that original Christianity had no doctrines and that doctrinal definitions watered down the genuine original Christian faith. See Adolf Harnack, *History of Dogma,* translated by Neil Buchanan (Boston, MA: Little, 1901).
12. Merlin D Burt, 'The Trinity in Seventh-day Adventist History', in *Ministry,* February 2009. https://www.ministrymagazine.org/archive/2009/02/the-trinity.html.
13. LeRoy Edwin Froom, *Movement of Destiny* (Washington, DC: Review and Herald, 1971), 146–47. Froom's comments reflect an apologetic agenda as he tries to show that only one in seven Millerite preachers were from an anti-trinitarian background. However, in the process he ignores the 'Christian' background of some of the listed pastors. Considering nineteenth century views, one should also keep in mind that all in Connexionist churches were not necessarily anti-trinitarian and some in traditional churches may have had Arian or semi-Arian views. For example, it would be interesting to check the views of other Millerites such as Stetson, or Wenham, or George Storr. Himes' prominent standing in Connexionism is reflected in his being called to write a description of 'Christian Connexion or Christian Churches', in *Encyclopedia of Religious Knowledge,* edited by BB Edwards (Brattleborough, VT: Fessenden and Co, 1838).
14. Knight, *A Search for Identity,* 31.
15. Ken McGaughhey, 'Seventh-day Adventist Roots VII', *Landmarks Magazine,* December 1998.
16. *Nation Master Encyclopedia* (nd), sv. 'White, James Springer', Retrieved February 13, 2009, from http://www.nationmaster.com/encyclopedia/James-Springer-White.
17. For example, Julian Kastrati, *Against Historical Adventists: The Whites and the Divinity of Christ.* Retrieved April 15, 2008, from http://juliankastrati.blogspot.com/2007_02_01_archive.html.

tion-shunning Connexionist background of the two leading Adventist pioneers. In fact, it is possible to postulate that the overall doctrinal development of Adventism, including its endorsement of, for example, the Sabbath, conditional immortality, or health reform, grew out of the general Restorationist spirit of the times.[18]

Restorationism and Trinitarian Churches

Very few, however, of the early Sabbath-keeping Adventists came from a Connexionist background, and one may with good reason ask why so many of those Adventist pioneers who came from traditionally trinitarian churches so easily gave up their trinitarianism. The reason might, of course, lie in the persuasiveness of Joseph Bates and James White, but a further possible reason can be seen in the impact restorationist antitrinitarian thinking had even within the established Protestant churches.

Traditionally, there had been a Unitarian base in Boston.[19] Unitarians, like Connexionists (or even the Millerites), had a distaste for organised churches, established creeds and trinitarian concepts.[20] In 1819 William Channing was catapulted to prominence for expressing Unitarian views in a sermon in Baltimore. His articles and speeches included strong opposition to the Trinity and appealed to those with a somewhat reformatory but at the same time liberal bent. Consequently many Congregationalist churches split off from their mother church to become Unitarian. Another example of a Unitarian challenge to traditional Christian thinking was Ralph Waldo Emerson's widely publicised 1838 speech at the graduation ceremony of Harvard Divinity School.[21]

---

18. David Millard, 'History of the Christians or the Christian Connexion', in *History of All the Religious Denominations in the United States,* edited by John Winebrenner (J Winebrenner, 1848), 164–170.
19. Unitarianism refers to belief in the oneness of God, strict monotheism and opposition to the doctrine of the Trinity, and represented other somewhat liberal theological views. See *Wikipedia,* sv 'Unitarianism' Retrieved 14 October 2008, from http://en.wikipedia.org/wiki/Unitarianism.
20. Unitarians shared the Connexionist and Millerite distaste for creeds and Church organisations. See *The Columbia Encyclopedia,* sixth edition sv 'Unitarianism'. Retrieved 27 April 2008, from http://www.questia.com/library/encyclopedia/unitarianism.jsp.
21. Chris Fisher, *A Brief History of Unitarian Christianity.* American Unitarian Conference. Retrieved 27 April 2008, from http://www.americanunitarian.org/fisherhistory.htm.

John W Gaston III has described how this 'liberal' doctrine was attractive to many Anglicans and Methodists in New England.[22] Thus, at the time Sabbatarian Adventism was formulating its beliefs, Arianism was making deep inroads in the traditionally trinitarian churches. It is no surprise therefore that in this setting even those among Adventist pioneers who came from a Baptist, Methodist, or Congregationalist background found it easy to shift to anti-trinitarian positions. A somewhat critical anti-orthodox mindset was thought to represent the radical values of Jesus better than traditional creeds and doctrines.

The theological ambience of the early nineteenth century incorporated this reaction against old Puritan conservatism. There was a strong reaction against the old theology and whether its origins lie in the restorationist movement or simply in tiredness with the carefully worded and argued dogmas of Protestant Orthodoxy is secondary. American Christians were ready to break new ground. It probably indicates a result of this trend rather than its cause, but it has been claimed that the least known and most important theological development of the turn of the nineteenth Century was the discontinuance of the more than one-hundred-year-old tradition of using Turretin's massive three volume *Institutes of Elenctic Theology* as the main textbook for systematic theology in most ivy league and other respectable American seminaries.

The Adventist pioneers may well have been wrong in their approach to the doctrine of the Trinity, but they seem to have sensed well the spirit of their times. It was not necessary to come from an Arian faith tradition to turn against trinitarianism.

The Present Truth Concept

Present Truth, a favorite theological concept in early Sabbatarian Adventism, represented the heart of the restorationist spirit in Adventism. This idea is poorly understood today because the restorationist spirit no longer impacts Christian churches or Adventism the way it did a century and a half ago.

It was no accident that James White chose *Present Truth* as the title of his pioneering publication. The concept implied two ideas. First, the belief

---

22. John W Gaston III, *A Theological History of Unitarianism.* American Unitarian Conference, 2000. Retrieved 28 April 2008, from http://www.americanunitarian.org/gastonhistory.htm.

that what is taught must be timely, absolutely relevant. This was affirmed by Daniel T Bourdeau:

> It is clear that we have reached the time when a flood of light is shining from God's word on the path of the just, and that this light relates to that great event which is immediately impending—the coming of the Lord, and to a preparation to meet it. This we denominate present truth, because it applies to the present time, and is adapted to the wants of the present generation; and it is through this truth that the last church will be sanctified.[23]

It would seem, therefore, that for some reason the doctrine of the Godhead, including the concept of the Trinity, had had its day in the minds of Adventist pioneers and was not considered vital any more.

For early Adventists a key indicator of what was relevant and *present truth* was biblical prophecy. They identified prophecies that related to the Sabbath and to many other doctrines. But they could not find a prophecy that related to the doctrine of the Godhead. Thus the issue could be brushed aside and it was possible to be an Adventist and an active anti-trinitarian (like James White or Uriah Smith) or trinitarian (like Ellen G White). Faith in the nearness of the second coming called them to proclaim the Sabbath, the state of the dead, or the Sanctuary, but not the doctrine of God. Adventist pioneers did, however, accept the possibility that there might have been biblical truths that were important at an earlier point in history but not part of today's *present truth*. This implied a hierarchy of biblical teachings. James White was therefore comfortable in stating that there is a truth for each epoch in World history, one for Peter's time and one for the last days.[24]

---

23. Daniel T Bourdeau, *Sanctification, or Living Holiness* (Battle Creek, MI: SDA Publishing, 1864), 13. Cf Ellen White's statement that 'In every age there is a new development of truth, a message of God to the people of that generation. The old truths are all essential; new truth is not independent of the old, but an unfolding of it. It is only as the old truths are understood that we can comprehend the new.' Ellen G White, *Christ's Object Lessons* (Washington, DC: Review and Herald, 1900), 127.
24. James White, untitled introductory note, *Present Truth* 1/1 July 1849, quoted in Fritz Guy, 'Mapping the Past: Exploring the Development of Adventist Theology—on Being Adventist in twenty-first Century Australia', Avondale College, September 2002. Retrieved 29 April 2008, from http://www.sdanet.org/atissue/doctrines/au2002conference/guy/guy-past.htm.

However, a further important meaning of the *present truth* concept was that only genuine and original biblical teachings represent truth and therefore nothing but an authentic truth could be so called. This was at the heart of restorationism. The search was not only for what was relevant but also for what was authentic. A doctrine formulated after the days of the apostles could never meet the criteria. Therefore, *present truth* implied a determination to reform the landscape of Christianity from the existing apostasy and formality into what was original.

Because of this foundational idea that true doctrine was not discoverable after biblical times, their view on the Trinity was also affected. They taught that the early church kept Saturday but 'Romanism' converted the day of rest to Sunday.[25] Similarly they saw conditionalism as a clear biblical doctrine which had been replaced by 'pagan' immortality of the soul. Baptism was seen in the same light. The negative development of Christian teachings was, they believed, confirmed by biblical prophecy and therefore, by implication, the doctrine of the Trinity must be questioned too, because it was not formulated until several centuries had passed from the time of the Apostles. Church councils and creeds had no authority for the early Adventists and they considered trinitarianism a post-biblical doctrine which had received its inspiration from Rome.[26]

Restorationism and Creeds

Another characteristic of restorationism was its distrust in historical creedal statements which were considered untrue and repressive in contrast to simple biblical confessions of faith. It was argued that over the centuries, due to pressure from a Greek rather than a Hebrew mindset, basic biblical ideas grew into intricate, carefully worded creeds. The creeds, it was believed, were theoretical and heretical and resulted in persecution. In contrast, the true New Testament message was rooted in the principles of freedom and practical love.

As a simple example one may claim that all Christians of all centuries could probably endorse an uncomplicated broad statement like 'Jesus is Lord' (Rom 10:9). The early Adventists clearly understood that issues became much more difficult when small details were brought into the

---

25. Malcolm Bull, and Keith Lockhart, *Seeking a Sanctuary* (New York: Harper & Row, 1989), 41.
26. Wikipedia, s.v. 'Seventh-day Adventist Eschatology', http://en.wikipedia.org/wiki/Seventh-day_Adventist_eschatology.

equation. As a historical case in point one may think of the trinitarian or christological debates centering on words like *hypostasis, homoousios, homoiousios, ousia, logos asarkos* vs *logos ensarkos* all of which were central to the development of trinitarianism. Not all church fathers understood these words in the same way and some suffered due to their inability to understand the words in line with their fellow Christians.[27]

For example, because he used the wrong word to express Christ's nature, Apollinaris of Laodicea, a staunch supporter of the Nicene Creed, ended up anathema. Nestorius made the mistake of refusing to use the word '*theotokos*' and his life might have been different had he sooner come across the term '*christotokos*' which he later used.[28] For the restorationist (Connexionist) thinking such minutely defined Christianity was totally unacceptable. They were persuaded that the Bible needed to be interpreted individually within a framework of freedom with the broadest possible formal definitions of doctrine—if any at all.

John Loughborough stated this rather bluntly: 'The first step of apostasy is to get up a creed..'[29] While this comment was made in the context of church organisation, it still reflects the spirit of the times. James White agreed when he declared. 'Now I take the ground that creeds stand in a direct opposition to the gifts.'[30] Expanding further, he explained: 'Let us suppose a case: We get up a creed, stating just what we shall believe on this point and the other, and just what we shall do in reference to this thing and that, and say that we will believe the gifts, too.'[31] Creeds, these pioneer Adventists believed, killed the pursuit for genuine, original faith.

Walter Scragg explained the early Adventist attitude: ' . . . they felt [Christian churches] had calcified their beliefs in . . . creedal statements, and [had] fought to defend those statements rather than embark on fresh

---

27. Bernhard Lohse, *A Short History of Christian Doctrine*, translated by F Ernest Stoeffer. (Philadelphia, PA: Fortress, 1985), 66-90.
28. Geoffrey W Bromiley, *Historical Theology, An Introduction* (Grand Rapids, MI: Eerdmans, 1978), 133.
29. 'Doings of the Battle Creek Conference, Oct. 5 & 6, 1861', in *Advent Review and Sabbath Herald*, October 8, 1861, 148.
30. James S White, quoted in Arthur L White, *Ellen G White: The Early Years*, volume 1 (Washington, DC: Review and Herald, 1985), 454.
31. Cf references to creeds in Fritz Guy, 'Uncovering the Origins of the Statement of Twenty-seven Fundamental Beliefs', Being Adventist, Avondale College, 2002. Retrieved, 10 April 2008, from http://www.goodnewsforadventists.com/home/skypage.php?keyid=235&parentkeyid=166

searches for biblical understanding and truth. The Reformation remained incomplete because it was held back by creeds.'[32]

At this point one may ask how well did the Adventist pioneers know church history and in particular the development of trinitarianism? On the one hand it could be argued that they were not totally ignorant because their views on prophetic interpretation suggested otherwise. Since the days of William Miller they had been inspired to study the rise and impact and meaning of the papacy. Furthermore, their sabbatarian convictions made them research church history for evidence on the change from Sabbath to Sunday. Likewise, some of their comments on creeds also implied some awareness of the trinitarian struggles of the first Christian centuries. On the other hand, while they refer to creeds and historical problems related to the Trinity, it is clear that they totally misunderstood the meaning of the Trinity and most of their historical comments were sweeping statements with little detail.

They rarely mentioned historical persons or details related to trinitarianism. When they did, it is difficult to see the relevance of what they wrote as their sources have not been available for this study. They did, however, regard Arius as a defender of biblical truth.[33] For example, John Loughborough alluded to the struggle between Athanasius and Arius.[34]

The culture and spirit of early Adventists (including those who had no Connexionist background) was so resolute against creeds that later on it was hard for James White to gain support even for the most basic and simple statement of faith needed at the time when the movement took its first organisational steps. If the simple confessional statement, 'Those who keep the commandments of God and the faith of Jesus', was too much for many of the early Adventists, it is no surprise that the long Trinitarian creeds were symbols of apostasy and spiritual repression for them.[35]

---

32. Walter RL Scragg, 'Doctrinal Statements and the Life and Witness of the Church', unpublished paper presented at workers' meetings in Vasteräng, Sweden and Manchester, England, between 24 August and 4 September 1981.
33. See, for example, DW Hull, 'The Bible Doctrine of Divinity', in *Review and Herald*, November 10, 1859; Erwin Gane, 'The Arian or Anti-Trinitarian Views'.
34. 'Doings of the Battle Creek Conference, Oct. 5 & 6, 1861', in *Advent Review and Sabbath Herald*, October 8, 1861, 148. Athanasios was banished five times and spent seventeen out of his forty-five years as the patriarch of Alexandria in exile. *Dictionary of Christian Biography*, sv, 'Athanasius', Michael Walsh, editor, (London: Continuum, 2001). Arius was twice exiled from Alexandria. See *Dictionary of Christian Biography*, sv, 'Arius'.
35. Fritz Guy, 'Uncovering the Origins of the Statement of the Twenty-seven Fundamental Beliefs'.

Adventist Views on Trinitarian History

It is important to understand clearly the historical argument Adventist pioneers used. For example, James White's reference to the 'old creed' in its context clearly rejected anything defined after the Bible and his restorationist approach guided him to accept only that which he believed to be genuinely biblical and original apostolic Christianity.[36] Others followed the same reasoning.

That the Trinity was identified as a Catholic doctrine is reflected also in DW Hull's statement in *The Review and Herald* in 1859. His two-part article on the doctrine of divinity comments on the Nicene Creed in an interesting way. He stated: 'The doctrine . . . was established by the Council of Nice [sic], AD 325, and ever since that period, persons not believing this particular tenet, have been denounced by popes and priests, as dangerous heretics. It was for disbelief in this doctrine, that the Arians were anathematised in AD 513.' Hull implied that what the papacy endorsed should be regarded un-biblical and what it condemned, the truth. He proceeded to connect the Trinity with papacy, the 'man of sin', and deplored the persecution of those who taught more biblically.[37] For the early Adventists the Trinity and apostasy came from the same source.[38]

It is true, of course, that the development of trinitarianism was a long and tumultuous road. It took almost three centuries for the doctrine of the Trinity to be formulated and a further three centuries were required to iron out the details and thus conclude a major christological controversy. It should be noted that the development and expressions of the Trinity were slightly different in the eastern and the western parts of the Holy Roman Empire because, as Rodney Stark persuasively argues, there were more Christians with Jewish background in the east and they, coming from a passionately monotheistic background, had a harder time in coming to terms with a concept like the Trinity.[39]

---

36. See, for example, James White's defence of Adventism as a turn to the true Bible message. *Bible Adventism*. A collection of Sermons by James White. Retrieved 29 April 2008, from http://dedication.www3.50megs.com/jswhite5.html.
37. DW Hull, 'The Bible Doctrine of Divinity'. See also, Erwin Gane, 'The Arian or Anti-Trinitarian Views'.
38. Cf Adolf Harnack, *History of Dogma*, 2:231, 257.
39. Rodney Stark, *The Rise of Christianity* (Princeton, NJ: Princeton University Press, 1996), 49ff.

Misunderstanding the Trinity

It is important to note that many early Adventist references to the Trinity confused trinitarianism with some of the major heresies related to the development of the Trinity. This may be indicative that in the end their knowledge of what the Trinity really meant was not very well founded. Docetism was a Gnostic heresy and extremely popular because Gnosticism was so widespread. It taught that Christ was a spirit and his body was an illusion that people were made to see.[40] Modalism, however, presented one God appearing in three forms. This was an attractive heresy because it made God understandable and it spread like wildfire during the third century and forced Irenaeus, Tertullian, Hippolytos and others to use all their persuasive powers to keep it at bay. Finally there was tritheism, popular in the eastern parts of the empire around the time of and after the Trinity had been defined in Nicea (325) and Constantinople (371). John of Damascus and Johannes Piloponus are usually cited as prime examples of this heresy.[41] JB Frisbie, Joseph Bates, John Loughborough and JM Sephenson are examples of early Seventh-day Adventist writers who expressed similar misunderstandings of the trinity to those found in the early Church.

Possible Docetism—JB Frisbie(1816–1882)

Joseph B Frisbie, an early Seventh-day Adventist minister, identified what he called the 'Sabbath God' and the 'Sunday God'. The biblical Sabbath God is not only a Spirit, but also a personal 'Being' with a face, hands, or other body parts. Referring to creedal expressions in the Catholic Catechism or Methodist literature he then defined the (non-biblical) 'Sunday God' and suggests that this Trinitarian God is a spirit only and not real and concrete because He is based on ideas which 'well accord with those heathen philosophers'.[42] Admittedly, Frisbie's argument is anything but clear and to classify it under Docetism is doubtful. But if the 'Sunday God' is spirit only, it is possible that he thought that for trinitarians not only God the Father but also Jesus was a somewhat unreal spirit being. In

---

40. For example Wikipedia, s.v., 'Docetism'. Retrieved 12 October 2008, from http://en.wikipedia.org/wiki/Docetism.
41. Ron Kangas, 'Modalism, Tritheism, or the Pure Revelation of the Triune God According to the Bible'. Retrieved 12 October 2008, from http://www.contendingforthefaith.org/responses/booklets/modalism.html
42. JB Frisbie, 'The Seventh day-Sabbath Not Abolished', in *Review and Herald*, 7 March 1854. Frisbie is cited by Gane in 'The Arian or Anti-Trinitarian Views'.

any case, Frisbie's understanding of the ontological definitions that relate to the Trinity was seriously flawed.

Modalistic Monarchianism—Joseph Bates (1792–1872)

Frisbie was not the only Adventist evangelist who totally misunderstood the Trinity. Joseph Bates wrote regarding his own conversion in 1827, 'Respecting the trinity, I concluded that it was impossible for me to believe that the Lord Jesus Christ, the Son of the Father, was also the Almighty God, the Father, one and the same being.'[43] In other words, he rejected the Trinity on the claim that it made the Father and the Son identical.

This was an important and typical early Adventist anti-trinitarian statement. However, Bates' argument is not against the Trinity but against the monarchianist concept that the Father and the Son are one and the same person. The statement does show that Bates' understanding of the Trinity was faulty and he condemned what the ancient church and all trinitarians had already condemned as a heresy,[44] because true trinitarianism specifically teaches that while the Father, the Son, and the Holy Spirit are one, they must also be distinguished as separate persons.

As a general comment related to trinitarian struggles one may observe that all trinitarian heresies were based on an effort to make an incomprehensible and unexplainable Christian God understandable. Adventist pioneers clearly preferred dealing with rationalistic ideas on the Trinity rather than the less understandable traditional view.

Tritheism–John Loughborough (1832–1924)

John Loughborough is another example of an Adventist pioneer who rejected trinitarianism through confusing it with something that all Trinitarians would reject as heresy. In 1861 he wrote that he could not believe in the Trinity because it implied the existence of three Gods. 'If Father, Son, and Holy Ghost are each God, it would be three Gods.'[45]

---

43. Jerry Moon, 'Early Adventists Struggle with the Truth about Trinity'. The same view was also presented by DW Hull, *The Bible Doctrine of Divinity*, Review and Herald, 17 November 1859; Gane, 'The Arian or Anti-Trinitarian Views'.
44. For example The expulsion of Sabellanians. See Bernhard Lohse, *A Short History of Christian Doctrine*, 58f.
45. JH Loughborough, 'Questions for Bro Loughborough', in *Advent Review and Sabbath Herald*, 5 November 1861, 184; Moon, *Early Adventists Struggle with the Truth about Trinity*.

While Loughborough's comments were not in any way related to Justin Martyr, an interesting parallel may be drawn with Loughborough's understanding of the Trinity and Justin Martyr's teaching. Justin was one of the first to explain the Christian God to a pagan audience. In his *Apology* he expressed a view on the nature of Christ and of the Holy Spirit and tried to refute the claim that Christians were atheists. After admitting that Christians indeed rejected false pagan gods he went on to affirm that they do not deny the true God who is the Father of all virtues. He then declared that 'Both him and the son who came forth from him . . . and the prophetic Spirit, we worship and adore . . .' What is confusing, and shows Justin's lack of grasp on the subject, is that in the Greek version he included angels and listed them before the Holy Spirit.[46] In fact the great apologist came close to tritheism or polytheism in some of his statements. Nevertheless, in his identification of Jesus Christ as the cosmic Logos, Justin contributed one of the important first steps towards the concept of the Trinity.[47] In addition to Justin Martyr, it is possible to create a list of a dozen church fathers who had difficulty in finding the proper expressions to explain the Trinity.

Biblical Study—JM Stephenson

Biblical arguments are beyond of the scope of this study. The following is, however, an illustration that some Adventist pioneer views on the Trinity were not only related to historical or prophetic arguments, but included biblical elements. JM Stephenson, who was for a time an Adventist preacher, tried to exegete biblical data related to the Godhead during the formative years of Sabbatarian Adventism (1854). He did this with forceful vigor. Discussing creedal language he claimed that Christ could not have had 'co-etaneous existence' with the Father for the simple reason that he is called the Son and is 'begotten'. If God is the 'supreme ruler' it would 'be impossible to have two Supreme Rulers at the same time'[48]

He then stated his belief that Jesus Christ was a created being. Referring to Colossians 1:15 he presented Christ as, 'the first-born of every

---

46. Alexander Roberts and James Donaldson, editors, *The Ante-Nicene Fathers: Translations of the Writings of the Fathers Down to A.D. 325* (Grand Rapids, MI: Eerdmans, 1988), 1:164. For example, Lohse translates his text in this way. Lohse, *A Short History of Christian Doctrine*, 43.
47. Adolf Harnack, *History of Dogma*, 2:208–13.
48. JM Stephenson, 'The Atonement', cited in Erwin Gane, 'The Arian or Anti-Trinitarian Views'.

creature'. This argument was then developed further with the claims that *creature* signifies creation and Christ cannot be the first born of every creature unless he was himself a created being.[49]

Seventh-day Adventists and the Trinity Today

Most Adventists had shifted from Arian views to trinitarianism by the end of the nineteenth century.[50] Today most Seventh-day Adventists, like their church, are fully committed trinitarians. Many are not only convinced that the Trinity is a fully provable biblical doctrine but also that it gives them the right to be called Christian in the true and full sense of the word.

---

49. JM Stephenson, 'The Atonement'.
50. For example, Ingemar Linden, 'Apologetics as History', in *Spectrum* (Autumn 1971). Retrieved 18 February 2009, from http://old.spectrummagazine.org/spectrum/archive01-05/3-4linden.pdf.

The Trinitarian Issue in Seventh-day Adventism

Gunnar Pedersen

The Trinity in early Seventh-day Adventism

Early Adventism reflects the anti-trinitarian polemics of the era of the Enlightenment Deism. Their understanding of the classical Trinity doctrine appears to have been defined by the polemics of the restorationist groups from which some of its key founders emerged.[1] Nevertheless, their Christology in general reflected the Nicene view that Christ in a pre-historic event was 'begotten' by the Father, that is, issued in some mysterious ways from the Father. While they thus affirmed this aspect of Nicene Christology yet in line with the restorationist anti-trinitarian polemics they held a hierarchical view on the relationship between the Father, Son and the Holy Spirit. Accordingly they tended to downplay the threeness of God and depersonalise the Holy Spirit as a power rather than a person.[2]

Whether or not early Adventists saw the finer distinctions in the Arian-Athanasian debate with regard to whether Christ through a pre-historic cosmic 'beggetting' held the 'same' nature or 'like' nature with the Father, with all its theological implications for defining his deity, may still be an open question. So on the question of whether or not early Adventists could best be described as semi-Arian or semi-Nicene the jury may still be out.

This challenging dogmatic position within early Adventism seems explainable in the context of the methodological ethos of early Adventists which was radical restorationist. In line with the American restoration-

---

1. The leading founders of Seventh-day Adventism such as Joseph Bates, James White and Uriah Smith all had a 'Christian Connection' background which echoed their anti-creedal and anti-trinitarian views. George R Knight, *Millennial Fever and the End of the World* (Boise, ID: Pacific Press, 1993), 298–303; Rolf J Pöhler, *Continuity and Change in Adventist Teaching* (Frankfurt am Main: Peter Lang, 2000), 27–30.
2. Pöhler, *Continuity and Change*, 37–42.

ist movement the early Adventists believed that Christianity was in need of being cleansed from past dogmatic errors and thus be restored to its pristine Apostolic biblical purity and the doctrine of the Trinity was no exception.[3]

Lately Adventist authors like Max Hatton and others[4] have argued that the Trinity could best understood as an ontological unity of three co-eternal beings. In support of this argument they are transcending the Christology of Nicea and the Adventist pioneers. They argue that the biblical term 'begotten' in the apostolic writings functions as a reference to Christ's historic incarnation rather than to an eternal pre-historic event in God's being as held by the Nicene Fathers and echoed by the pioneers of Adventism. However, Hatton and others, by challenging the dogmatic interpretation of the biblical concept 'begotten', do not necessarily opt for three-theism rejecting an inner ontological unity of the Trinity; however they argue that the rationale for this unity lies in the mystery of God's inner being and thus transcends the sphere of divine revelation and human comprehension.[5] However their modification of the Nicene explanation regarding the inner ontological unity of God has added fuel to the present trinitarian debate among Adventists raising accusations of three-theism.[6]

The founders of Adventism opted for the view that Christ's deity is derived from the Father in a pre-historic event in God's being. This is the prime christological argument used by the Nicene Fathers to define the deity of Christ and thus the inner unity of God while manifesting himself as a trio. The main theological concerns, currently causing some debate within Adventism thus appear to be centred in the issue of whether 'Christ is the pre-existing begotten son of God' and thus conceptually hold the status as Son from some 'moment' in eternity or whether 'Christ in his

---

3. Pöhler, 27–30; George R Knight, *A Search for Identity: The Development of Seventh-day Adventist Beliefs* (Hagerstown, MD: Review and Herald, 2000), 112; Woodrow W Whidden, Jerry Moon, and John W Reeve, *The Trinity: Understanding God's Love, His Plan of Salvation, and Christian Relationships* (Hagerstown, MD: Review and Herald, 2002), 186–88.
4. For an introduction to the current debate in Adventism see Max Hatton, *Understanding the Trinity* (Grantham: Autumn House, 2001).
5. Ibid, 76.
6. The debate concerning whether or in what sense Christ is to be seen as 'begotten' and whether or not this concept refer to an inner ontological unity in the Godhead is a biblical question and not a dogmatic on. To challenge the traditional interpretation of this concept does not necessarily lead to three-theism nor does necessarily lead to a subordinationist view regarding the Godhead. The doctrine of the ontological oneness and equality in the Godhead does not rest on the possible meaning of one biblical semantic phrase but on a whole range of biblical texts and themes that may logically affirms this doctrine.

pre-existence was un-begotten just like the Father and thus not conceptually holding the position as Son until his incarnation.

The Historical-Theological Issues

Historically, the christological-trinitarian controversy started within Alexandrian Christianity as it gradually adopted a Platonic world-view in place of a Mosaic one and sought to reinterpret Christianity and thus the Biblical teachings about God and cosmos in terms of platonically informed cosmology.[7] Not only does the platonic world-view assume that the human mind has direct access to the deepest secrets of the universe including the mind of God it also poses a radical dualistic disjunction between God and the material world. Thus the incarnation of the truly divine was rationally speaking impossible.

Origin's platonically informed Logos Christology was designed as a resolution of the cosmological dualism between God and the material world. However this idea appears to be the source of the problems that exploded in the christological and trinitarian controversies arising within Alexandrian Christianity. The Alexandrians interpreted the biblical idea of Christ's mediation as a cosmic mediation bridging the gap between divine and material worlds. Christ's role was not so much to bridge the gap between fallen humanity and a holy God but rather to bridge the inherent metaphysical divide in the cosmos. The heresies that arose in the third and fourth century appear to have been so many attempts to rationally explain the position and function of Christ as an intermediate being in the context of a platonically informed cosmology. The Church Councils may have managed to fight off the many attempts to see Christ as semi-divine but in the process of emphasising his divinity they appear to have partly lost sight of the mediatorial redemptive significance of Christ's humanity as a fall-out of the struggle.[8]

The Nicene Council debated whether or not Christ's deity should be defined in terms of **same** substance or **like** substance with the Father. The Nicene Council opted for the formulation 'same substance' and thus they sought to emphasise the ontological sameness of Christ with the Father

---

7. For a brief overview of the ancient christological controversy see Alister E McGrath, *Christian Theology: An Introduction* (Oxford: Blackwell, 1994), 330–46.
8. For discussion of the implications of the Arian controversy on Christ's role as redemptive mediator see Josef A Jungmann, *The Place of Christ in Liturgical Prayer* (London: Geoffrey Chapman, 1989), 161–62, 176–77.

and thus their essential coequality and oneness. The Church Fathers clearly tried to provide a rational explanation for why there is only One God and not three gods in a polytheistic hierarchy despite God's dual or triple manifestation as Father, Son and Holy Spirit at the time of the incarnation. The rationale for this sameness and oneness and co-equality and thus the inner ontological unity in God was grounded in their argument that Christ was pre-existently 'begotten', from eternity, that is, Christ issued from the Father and thus there was analogically speaking a Farther and Son relationship within God even before the incarnation.

One could question whether this idea of a cosmic 'begetting' is a necessary argument for maintaining the essentially ontological unity and oneness of God despite his manifestation as a Trio. Thus the formulations of the Patristic Councils could be seen as an attempt to provide an explanation that seeks overcomes the major rationalistic objections of the human mind to the idea that something can be one and three at the same time.

This historic controversy regarding the attempts to rationally explain the identity of Christ and thus the mysterious inner being of God poses an even more fundamental question regarding the adequacy of human speech in describing the divine mystery. Is the true nature of the divine being a mystery beyond the human cognitive rational capabilities? Should the divine dimension be respected as an inexplicable mystery that transcends the limits of human rationality? Is it legitimate to insist that God's being must be explainable in terms of human analogies and rational categories as was the case in the platonically informed Christianity of Alexandria? Could it be that the human desire to probe into the mysteries of God's eternal being is the real cause of the endless and often meaningless disputes over Christ's divinity and the question of the Trinity?

Adventist Epistemology

The confessional position of Seventh-day Adventists is that Scripture is their only 'creed'.[9] From this principal it is evident that for Adventists, scriptural revelation is not only the source, but also the norm by which beliefs and experience are tested. This implies that doctrine, faith and ex-

---

9. *Seventh-day Adventists Believe. A Biblical exposition of Fundamental Doctrines*, second edition (Boise ID: Ministerial Association, General conference of Seventh-day Adventists, 2005), 5. See also Knight, *A Search for Identity*, 30–31. The Adventist Church has established a formal process by which doctrinal confessional changes can be facilitated and by which such a common consensus can be expressed formally.

perience are subject to the benchmark of scriptural revelation as the ultimate criterion of truth. Thus revelation is not only the ultimate source of knowledge of God but revelation itself sets the limits to what humans can know about God. Thus Adventism confesses a Hebrew epistemology rather than Greek one. The radical implication of such an epistemological principle is that 'human reason' cannot serve as the ultimate source or benchmark for the truth about God. Furthermore, Adventist epistemology limits such normative revelation to the biblical canon: a principle which in turn excludes any human ecclesiastical magisterium, council, tradition or confessional statement from functioning as the ultimate canon of truth about God.

While the ecclesiastical traditions and teachings of the past are formative in sharpening the key theological questions and issues, they are not considered to be normative in Adventism. So if Adventism does not fully agree in detail with the council of Nicaea, Chalcedon or the teachings of the Adventist pioneers it does not mean that they are necessarily on a wrong track in terms of their epistemology. Given such methodologically premises, one should listen carefully to the insight of the past and should only reform the tradition if it falls short of Biblical revelation. However, according to the preamble to the Fundamental Beliefs of Seventh-day Adventists, if any historic teachings falls short of Biblical insights they should be revised according to the methodological ethos of Adventism. So if biblical revelation takes the reader beyond the insights of the Adventist pioneers and the Patristic Councils, it should cause no fundamental concern. It would be unfaithfulness to the real methodological ethos of Adventism if one does not follow the lead of Scripture.

The point being that because it can be demonstrated that while some of the past and present Adventist publications on any topic—in this case the topic of the Trinity—may fall short of the full biblical testimony, it does not necessarily imply that the church is in the process of apostasy. Given the process of doctrinal revisions in the Adventist Church any serious view must gain a sustained and prolonged support in the community of faith before it will ever enter into the church's fundamental articles of faith; even when that happens such views can still be changed over time as the official 'fundamental beliefs' in Adventism may be best defined as a current communial consensus on biblical teachings rather than a final word.

So even if several leading persons in the past, present or future propose certain view and even if such views receives administrative support and is disseminated in church publications it does not make it normative Adventist beliefs. Church leaders and theologians do not constitute a 'magisterium' of infallible interpreters whose formulations must be adopted by the faithful. The Adventist Church does not have an ecclesiastical or academic order of people who decides the truth. The leaders and teachers in the church are naturally influential and can facilitate a debate and thus lead the church towards deeper insights that might eventually be reflected in the fundamental beliefs of the church. However, no-one's conscience is ultimately bound by such confessional statements, not even the Church's official articles of faith. Such a concept of doctrinal authority is not universally accepted in the Christian world; a world in which a magisterium, tradition, councils, scholars or charismatic persons defines creeds and articles of faith implying that the 'leadership' of the church tends to be the final authority on truth.

Finally, the Adventist church in its 'fundamental beliefs' formally honours the reformation position that every man has the right and duty to study Scripture and interpret it for himself. This does not mean that every man necessarily has the ability to study Scripture let alone an ability to infallibly interpret Scripture due to the human cognitive and cultural limitations; nevertheless he has the right and duty to acquire such skills and to study and interpret scripture in dialogue with the community of believers as a whole and thus to participate in a common search for an understanding that feeds into and informs the public confessions of the community.

The Biblical Data and the Biblical World-View

The scriptural testimony about Jesus poses a central methodological challenge. How are the readers to understand the apostolic assertions about Christ's alleged divinity? Methodologically speaking, later generations naturally approach the topic of the Trinity from the horizon of the mature doctrinal definitions as they have developed over time in the Christian tradition and as such the dogma sets the agenda, defines he issues and forms our linguistic formulations. What is often ignored is the fact that the dogma matured over time firstly in the flow of biblical revelation and secondly in the context of a platonically influenced ecclesiastical tradition which implies that this doctrine is the outcome of not only a revelatory but also a post-revelatory process.

The trinitarian issue seems absent in Old Testament times as the authors emphasised the oneness of God in contrast to polytheism. Even in

New Testament times the inclusion of Christ into biblical monotheism and thus making him an object of faith and worship did not seems to cause a major problem until Christianity moved into a platonically informed environment, which hermeneutically speaking demanded a human rational explanations for the incarnation and thus for the mysteries of God's being. There appear to be a fundamental hermeneutical divide between the Hebrew and the Greek mind. The Hebrew mind operates in the context of a world view and thus an epistemology in which divine revelation is seen as the supreme source and benchmark of knowledge of God, while the Greek mind operates within a world view horizon and thus an epistemology in which the mind is seen not only as the source of knowledge of ultimate reality, but also as the benchmark for such truth. Any 'truth'—even a truth of revelation—must therefore conform to the Canons of reason according to the Greek mind.

However, from an Adventist methodological perspective it seems necessary to ask a biblical theological question such as: Why did Jesus and the Apostles use such terminology and what did they mean by such language? It must be remembered that both Jesus and the Apostles spoke in the context of the larger Old Testament narrative horizon with its Davidic and Messianic kingship language. They did not think in terms of the horizon of the Creeds of Nicaea and Chalcedon or later church dogmatics. Thus the Adventist methodology demands that one needs to go back and rethink this dogma in terms of the biblical first principles including the biblical story line and thus rediscover its rationale and meaning within the flow, sphere and horizon of biblical revelation itself.

In 'biblical theology' the progressive nature of God's self-revelation is axiomatic and thus deeper meanings could be expected to emerge as God discloses more of himself through his progressive self-revelation climaxing in the person of Christ. Thus a deeper meanings might develop over time in the usage of such relational terminology as Father, Son and begotten; meanings that could only be disclosed as the full identity of the ultimate son of David would be finally revealed in the Apostolic story.

However, there is a need methodologically speaking to trace the usage of such language within the biblical story-line in order to contextually understand how the New Testament authors used such expressions. In the Old Testament the Father-Son language was explicitly applied to the Davidic Dynasty and thus defined the position and relationship between God and the King —'I will be to him a Father and he shall be to me a Son' (2 Sam 7:14); a formulation that will be repeated in terms of Davidic/

Messianic kingship and kingdom promises throughout the Old Testament narrative (Ps 2:7–12; 89:26–28) and applied to Jesus by the New Testament authors (Acts 13:32–33; Heb 1:3–6). So to be called the Son of God does not necessarily refer to deity but to a divine appointment to the Davidic and Messianic kingship office.

Furthermore, when Luke traced the human genealogy of Jesus, he reverts all the way back to Genesis saying 'son of Adam son of God'. (Luke 3:38) Here the expression Son of God is clearly a reference to the position of Adam. In terms of the Old Testament Adam and Messianic kingship theology the term 'Son of God' seems to refer to the status and relationship of a particular human being to God. The textual issue thus is: do the New Testament authors use the term exclusively in the above sense or does the New Testament revelation infuse this term with deeper meaning? So the core question from a biblical theological point of view concerns the New Testament usage of such terms as 'Father, Son', 'Son of God', 'begetting' and 'firstborn'. While such language seems to refer to Jesus' true humanity as the new Adam and the Messianic king does it also refer to his pre-historic identity?

On biblical ground it could clearly be legitimate to ask the question as to whether or not the Father-Son language and the begetting language are somehow connected with the historical event of the incarnation. If indeed, as asserted by John and Paul, one of the heavenly 'trio' fused with humanity for time and eternity then he is indeed assuming a position and a relationship to the rest of the Godhead which is uniquely that of sonship in the Adamic and Davidic kingship sense as he assumes the position of humanity. This is not a role play this is the formation of a new reality as he took on a new identity in order to become a human Saviour and Lord. So a substantial case could be made for arguing that the son-ship language refers to the new identity assumed through the incarnation. So concerning the question as to whether or not this New Testament application of Old Testament Adamic and Messianic kingship language could refer to more than Christ's humanity and thus to a pre-historic identity the jury may still be out.

The issue of whether or not the biblical idea of 'begotten' is a reference to a pre-incarnational divine event or a reference to the historic divine event in the incarnation is not an issue to be settled by the Canons of human reason but on the premises of biblical theology proper. Biblical theology proper proceeds on the premises that the subject matter is God and that the epistemological source and benchmark of truth about God is God's Self- revelation as manifested in Scripture and not in human reason.

Given the first principles of the biblical world view, the interpreter must thus be aware of his creaturely limitations epistemologically speaking, as he only has access to the dimension of reality to which he belongs. Thus the human creaturely dimension will naturally set the limits for what humans can understand about God's eternal being. Even if God wanted to inform humans about his inner ontological being, humans could probably not comprehend it as there may be no analogies from the order of creation by which this could be made comprehensible. Thus even the scriptural analogies taken from the world of humanity can only be parabolic in scope without a full literal correspondence. Such speech will always be: It is like this but always much more!

The long standing debates and controversies about the Trinity have always been centred in the seemingly irrational nature of the assertion that God has the dimension of singularity (One) and plurality (Three) simultaneously and the attempts to provide a rational explanation for this seeming irrationality. Actually there is no language by which to speak of such mysterious dimensions of God and there are no analogies from the material order by which such a dimensional reality can be fully comprehended.

In a biblical world-view context nobody should be surprised by this fact. Even in natural world phenomena's are observed for which Science have no analogies by which fully to explain what is observed. Accordingly scientists describe observed natural phenomena by complementary models.[10] However, the field of science was apparently not the first one to use this explanatory principle the Church Fathers seems to be doing it in their talk about God long before science ever did. The issue of God's singularity (One) and Plurality (Three) poses a logical challenge of a similar fashion. This phenomenon of speech in the confessional statements of the Fathers appears to represent a usage of two complementary models by which to

---

10. The phenomenon of light poses such a problem. Science describes light both as particles and waves two assertions that are conceptually incompatible. Light appears to behave in terms of what we know as particles but also as waves. The truth is that we do not fully understand what light is and thus this physical phenomenon apparently transcends our present comprehension. So science describes what it observes by two incompatible models and analogies. In the world of science this explanatory approach is called the principle of 'complementarity'.

speak about a divine reality that transcends human comprehension and language.

Concluding Remarks

Attempts to formulate a rational coherent theory about the inner being of God often either end up emphasising the plurality at the expense of unity or the singularity at the expense of co-equality. Either case produces a theology that falls short of the biblical assertions and the glory of God. The sphere of the created order has been searched in vain in to find analogies by which we can comprehend such a mystery only to be challenged by an Old Testament prophet who said: 'To whom then will you compare me?' (Isa 40: 25). We can confess the singularity and plurality of God based on his self-revelation but cannot provide explanation that will fully satisfy human reason. All attempts to use analogies even human analogies will fall short of the full truth about God's being. Given the first principles of the biblical world-view even to attempt to give a rational explanations looks suspiciously like an attempt to form in words what idol makers have always been attempting through material form.

The trouble seems to start when we rationally attempt to explain what God is in himself, that is, try to provide an explanation that will satisfy the human demand for a rationally satisfactory answer. If such a criteria is not demanded in the field of empirical scientific study of nature, why should it be demanded in the metaphysical field of divine revelation. We can confess that according to biblical revelation there is a mysterious ontological inner unity in the divine trio but we cannot rationally explain it unless there is a clear biblical revelation. So when we speak of God on biblical premises we can only know what has been revealed and to the degree that is has been revealed and in the manner that it has been revealed. So our theological reflections may only be able to speak confessionally about the mysteries being of God in terms of the principle of complementarity. That observation does not make human theological speech about the dimension of deity irrational but like in natural science one only affirms its limitations.

The key concern of this chapter has been to focus on some critical methodological issues highlighting why humans due to creaturely limitations must be extremely cautious in their speech about God's mysterious inner ontological being as this constitutes a speech about a dimension that seems to transcend the human field of investigation. This chapter proposes a revival of a genuinely biblical theological approach as the way forward not only in this particular dogmatic issue but in all other dogmatic issues. After 1700 years of a Hellenistic rationally informed theology including the Enlightenment critical approaches, subjecting the biblical assertions about God to the canons of human reason, biblical theology proper is almost dead. The methodological task is again to restore it to its full apostolic glory. From that vantage point it might be discovered that the classical struggle over the 'divine trio' is biblically speaking a non-issue.

Despite what God has revealed about himself he remains the mysterious other, a dimension radically different from anything created according to biblical first-principles, which sets the limits for our capacity to fully know and comprehend God and thus God's eternal inner being may thus forever remain God's secret. According to the biblical revelation we can know enough of his character as a being of boundless love and that in God there is no dark side and thus we can respond appropriately to him in trust. The only proper response to God according to Scripture is at the end of the day to give glory to God and worship him and thus recognise one's own limitation as creatures.

As long as a core confession regarding God's self-revelation as a divine trio with an inner ontological unity of being can be maintained on biblical New Testament grounds, and that one in this divine trio took on a human identity through the incarnation, then this question should not turn into a contentious church splitting issue. We should always examine ourselves as to whether or not we are deifying our own reasoning powers by our demand that even the mysteries of God's inner being must conform to our cognitive abilities and comprehension. With the Apostles we should go all the way to the summit of divine revelation and behold the glory of the Lord and bow in worship for the great I AM, but regarding the mysterious inner being of God—silence would be eloquence.

John Harvey Kellogg's Concept of the Godhead

John Skrzypaszek

Introduction

This chapter examines John Harvey Kellogg's[1] understanding of the Godhead within the context of his steadily developing views which were seen by the many contemporary leaders of the Seventh-day Adventist Church as views akin to pantheism.[2] After the first official presentation of his ideas at the 1897 General Conference of Seventh-day Adventists in Lincoln, Nebraska, Kellogg's views peaked in his book *The Living Temple* (1903).[3]

---

1. John Harvey Kellogg (1852–1943) was a physician, surgeon, administrator, educator, author, a great inventor and entrepreneur, a health promoter and a tireless leader. He was born into a Seventh-day Adventist Home. After completing high school and with the encouragement and support of James and Ellen White, he commenced studies at the Bellevue Medical College in 1872. After his graduation, he assumed the leadership role of the Battle Creek Sanitarium and remained there until his death in 1943. As a promoter of healthful living, he was instrumental in establishing the Adventist health care. In 1903 he published a book entitled *The Living Temple* in which he expressed views, believed by the church leadership and Ellen White, to be akin to pantheism. The emerged conflict severed his relationship with the leaders of the Seventh-day Adventist Church and finally it led to the loss of his church memberships in 1907. Richard W Schwarz, *John Harvey Kellogg: Pioneering Health Reformer* (Hagerstown, MD: Review and Herald, 2006), 13–231.
2. Richard W Schwarz, 'The Kellogg Schism: The Hidden Issues', in *Spectrum* (Autumn 1972): 23. See also, Ellen White, Letter 259, 23 June 1904; Letter 242, October 1903. In both letters, one to the Conference Presidents and the other to Physicians and Ministers, Ellen White uses the phrase 'scientific terms which are akin the pantheism' and Kellogg's writings in which 'his tendencies towards Pantheism have been revealed'. The *Noah Webster's 1828 American Dictionary* defines pantheism as follows: PANTHEISM, n [Gr all, and God, whence theism]. The doctrine that the universe is God, or the system of theology in which it is maintained that the universe is the supreme God; PANTHEIST, One that believes the universe to be God; PANTHEISTIC, confounding God with the universe.
3. John, Harvey Kellogg, *The Living Temple* (Battle Creek, MI: Good Health Publishing Company, 1903), 15–36. The introductory chapter, 'The Mystery of Life,' in which

Eventually, at the 1905 General Conference, while reacting to Kellogg's insinuation that 'she believed and taught the same things,' as presented in his book, one of the leading Adventist pioneers, Ellen White referred to her early encounter with Kellogg's views.

> This subject has been kept before me for the past twenty years, yea, for more than twenty years. Before my husband's death, Dr. Kellogg came to my room to tell me that he had great light. He sat down and told me what it was. It was similar to some of the views that he has presented in *The Living Temple*.[4]

It appears that over a period of sixteen years, before he openly shared his views in 1897, Kellogg explored new thoughts, which according to Ellen White were 'similar to some views that he presented in *The Living Temple*'. Without reference to any specific details, she claimed that his views were not new for she met them in the early stages of her ministry in Vermont, New Hampshire and Massachusetts.[5] She made it clear that 'those theories were wrong' and led to 'making God a nonentity and Christ a nonentity'.[6] Three issues emerge from Ellen White's assessment.

First, Ellen White's reaction to Kellogg's early *new ideas* warrants the need for an exploration of the background and influences, which birthed his views of the Godhead. Second, with the recent upsurge of interest on

---

Kellogg expressed his theological views generated considerable concerns among church leaders.

4. Ellen White, Ms 70, 1905. James White died on August 6, 1881. Although the historical data lacks a detailed reference to this meeting, the discussion between Kellogg and Ellen White may have occurred before James' death and Kellogg's publication of the book *Harmony of Science and the Bible* (1879), circa 1880, 1881. In 1885, in her letter to the Directors of the Sanitarium at Battle Creek. Ellen White shared the following words of caution: 'I was not willing that this should come to those who might use it to the Doctor's injury, but now I must write it out. I was shown that he had been in danger, great danger, in the past, of making shipwreck of faith by exalting science above the God of science. He has not a clearly defined position in reference to his faith, and should be guarded, or he will certainly wander in the mazes of scepticism.' Ellen White, Lt 1, 1885.
5. In tracing Ellen White's early views of the trinity Moon refers to the early post-disappointment period of 1845 where former Millerites 'spiritualised' the biblical teachings, which in turn led to fanatical practices. Jerry Moon, 'The Adventist Trinity Debate, Part 2: The Role of Ellen G White', in *Andrews University Seminary Studies* 41 (2003): 277-9.
6. White, Ms 70, 1905.

the subject of Trinity, some groups claim that Kellogg's trinitarian view, which Ellen White condemned in 1905, is the same view of the Trinity later accepted by the church. Others argue that she spoke out specifically against Kellogg's Trinity doctrine that was fundamental to his theology.[7] Such conclusions are supported by Kellogg's defensive and reactionary statements from his correspondence to General Conference President George I Butler (1903, 1904), College Professor William W Prescott (1904) and Daniel's letter to WC White (1903).[8] Because of such claims, it is essential to explore Kellogg's beliefs. Third, as Moon notes, even though a number of Seventh-day Adventist writers explored a progressive shift among the church pioneers from the anti-trinitarian to the trinitarian position 'only Froom addresses the trinitarian issues associated with the Kellogg crisis'.[9] Therefore, it is important to examine the development of Kellogg's ideas and its impact, if any, on Seventh-day Adventism's journey from the anti-trinitarian to the trinitarian position.

This chapter interacts with the following material: Kellogg's book, *Harmony of Science and the Bible on the Nature of the Soul and the Doctrine of the Resurrection of the Dead*, his presentations during the 1897 General Conference and his last publication, *The Living Temple*. As well as, because of the claims which incorporate Ellen White's reactions to Kellogg's views, it is necessary to bring into the discussion her understanding of the Godhead.

Understanding the Background to Kellogg's View of God: *Harmony of Science and the Bible* (1879)

In 1879 Kellogg published his book entitled *Harmony of Science and the Bible on the Nature of the Soul and the Doctrine of the Resurrection of the*

---

7. Jerry Moon, 'The Adventist Trinity Debate', 289. Also, see Allen Stump, editor 'Did Ellen G White Speak Against the Trinity Doctrine', in *Old Paths* (April 2008): 8-9. Stump suggests that Ellen White not only spoke against false views of God, she specifically spoke out against Kellogg's trinity doctrine that it was fundamental to his theology.
8. Butler (Letter, October 28, 1903; Letter 21 February, 1904); Prescott (Letter 25, 10 October, 1903); Daniel's letter to WC White (Letter 29, October 1903). This paper will argue against the position that Kellogg changed his views to accept a trinitarian position which Ellen White spoke against.
9. Jerry Moon, 'The Adventist Trinity Debate, Part 1: Historical Overview', in *Andrews University Seminary Studies* 41 (2003): 113. Moon suggests that the three periods: (1) anti-trinitarian Dominance, 1846-1888; (2) Dissatisfaction with anti-trinitarianism, 1888-1898; and (3) Paradigm Shift, 1898-1913 were discussed by Gane, Holt and Froom, and the 1888-1957 period by Merlin Burt.

Dead. As stated in the preface, he published it as 'the outgrowth of an address delivered by request before the Seventh-day Adventist General Conference, October 8, 1878'.[10] Kellogg stressed that 'the views presented may be new to many and at first may appear somewhat fanciful'.[11] While justifying his new approach to harmonise science and the Bible, his words suggest an awareness of existing prejudice against *some* of his ideas by 'those who held opposite views on *some* of the subjects'.[12] The report from the 1878 General Conference supports such opposition. It was resolved that 'justice to the doctor and the Institute under his care demand that he should have the privilege of making his sentiments known'.[13] James White, who chaired the meetings, received the following resolution.

> The impression has gone out from some unknown cause that JH Kellogg, MD holds infidel sentiments, which does him a great deal of injustice, and so endangers his influence as physician-in-chief of the Sanitarium.[14]

It appears, the referred 'infidel sentiments' involved issues other than discussions about the Godhead. As Burt indicates, up to 1890 the Adventist sentiments were anti-trinitarian and the significant leanings towards trinitarianism did not emerge until the 1888 General Conference in Minneapolis.[15] Possibly fears other than anti-trinitarianism raised the prevailing opposition against Kellogg's 'infidel sentiments'.

The issues and challenges experienced by the early Adventists cannot be isolated from the religious, societal, scientific and political trends which weaved their way through nineteenth century America.[16] In other

---

10. JH Kellogg, *Harmony of Science and the Bible on the Nature of the Soul and the Doctrine of the Resurrection of the Dead* (Battle Creek, MI: Review and Herald, 1879), iii.
11. *Ibid*.
12. However, he mentions that it presented 'fascinating new terms and concepts' Le Roy Edwin Froom, *Movement of Destiny* (Washington DC, Review and Herald, 1971), 349.
13. James White, *The Advent Review and Sabbath Herald*, 17 October, 1878, 1.
14. *Ibid*. In view of the accusations against him, Kellogg was given the privilege 'to make his sentiments' known to the assembled delegates. An added note states that on October 6, Dr Kellogg addressed a large audience 'on the harmony of science and the Bible for which the congregation tendered him a vote of thanks'.
15. Merlin Burt, 'History of Seventh-day Adventist Views on the Trinity', in *Journal of the Adventist Theological Society* 17 (2006): 126. He attributes the shift to the new emphasis on Jesus and the plan of salvation (128).
16. Jonathan Butler, 'When America Was 'Christian', in *The World of Ellen G White*, edited by Gary Land (Hagerstown, MD: Review and Herald, 1987), 97–110. In his brief

words, to grasp the meaning of certain internal issues it is important to consider the influence and impact of 'the social, intellectual and religious upheavals of the late-nineteenth century America'.[17] Bruce Shelley suggests that 'evangelical liberalism' threatened the theological foundations of the nineteenth century Protestant churches.[18] This school of thought promoted the notion that 'Christian theology had to come to terms with modern science if it ever hoped to claim and hold the allegiance of the intelligent men of the day'.[19] Proponents of this view claimed that 'faith had to pass the test of reason and experience'. Further, 'man's mind was capable of thinking God's thoughts after him' and 'the best clues to the nature of God were human intuition and reason'.[20] Shelley describes the prevailing views in the following words: 'The universe was one grand, harmonious machine or perhaps an extremely complex growing organism. Whatever the image—a watch or a plant—the point is unity, harmony, coherence.'[21]

Naturally, liberal views, which promoted scientific study of the Bible, human reason and search for God's immanence outside the Bible, became an object of concern among the Adventist writers. As early as 1861 JN Loughborough defended the superiority of the Bible arguing that reason and nature were not trustworthy.[22] He argued: 'This professed revelation

---

overview Butler refers to the impact of Protestant Liberalism with its accommodation to new science which provoked a reaction from the conservative segments of Protestantism, 106–7.

17. *Ibid*, 110.
18. Bruce Shelley, *Church History in Plain Language* (Nashville, TN: Thomas Nelson, 1995), 396. Hinson, however, points out that the American theological liberalism had roots in European as well as American soil—Schleiermacher, Ritschl, Troelsch, the Religions Geschichtliche Schule, Harnack and others. Also, he refers to the works of the influential American theologian and father of American religious liberalism, Horace Bushnell (1802–1876). Glenn E Hinson, 'Baptist Contribution to Liberalism', Baptist History and Heritage Society (1 January, 2000): http://www.encyclopedia.com/doc/1E1-Bushnell.html (18.4.2008). In his 'Dissertation on Language as Related to Thought' Bushnell expressed a challenging view of Trinity. He claimed that the Godhead is the instrumental three—three simply as related to our finite apprehension, and the communication of God's incommunicable nature. Also see, Fred Kirschenmann, 'Horace Bushnell: Orthodox or Sabellian', in *Church History* 33 (March 1964): 49–59.
19. *Ibid*. Also, see Stanley J Grenz & Roger E Olson, *20th Century Theology: God & the World in a Transitional Age* (Downers Grove, IL: InterVarsity, 1992), 53. In the late nineteenth century Christianity seemed constantly to be losing ground to the secular science.
20. *Ibid*. Also see Ronald, L Numbers, 'Science Falsely So-Called: Evolution and Adventists in the Nineteenth Century', in *JASA* 27 (March 1975): 19.
21. Shelley, *Church History*, 397.
22. JN Loughborough, 'Guidance and Nature', in *Review and Herald* (5 November 1861):

from nature as we have already intimated is to a great extent imaginary, and for this reason has led men to believe in no God or to believe that everything is God.'[23]

Later in 1884 Ellen White wrote in *Signs of the Times* on the topic of Science and Revelation. She argued that great minds, if not guided by the Bible, 'become bewildered in their attempts to investigate the relations of science and revelation'.[24] Further, she pointed out the dangers of losing trust in the reliability of the Bible history and inspiration.[25]

Ronald Numbers infers that Kellogg's book surfaced as the result of the tension between science and religion.[26] Therefore, it is possible to assume the early opposition against Kellogg's views emerged from the reactionary attitudes among the Adventists against free and independent thinking or, as Kellogg expressed it, an open-minded approach to truth seeking.[27] Possibly such modern freethinking would have been tagged as infidel sentiments.

The reality of this tension became obvious in Kellogg's defensive remarks. He argued that religionists used 'a bigoted, unreasoning, dogmatic faith . . . holding the Bible as unimpeachable authority on all subjects'.[28]

---

177. It appears that Loughborough was responding to arguments which claimed that 'nature is the *only* guide and in fact the only revelation that God has made to his creatures' (Emphasis added).
23. *Ibid*.
24. Ellen White, *Signs of the Times*, 13 March 1884.
25. *Ibid*. Ellen White wrote 'There should be a settled faith in the divinity of God's holy word. The Bible is not to be tested by men's ideas of science, but science is to be brought to the test of this unerring standard.' At this early stage Ellen White foresaw the dangers of 'doubts in the reliability of the Old and New Testaments' and 'doubts in God's existence'.
26. While 'most of the leaders of the mainline Protestant churches of the nineteenth century, who even before 1859 had abandoned belief in the literality of the Mosaic story of creation, Adventist writers defended both the historical and scientific accuracy of the first chapters of Genesis', in Numbers, 'Science Falsely So-Called', 18.
27. Kellogg, 'Harmony and Science', iv. Further, it appears that the influence of the Protestant liberalism effected Kellogg's view of the traditional interpretation of Adventist theology. As Schwarz points out 'The denominational leadership had grown apprehensive of the doctor's tendency to regard large portions of the Bible as figurative particularly those prophetic sections on which Adventist scholars built much of the church's theology', Richard W Schwarz, *John Harvey Kellogg: Pioneering Health Reformer* (Hagerstown, MD: Review and Herald, 2006), 187–8.
28. *Ibid*, 10, 11. Also, Shelley points out that Liberal thinkers claimed that a 'Christian should keep his mind open to truth from any source. New facts may well change traditional beliefs that rest on no more than customs and time' and that 'unexamined faith is not worth having'. Shelley, *Church History*, 396.

He cried out for an open-minded approach to truth seeking. He stated that, 'His only desire is to aid if possible, those who are seeking for truth to find the gem in its purest, clearest and consequently beautiful form.'[29] Kellogg claimed that truth about God stemmed both from nature and from inspiration. His statements were emphatic. 'The truth of nature is God's truth just as are the truth of inspiration; for God is the author of nature.'[30] He argued against 'bigoted, unreasonable zeal of the religionists' and 'the blustering arrogant assumptions of the scientists.'[31] His stress on open-minded search for 'conceptions of God' included nature where one can explore God's greatness, beneficence and his infinite power. In all his freethinking, Kellogg did not disagree with special revelation. He claimed, 'It is only through the inspired book that we learn the fullness of his attributes and our whole duty as the creatures of his hand.'[32]

However, his affinity with the wonders of nature and openness to scientific reasoning stood in direct conflict with the orthodox view of the transcendent God. On the other hand, the idea of a God 'somewhere beyond the universe' was not acceptable to modern man. Modern thinkers explored God's immanence as his 'dwelling in the world and working through nature.'[33] While defending ably the biblical view on the nature of the human soul and the resurrection, Kellogg swayed away from the traditional reasoning. He began to create a philosophical maze of nature's wonders to describe the mysteries of God. In his search for God's immanence he followed the thoughts of the contemporary thinkers of his day. He claimed.

> A man who studies nature truly seeking by patient observation to solve her mysteries and discover the curious wonders can never become an infidel. Every step as he advances brings him deeper into the mysteries of the Almighty. Every new discovery opens to Him broader views of wisdom and goodness of the author of existence. His ideas of the God of nature, of the universe, of truth and purity enlarge; self-

---

29. Kellogg, 'Science and the Bible', iv.
30. *Ibid*, 29.
31. *Ibid*.
32. *Ibid*.
33. Shelley, *Church History*, 396.

sinks into insignificance. Surely there is nothing dangerous in this.[34]

Before proceeding further, let us briefly consider the early stages of Kellogg's journey. While rescuing God from the 'bigoted unreasoning, dogmatic faith in the infallibility of the ancient doctrines supposed to be based on inspiration', maybe even unintentionally, Kellogg placed God under the scrutiny of human reason. Furthermore, his search for God's immanence followed the reactionary spirit of his time towards orthodoxy and authoritative theology. The new theological reflections viewed theology as 'human reflection on human experience of God'.[35]

It must be said that Ellen White did not oppose intellectual reasoning and the development of intellect. To the contrary, as early as 1872, she encouraged intellectual growth. She said, 'The truth of the divine word can be best appreciated by an intellectual Christian'.[36] However, Kellogg's heightened emphasis on the intellectual understanding of God through the wonders of nature shifted human views of God to abstract, theoretical and impersonal definitions. In other words, God's personality vanished in the vastness of 'the wonders and beauties of nature' and the struggles of the human mind which 'trembles as it attempts to grasp a concept of the infinitude of life'.[37] In the milieu of that time, 'spiritualising' implied the process of 'identifying the supernatural and the spiritual' and linking 'the spiritual with human consciousness, the intellectual and emotive side of man'.[38] According to Moon such spiritualising transformed what was intended to be literal into non-literal, spiritual and mystical.[39] Because of her early experiences, Ellen White warned Kellogg of the dangers of developing such speculative ideas. Furthermore, her description of Kellogg's reac-

---

34. Kellogg, 'Harmony and Science', 30.
35. Grenz & Olson, *20th Century Theology*, 44. On Schleiermacher's influence on American theologians. see Fred Kirschenmann, 'Horace Bushnell: Orthodox or Sabellian', *Church History*, 33 (March 1964): 49–59.
36. Ellen G White, *Testimonies for the Church,* volume 3 (Mountain View, California: Pacific Press, 1948), 160. In 1872 she stated: 'Ignorance will not increase the humility or spirituality of any professed follower of Christ.' Further she promoted the value of education and the understanding of true science. In 1882 she wrote, 'The only safety for the people now is to feel the importance of combining religious culture with general education, that we may escape the curse of unsanctified knowledge. Every effort should be made in the education of youth to impress their minds with the loveliness and power of the truth as it is in Jesus.' Ms 4, 1882.
37. Kellogg, *Science and the Bible*, 222.
38. Shelley, *Church History*, 396.
39. Moon, 'The Adventist Trinity Debate', 277.

tion to her counsel is worth mentioning. 'As I talked about these things, laying the whole matter before Dr Kellogg, and showing him what the outcome of receiving these theories would be, he seemed dazed.'[40]

If Kellogg's early theories were shaped by a genuine pursuit of God's immanence found in nature and human experience then one can understand his 'dazed' reaction to Ellen White's advice. No wonder that he remarked, 'Surely there is nothing dangerous in this'. However, Ellen White's reference to the 'nonentity' of God and Christ meant more than abstract definitions.[41] As shown by Whidden, Moon, and Reeve at the time of her meeting with Kellogg, circa 1890, 1891, while he presented his new ideas, she had a well-set and progressively growing understanding of the Godhead.

- 1850—Christ and the Father are personal beings with tangible form (*Early Writings*, 54, 77.
- 1869—Christ is equal with God (*Testimonies*, volume 2, 200)
- 1872—Christ was not created (*Review and Herald*, 17 December 1872)
- 1878 - Christ was the 'eternal Son' (*Review and Herald*, 8 August 1878; letter 37, 1887, in *Manuscript Releases*, volume 15, 26; *Youth's Instructor*, 31 August 1887; *1888 Materials*, volume 1, 29; *Review and Herald*, 8 February 1898; *Review and Herald*, 5 April 1906.[42]

Her knowledge of God and Jesus was not theoretical, based on specific definitions, but *wholistically experiential*.[43] As early as 1850, she described

---

40. Ellen White, Ms 70, 1905.
41. It appears that Ellen White had a clear understanding of what she meant by nonentity. 'And truly our fellowship is with the Father, and with his Son Jesus Christ.' All through the Scriptures, the Father and the Son are spoken of as two distinct personages. You will hear men endeavoring to make the Son of God a nonentity. He and the Father are one, but they are two personages. Wrong sentiments regarding this are coming in, and we shall all have to meet them.' *Review and Herald*, 13 July 1905. This statement was taken from Ellen White's talk presented at the General Conference on May 25, 1905.
42. Woodrow Whidden, Jerry Moon, and John W Reeve, *The Trinity: Understanding God's Love, His Plan of Salvation and Christian Relationship* (Hagerstown, MD: Review and Herald, 2002), 208.
43. The term 'wholistically experiential' includes the concepts such as a progressively growing biblical view of the Godhead, and understanding based on her visions and knowledge derived from her personal experience of God's presence in human life. This concept is expressed by Ellen White in a letter written to Kellogg in 1903 where she said, 'What we most need is an experimental knowledge of God, as He revealed in His Word. Such knowledge would enable us to see our imperfection of character and

her early vision of God and Jesus. 'I gazed on Jesus' countenance and admired His lovely person'. She continued. 'The Father's person I could not behold, for a cloud of glorious light covered Him. I asked Jesus if His Father had a form like Himself. He said he had, but I could not behold it, for said He, "If you should once behold the glory of His person you would cease to exist"'.[44] In 1870 she spoke about the Son's distinctive personality and equality with the Father.[45] Stressing the unity of purpose between the Father and the Son, she wrote, 'His Son would carry out his will and all his purposes, but would do nothing of himself alone, The Father's will would be fulfilled in him'[46]

On the other hand, Kellogg's search for God's immanence and its relationship to human experience eventually forced him to seek God outside his self-revelation through Jesus and the Bible. It forced him to define God in *abstract, technical, impersonal and mythical* terms rather than a 'loving,

---

our ignorance of our Lord and Saviour Jesus Christ . . .' Ellen G White to JH Kellogg, Letter 232, 1903. Further, the words she wrote in 1905 illustrate this point. 'We cannot present any correct representation in words of God's glory and majesty. It is beyond expression. But we can enjoy the contemplation of God, and the sense of His presence. We can know of Him all that human beings can bear. We can talk with Him in prayer. At times when our faith goes out to Him completely, we can converse with Him, and by faith endure the seeing of the Invisible. Faith reveals Him, and we can contemplate all that we can endure. When in times of trouble and perplexity we trust Him fully, we have a living sense of His cheering, all-pervading presence and power. We realise that the Lord is indeed our strength and our portion forever. We can be one with Christ in God.' Ellen White, Ms 126, 1905.

44. Ellen White, *Early Writings* (Washington DC: Review and Herald, 1882), 54, 77, 99. 'I have often seen the lovely Jesus, that He is a *person*. I asked Him if His Father was a person and had a form like himself. Said Jesus, "I am in the expressed *image* of My Father's *person*"'. 77.

45. Ellen White, *The Spirit of Prophecy*, volume 1 (Battle Creek, MI: Steam Press, 1870), 17. Also as early as 1870 Ellen White wrote about the equality and distinctive personality of the Father and the Son. 'The great Creator assembled the heavenly host, that he might in the presence of all the angels confer special honor upon his Son. The Son was seated on the throne with the Father, and the heavenly throng of holy angels was gathered around them. The Father then made known that it was ordained by himself that Christ, his Son, should be equal with himself; so that wherever was the presence of his Son, it was as his own presence. The word of the Son was to be obeyed as readily as the word of the Father. His Son he had invested with authority to command the heavenly host. Especially was his Son to work in union with himself in the anticipated creation of the earth and every living thing that should exist upon the earth. His Son would carry out his will and his purposes, but would do nothing of himself alone. The Father's will would be fulfilled in him.'

46. Ibid.

caring and personal Being'.[47] However, as LeRoy Froom suggested, Kellogg's views were not yet fully developed.[48] The report of the 1878 General Conference meeting included a note about Dr Kellogg's presentation of the topic on 'the harmony of science and the Bible' to a large audience 'for which the congregation tendered him a vote of thanks'.[49]

Expanding Views: Kellogg's Presentations at the 1897 General Conference in Lincoln, Nebraska

At the minister's meetings preceding the 1897 General Conference, Kellogg presented six lectures. The topics included themes such as 'God in Man', 'God in Nature', and 'The Work of God'.[50] By this time, he had developed strong convictions about health reform. In a letter written to Ellen White in 1898, he wrote. 'Those who meet the Lord when he comes will be above the power of disease as well as the power of sin and they will reach this condition by obedience to the truth.'[51] Kellogg believed 'the healing of disease is the completion of the work of forgiveness . . . and the evidence of God's forgiveness and moral healing.'[52] Such a conclusion swayed his mind towards perfectionism and in effect it coloured his understanding of the Godhead. Schwarz notes that 'Adventist history is replete with individuals who fasten onto a particular aspect of doctrine and seek to make all else subservient to it.'[53] Kellogg is a classic case study. He encapsulated his theology in a question. 'How do we know that God is in us?'[54]

Concerning Kellogg's attempts to answer this question, we should note the following. First, in his six presentations, he did not refer to the Holy Spirit. In fact, his view of God's presence both in nature and in man, de-

---

47. Moon, 'The Adventist Trinity Debate', 278. Also see, Woodrow Whidden, Jerry Moon, and John W Reeve, *The Trinity*, 206–7.
48. LeRoy Edwin Froom, *Movement of Destiny* (Washington, DC: Review and Herald. 1971), 349.
49. *The Advent Review and Sabbath Herald*, 17 October 1878.
50. The presentations were recorded in the 1897 *General Conference Bulletin Daily* February 15 – March 8, cited below as *GCB*.
51. Ellen White, Letter to Kellogg, 28 June 1898.
52. *Ibid.*
53. Schwarz, 'The Kellogg Schism', 24.
54. *GCB*(1878), 78.

fined as an 'intelligent power'[55] made ineffective the biblical role and purpose of the Holy Spirit.[56]

Second, referring to Christ, Kellogg failed to speak about his pre-existence. He argued. 'there is only one God, there is only one kind of divinity'.[57] He stated that Jesus was divine, but he merged the view of divinity with his conception of the 'image of God'. This conception was explained as follows. 'The image of God means that God put into the mass of clay, out of which man was made, everything of God that it is possible to manifest through human form.'[58]

He reasoned, 'Adam was created in the first place in the image of God, the perfect man' and because of the fall 'God manifest in flesh', appeared in Christ, the second Adam. He inferred that 'in Christ we have the same sort of image of God as in the first Adam'.[59] Kellogg made a distinction between Christ's divinity and man's divinity by saying that 'Christ was divine in an unmeasurably larger and more perfect sense than man'.[60] However, he concluded that 'we have in man the same image of God and the same divinity as in Christ'.[61] It appears that Kellogg's reasoning reflects the thoughts of classical liberalism. Commenting on this school of thought Millard Erickson points out that in contrast to the traditional orthodox view, 'it pictures human nature as in itself containing God' for 'there is a spark of the divine within man'.[62] The liberal views placed an emphasis on

---

55. *Ibid*, 94.
56. John 16: 5-15; Galatians 5:22-25.
57. GCB (1897), 77.
58. *Ibid*, 77.
59. *Ibid*.
60. *Ibid*.
61. *Ibid*.
62 Millard J Erickson, *Christian Theology* (Grand Rapids, MI: Baker, 1985), 305. Both Arthur White and LeRoy Froom refer to Kellogg's contact with Dr AH Lewis, a Seventh Day Baptist and editor of the *Sabbath Recorder* who was a keen promoter of pantheism. Both suggest that Lewis who visited Kellogg's home in Battle Creek was probably instrumental in enhancing Kellogg's views. However, As evidence for his assertion, Froom quoted from a letter he had received from Dr SPS Edwards who was related to Dr Lewis, and attested to Lewis's confusion on a number of theological issues, including pantheism. Froom concluded that 'whether—had first influenced Kellogg along these lines or visa versa is not known and is immaterial. But this situation throws light on the Kellogg position', Froom, *Movement of Destiny*, 352. Arthur White, *The Early Elmshaven Years 1900-1905* (Washington, DC: Review and Herald, 1981), 281-2. This chapter, however, takes the position that Kellogg's views were shaped by a wider range of contemporary thinkers of his time. For example in describing the classical liberalism view of miracles Millard Erickson points out that 'miracle is simply the religious name for event. Every event, even the most natural

the development of 'the potential divinity of man' and on the amplification of the divine presence within human life.[63] Such views would harmonise with Kellogg's tendency towards perfectionism. By defining redemption as 'restoration of the image of God in man which Adam lost by sin', Kellogg followed a similar thought pattern. [64] Therefore, he saw redemption as 'restoration of those godlike attributes which were given to Adam and which were reproduced in the second Adam'.[65] The seeds of such inherent divinity present in man paved the pathway towards development of 'the same perfection we see in Christ'.[66] In all his reasoning Kellogg made no room for Christ as mediator, the eternal son, equal to God yet a distinct personality. Rather, Christ appears as the divine expression of God's human qualities otherwise invisible in this world to 'show us the humanity of God'.[67]

Third, Kellogg argued 'we do not see in Jesus Christ everything of God' for Christ only 'shows the human side of God' and not the divine.[68] Even though, he claims that one can only get acquainted with God through Jesus Christ, such knowledge was limited. Clearly Kellogg's search for the immanence of the transcendent God moved beyond God's revelation through Jesus Christ and the Bible. He claimed. 'What a wonderful thought, that this mighty God that keeps the whole universe in order, is in us and in everything.'[69] To Kellogg God's personality became an 'intelligent power' which kept everything in action. In other words, immanence meant that 'God was in nature'.[70] For example, Kellogg defined God as 'intelligent presence', 'all wise presence', 'all powerful presence', 'force that holds all things together', and a God-force present 'in us'.[71] In effect, within

---

and unusual becomes a miracle as soon as the religious view of it can be dominant', Erickson, *Christian Theology*, 304. It appears that Kellogg expressed similar thoughts when he stated: 'The miracle of being, the miracle of existence, the miracle enacted in our bodies . . . all these are greater miracles than Christ ever did.' GCB (1897), 78.

63. Erickson, *Christian Theology*, 305
64. GCB (1987), 78.
65. Ibid.
66. Ibid, 78.
67. Ibid, 77.
68. Ibid, 81.
69. Ibid, 83.
70. Ibid, 72.
71. Valentine shows that Kellogg used other descriptive terms such as 'nature is simply a philosophical name for God' or 'sunshine is a true Shekinah, the real presence', 'God is not behind nature, nor above nature, he is nature'. Gilbert Valentine, *The Shaping of Adventism: The Case of WW Prescott* (Barrier Springs, MI: Andrews University Press,

the wonders and mysteries of nature, God lost his independent status and distinct personality. Couched in terms similar to Schleiermacher's perception that God was 'the absolute, all determining, suprapersonal power immanent in everything but beyond all the distinction . . . '[72] The main thrust of Kellogg's view therefore was the need and presence of an innate power in human life. Here, Ellen White's previous warning on making God a nonentity seems so fitting. For her 'Christ and the Father are continually working through the law of nature' but nature was simply God's servant.[73] She pointed out that 'All through the Scriptures, the Father and the Son are spoken of as two distinct personages'.[74] For Kellogg, God was in nature. Such a view of God's immanence implied that 'a universal presence, an intelligent presence, an all-wise presence by the aid of which every atom of the universe is kept in touch with every other atom'. He inferred that such acts, 'can be nothing else than God himself' and so 'this same God is in us and in everything'[75] Here, Kellogg merged God's 'distinct personage' with an the idea of a mystical identity.

Further, his Kellogg's reductionism of Christ's deity divested him from the objective nature of the atonement. It is of interest to note that at the 1905 General Conference Ellen White referred to man's endeavours 'to make the Son of God a nonentity'.[76] It may be suggested that just as God's personality lost its distinctiveness among the descriptive wonders of his presence in nature, so Christ's divinity lost its distinctive individuality in the maze of philosophical assumptions. Thus, in the plan of salvation, he became a nonentity. Valentine comments correctly. 'If man could become like the divine simply by conforming to divine and natural law, there was

---

1992), 164. Furthermore, at the General Conference in 1901, Kellogg continued to define God as the intelligence that is 'present in the plant, in all vegetation', and 'God in the sunflower'.

72. Grenz & Olson, *20th Century Theology*, citing Schleiermacher, 49.
73. *GCB* (1897) 78. During his presentation 'God in Nature' Kellogg relied heavily on Ellen White's article 'God in Nature' (MS 4, 1882). In this article she stressed that Christ and his Father are continually working through the laws of nature. She said, 'God does not annul his laws, but he is continually working through them, using them as his instruments. They are not self-working'. However, Kellogg used her article as a supportive springboard for his personal views stressing God's presence in nature (GCB, 72–76).
74. Ellen White, *Review and Herald*, 13 July 1905.
75. *Ibid*, 83.
76. Ellen White, *Review and Herald*, 13 July 1905.

no need for divine power to help. There was no need for Christ's substitutionary death.⁷⁷

In other words, there was no need to understand and define the essence of Christ's deity and distinct personality as equal to God. He simply became a historical figure for reflections and inspiration of what people could become. Kellogg claimed 'Man may not be godlike in all things, but he may in all things be Christlike'.⁷⁸

It is of interest to note that at the opening meeting of the 1897 General Conference, the constituency listened to Ellen White's letter from Cooranbong written on January 10, 1897. In her greetings she pointed to the need of the Holy Spirit and the need to refocus on Jesus.

> The whole multitude of them that believed were of one heart and one mind, we understand that the agency of the Holy Spirit was doing its work on the human heart. Until the Holy Spirit is accepted and allowed to do its office work upon the heart, each individual will strive to become a center of influence for himself. But we know in our experience, that harmonious subordination to the Spirit of God is rest, and peace, and joy.⁷⁹

While Kellogg failed to refer to the Holy Spirit, Ellen White stressed his active role on human hearts. Her view of the Holy Spirit was reemphasised in The Desire of Ages (1898) when she wrote: 'The Spirit was to be given as a regenerating agent, and without this the sacrifice of Christ would have been of no avail.' She then added: 'Sin could be resisted and overcome only through the mighty agency of the Third Person of the Godhead, who would come with no modified energy, but in the fullness of divine power.'⁸⁰

Kellogg's Views in *The Living Temple*

This study does not intend to explore the complexities associated with the attitudes and leadership tensions which eventually lead to Kellogg's severance from the church.⁸¹ It should be noted, however, that Kellogg's

---

77. Valentine, *The Shaping of Adventism*, 162.
78. GCB (1897), 78.
79. *Ibid*, 97. Letter, 10 January, 1897. EG White, Sunnyside, Cooranbong.
80. Ellen White, *Desire of Ages*, 671. See also Moon, 'The Adventist Trinity Debate', 278.
81. Schwarz, 'The Kellogg, Schism', 23–39.

nonconformist, creative, freethinking spirit stood in direct contrast to the conformity and traditional orthodoxy of the church leadership.[82] Without any doubt question, the spreading influence of his views troubled many. The publishing of *The Living Temple* was a capstone which precipitated the final stage in the Kellogg drama. Those parts of the book which dealt with human physiology were of no concern. It was the introductory chapter, which expressed his theological reflections, that triggered reactionary responses. However, in contrast to his previous presentations, Kellogg expressed an affirmative statement about his belief in a personal God and he referred to God's Spirit. A question arises therefore whether such references imply that Kellogg upheld trinitarian views.

As in his previous presentations, the expressed views disclose a determination to affirm the continuity of the search for God's immanence. Kellogg wrote. 'One of the saddest mistakes man has made is in putting God so far away from himself.'[83] He aimed to close this gap by highlighting the presence of an infinite Intelligence continuously 'working, controlling and creating for man's good'.[84] Such activity was not distant but took place in man and in nature. This led him to argue that 'God is the explanation of nature not a God outside of nature, but in nature'.[85] Further, God's presence reveals itself 'through and in all the objects, movements, and varied phenomena of the universe'.[86] With such views in mind, and as suggested by Moon, most probably responding to his prepublication critics, Kellogg referred to the personality of God and God's Spirit.[87] One wonders, how to understand his statements.

First, he dealt with the objection that, 'God may be present by His Spirit or by his power but certainly God himself cannot be present everywhere all at once'.[88] He argued 'how can the power be separated from its source?' Second, he said that 'where God's Spirit is at work, where God's power is

---

82. Alonzo L Baker, 'My Years with John Harvey Kellogg', in *Spectrum* (Autumn 1972): 43. Schwarz suggests that one underlying reason for reactionary responses might be that: 'In Kellogg's day most Adventist ministers lacked the advantage of much formal education beyond grammar school. This lack contributed to the doctor's feelings of superiority toward his ministerial colleagues.' Schwarz, 'The Kellogg Schism', 26.
83. John Harvey Kellogg, *The Living Temple* (Battle Creek, MI: Good Health Publishing Company, 1903), 35.
84. *Ibid*, 36.
85. *Ibid*, 28.
86. *Ibid*.
87. Moon, *The Trinity Debate*, 292.
88. *Ibid, The Living Temple*, 28.

manifested, God is actually and truly present'.[89] It appears that Kellogg merged God's Spirit and power into one entity which equalled God's presence. He concluded, 'There is about us, an infinite, divine, though invisible Presence'.[90] Rather than explaining God's presence through the delegated role and work of the Holy Spirit,[91] he described it in an impersonal and mystical language. He used terms such as 'a tree maker is in the tree', 'a flower-maker in the flower' and 'shoemaker in the boot'.[92]

Further, Kellogg argued against claims which may suggest that his views destroy God's personality. He answered that he believed in a personal God for such belief in an 'infinite, divine, personal being is essential religion' and 'belief in a personal God is the very core of the Christian religion'.[93] One must not therefore discard the notion that Kellogg believed in a personal God. However, the term 'personal God' needs redefinition for he operated from a different world view. In contrast to the orthodox views of his time, which described God's status independent of the creation, for Kellogg God was at work 'everywhere and through everything that occurs'.[94] In the language of classical liberalism such a God could be perceived as a personal God, but not anthropomorphically.[95] Kellogg ar-

---

89. *Ibid*. In 1897, Kellogg expressed a similar view. 'Why should any one try to minimise the power of God, or to claim that the power is divided between him and another being?' He expressed this view while defending God as 'the only supreme, absolute, the only God, the only ruler in the universe' *GCB(1897)*, 84.
90. Kellogg, *The Living Temple*, 29
91. It's interesting to note that in 1907 in his letter to Elder Horn, Kellogg affirmed his belief in a personal God and in Jesus Christ as the only hope for salvation. Also he affirmed his belief in Sabbath and in the Bible as the word of God. However, again, he did not make any reference to the Holy Spirit. John Harvey Kellogg, December 8, 1907. Letter to Elder ID Horn. On the other hand, in a letter written to Butler, on October 28, 1903, Kellogg seems to defend his position by arguing that he was misunderstood by Ellen White. JH Kellogg to GI Butler, October 28, 1903. Also see, Moon, 'The Trinity Debate', 283–4.
92. Kellogg, *The Living Temple*, 29. At the General Conference of 1901, Kellogg referred to 'God's presence in the sunflower', 'an intelligence that is present in all plants', 'God-life operating in the body cells'. He argued against the concept of God's transcendence by suggesting that every single act is the creating act of God's power in the human body. *GCB (1901)*.
93. Kellogg, *The Living Temple*, 29. It is of interest to note Bushnell's understanding of God's personality. ' . . . a little reflection will show us that the word "person" thus applied is only a figure derived from our finite human personality, and is, in fact a strictly finite word.' Kirschenmann, 'Horace Bushnell', 55.
94. Erickson, *Christian Theology*, 304.
95. Grenz & Olson, *20th Century Theology*, 48. According to Schleiermacher God is not thought to be as a great humanlike being who rules the world from afar. It is of interest

gued, 'We do not see in Jesus Christ everything of God' for 'Christ shows the human side of God'.[96] He moved on to redefine God's personality from the perspective of his world-view. God 'the All-Energy, the infinite Power, an all-pervading Presence' was too vast for the human mind to grasp.[97] To Kellogg the presence of such power was nothing less than 'the power which builds, which creates, it is God himself, the divine Presence in the temple'.[98]

Here Kellogg's view of God's personality changed into abstract, mystical and impersonal terminology. Commenting on the dangers of searching for God's immanence when carried to an extreme, Erickson points out, it resembles pantheism where both nature and God do not have an independent status.[99] It seems that while building his own view of the Godhead, Kellogg blurred the distinctive personality of God the Father, God the Son and God the Holy Spirit. Moon identifies Kellogg's problem as follows

Kellogg hinted in *The Living Temple* that the concept of a personal God was an (ultimately unfactual) construct for the benefit of immature minds, implying that intellectuals like himself could perceive the reality beyond the anthropomorphic accommodation.[100]

In a letter written to Kellogg in 1903 Ellen White expressed her concerns stating the book 'introduces that which is naught but speculations about the *personality of God and where His presence is*'.[101] Further, she stated that 'the personality of the one does not do away with the necessity for the personality of the other' and she encouraged Kellogg to concentrate on the value of Christ's pre-existence.[102]

---

to note that in *The Living Temple* Kellogg uses the biblical anthropomorphic images to conclude that: 'Discussion regarding the form of God are utterly unprofitable ... In the presence of such questions like these we have only to acknowledge our foolishness and incapacity, and bow our heads with awe and reverence in the presence of Personality, and Intelligent Being to the existence of which all nature bears definite and positive testimony, but of which is as far beyond our comprehension as are the bounds of space and time.' Kellogg, *The Living Temple*, 32–33.

96. *GCB* (1897), 81.
97. Kellogg, *The Living Temple*, 29–30.
98. *Ibid*, 52.
99. Erickson, *Christian Theology*, 303.
100. Moon, 'The Adventist Trinity Debate', footnote, 65.
101. Ellen White, Letter 232, 1903.
102. *Ibid*.

Summary of Kellogg's view of the Godhead

This chapter takes the position that Kellogg's views of the Godhead reflected a trend distinct from the denominational journey from the antitrinitarian to the trinitarian position. Rather, his views echoed the sentiments of the liberal thought-leaders of his time—the search for God's immanence. As shown in figure 1, such a journey places God in the hub of human experience subjecting Him to views which stem from human reason rather than the Bible. If one considers the possibility of Kellogg's empathy with the theological and philosophical trends of his time, one must not discard the likelihood of Bushnell's influence.[103] Bushnell stressed the presence of the divine in humanity and nature and on internal Christian experience. One wonders, whether such thoughts influenced Kellogg to the point where he failed to explore the full dynamism of the biblical view of the Godhead and its relationship to Christian experience. Thus, he developed ideas about the personality of God and Christ considered misleading by Ellen White and most of his Adventist contemporaries. [104]

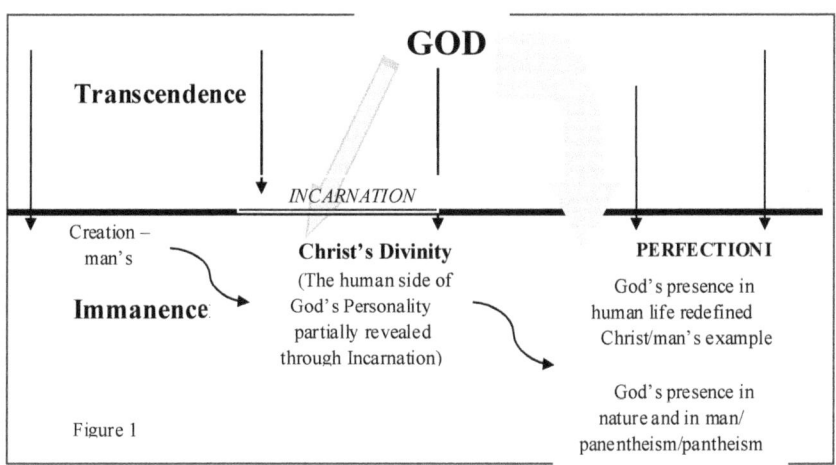

Figure 1

Although Kellogg's view leans towards modalism and sabellianism, it does not originate from his effort to define the mystery of the Godhead. He does not explore themes such as Christ's pre-existence, his deity in substance or consubstantiality with God. Grenz points out correctly that to the nineteenth century liberal thinkers such terms became 'unintelligi-

---

103. Horace Bushnell (1802–76) He was an American Congregational minister who wrote *Christian Nurture* (1847) and *God in Christ* (1849).
104. Ibid.

ble'[105] Rather, his references to God and Christ flow from his attempts to show the reality of God's presence, or the presence of his power, in human life. He viewed the incarnation *only* as God's way to display the human characteristics of his personality. At the same time he argued that such revelation was limited.[106] God had to be 'discovered in the beauty of the universe above, beneath, and all about us'.[107] Kellogg's view that God had both a human and a divine side to his personality introduced the idea of personality dualism. On the one hand were God's revealed human traits, and on the other hand was the mystical wonder of the divine greatness. Here, Kellogg reflects the nineteenth-century Hegelian view of the Absolute, a great-spirit or mind, yet with 'no personal self-consciousness, no personality to which one can relate'.[108] Such dualism is contrary to the biblical view where God is revealed as personal 'an individual being, with self-consciousness and will, capable of feeling, choosing, and having a reciprocal relationship with other personal and social beings'.[109] The characteristics of God's omnipotence, omnipresence and omniscience relate to his identity as God. However, this otherness, which is beyond the scope of any anthropomorphic terminologies, does not nullify the essence of his distinct personality. As a God of love, he shows his acts of love. As a relational Being, who feels, hears and understands, He enters into a relationship with people. The Biblical view of God's otherness does not change his personality into an 'abstract, unknowable being, or a nameless force'.[110] However, Kellogg's reinterpretation of God's personality as a universal, suprapersonal power immanent in everything, reshaped God into everything but beyond all distinction. In that sense, God became a nonentity.

Similarly, by equating Christ's divinity with human divinity before the fall, Kellogg reduced Christ's role to a 'religious and ethical ideal of humanity'. [111] Such reductionism made Christ different from other human

---

105. Grenz & Olson, *20th Century Theology*, 59.
106. GCB (1897), 77.
107. *Ibid*, 82.
108. Erickson, 268.
109. *Ibid*, 269.
110. *Ibid*.
111. Grenz & Olson, *20th Century Theology*, 59. While Kellogg limited incarnation to the revelation of God's human qualities, in 1903 Ellen White wrote, 'Christ converted all nature into an index to illustrate His greatness, His goodness, His love. Water, air, light, life – these Christ used to illustrate His work and His character.' Further she said, 'Christ would heighten our conception of His exalted character, His preexistence and His prospective glory.'" Ellen White, Letter 232, 1903.

beings in degree only and not in kind. Kellogg claimed, 'Christ was divine in an unmeasurable larger and more perfect sense than man and yet we have in man the same image of God and the same divinity as in Christ'.[112] Further, by associating the Holy Spirit with God's power without any reference to his personality and role within the Godhead, Kellogg was able to replace the presence of God's appointed comforter and helper with his own focus on human effort. Kellogg's view of the Godhead emerged from the spiritualised intellectualising through which the literal personality of God, as revealed in Scripture, changed into speculative nonentity. Also, his view of Christ's divinity lost its distinctive uniqueness in the maze of reductionistic philosophical assumption and became a nonentity. Lastly, Kellogg's panentheistic[113] view of God replaced the distinctive role of the Holy Spirit in human life.

Kellogg's views reached its their peak in the years 1903–1905. During these same years, Ellen White upheld a balanced view of the Trinity. As Moon suggests, 'it showed God as including three individual personalities, who in nature, character, purpose and love are one'.[114] As shown below, her views expressed a relational unity within the Godhead.[115]

---

112. *Ibid.* See also Grenz & Olson, *20th Century Theology*, 50 for critical comment on Schleirmacher's overemphasis on immanence.
113. This chapter takes the position that Kellogg's views of God reflect the views of panentheism rather than pantheism. As pointed out previously, Ellen White referred to his views as 'akin to pantheism'. In contrast to pantheism which claims the 'universe is the supreme God' or that 'God and everything that exists are identical'. Panentheism expresses the thought that 'God is in everything'. Erickson, *Christian Theology*, 307. ST Franklin suggests that panentheism is 'the doctrine that God includes the world as part of his being, that is, the world is God, although God if more than the world', in *The Concise Evangelical Dictionary of Theology*, edited by Walter A Elwell (Grand Rapids, MI: Baker Book House, 1991), 368.
114. Moon, 'The Adventist Trinity Debate', 285.
115. *Ibid.*

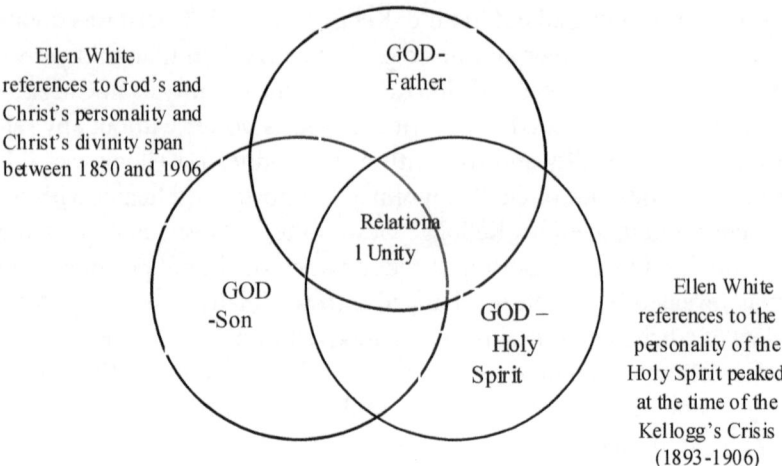

Figure 2

Although, as early as 1850 Ellen White made reference to the distinct personalities of God and Christ, with time, her definitions become more transparent and her reference to the personality of the Holy Spirit peaked during the Kellogg crisis.[116] In 1901 while speaking about human struggle between good and evil she referred to the promise of divine help.

> But they were not left to fight the battles in their own human strength. The angelic host coming as ministers of God would be in that battle. Also there would be the eternal heavenly dignitaries—God, and Christ, and the Holy Spirit—among them with more than mortal energy, and would advance with them to the work, and convince the world of sin.[117]

Then in 1905, she referred to the three persons of the heavenly trio.

> The Son is all the fullness of the Godhead manifested. The Word of God declares Him to be 'the express image of His person'. 'God so loved the world, that He gave His only begot-

---

116. Ellen White references to the personality of God, Ms 83 (1902); Ms 124 (1902), Letter, 233 (1904); Ms 21 (1906): Personality of Jesus, Ms 58, (1900); Ms 140 (1903); Ms 83 (1903); Letter, 233, 1904; Ms 116 (1905); Letter 233 (1904); Ms 116 (1905); Ms 21 (1905); Letter 52 (1906): Personality of the Holy Spirit, Ms 93 (1893); Letter 119 (1895); Letter 233 (1904); Ms 20 (1906); Ms 21 (1906).
117. Ellen White, MR, 1213, 1990, 204.

ten Son, that whosoever believeth in Him should not perish, but have everlasting life.' Here is shown the personality of the Father. The Comforter that Christ promised to send after He ascended to heaven, is the Spirit in all the fullness of the Godhead, making manifest the power of divine grace to all who receive and believe in Christ as a personal Saviour. There are three living persons of the heavenly trio; in the name of these three great powers—the Father, the Son, and the Holy Spirit—those who receive Christ by living faith are baptized, and these powers will co-operate with the obedient subjects of heaven in their efforts to live the new life in Christ . . .[118]

By 1906, Ellen White had a well-defined understanding of the relational unity between the Father, the Son and the Holy Spirit and she spoke of three distinct personalities of the Godhead. In other words, from her trinitarian position, she reacted to Kellogg's abstract, technical, impersonal view of God's personality and to his reductionistic view of Christ. On this journey, Kellogg viewed and defined the Godhead from the hub of universal human experience and through his lenses of perfectionism. Here, his views differed to Ellen White's understanding of God which included the three individual personalities of the Godhead, who in nature, character and purpose and love are one. Although in his later responses to Butler and Prescott Kellogg affirmed his belief in a personal God and Jesus Christ and denied any affiliation with pantheism, this did not necessarily imply that he changed his understanding.[119] As, suggested from his stance,

---

118. Ellen White, *Special Testimonies*, Series B, 7, 1905, 62–63.
119. In a letter written to Prescott on October 25, 1903, Kellogg stated. 'Since leaving Washington, I have been thinking over the letter from Sister White addressed to you in relation to the personality of God, and I think I can see where the difficulty is. Sister White says it is not proper to say God himself is in the tree; at the same time she says that God is Spirit, and his life is in the tree and that his presence is in the tree. You, Elder Daniells and others have spoken about a fine line of distinction, but I could not see what it was, but this statement by Sister White makes it clear to me. The difference is this: When we say God is in the tree, the word "God" is understood in the most comprehensive sense, and people understand the meaning to be that the Godhead is in the tree, God the Father, God the Son, and God the Holy Spirit, whereas the proper understanding in order that wholesome conceptions should be preserved in our minds is that God the Father sits upon his throne in heaven where God the Son is also; while God's life or Spirit or presence is the all-pervading power which is carrying out the will of God in all the universe. The whole thing is now clear to my mind. I confess it was not quite clear before, and I felt a distrust and an uneasiness with reference to the matter, though I could not for the life of me see where there was an error.' October 25, 1903, Letter Kellogg to Prescott. Some tend

he could still refer to God as a personal God but not in the sense of the trinitarian completeness.

---

to suggest that at this point Kellogg experienced a change to a trinitarian position which Ellen White refuted. However, a careful examination of his statement shows that he defined the Holy Spirit as God's extended life or power which equal God's presence. He does not seem to define the Holy Spirit in terms of personality. In his letter to WC White, Daniells quoted Kellogg expressing similar thoughts. 'He told me that he believed in God the Father, God the Son, and God the Holy Ghost; and his view was that it was God the Holy Ghost, and not the Father, that filled all space, and every living thing.' Lt, Daniells to WC White October 29, 1903. It seems to me that Daniells misquoted or misunderstood what Kellogg was saying. It we are to take Kellogg's statement for what it reads, it may be argued that his view of the Holy Spirit does not reflect the understanding upheld by Ellen White. As shown in the analysis of his statement from the Living Temple, it appears that Kellogg merged God's Spirit and power into one entity which equaled God's presence. He concluded, 'There is about us, an infinite, divine, though invisible Presence'. Rather than explaining God's presence through the delegated role and work of the Holy Spirit, he described it in an impersonal and mystical language. In other words the Holy Spirit as God's extended life or power which equal God's presence rather than personality. He does not speak about the Holy Spirit in terms of his personality. However, Daniells was certain that Kellogg's 'seeming change' was a political ploy. As he suggested the Doctor and several of his associates talked 'how it would be possible to get the stamp of orthodoxy upon the book' where it was suggested that 'the first step to take was to get Daniell's and Prescott to fix it'. Daniells to WC White 29 October 1903. Also, Ellen White did not buy into Kellogg's seeming change for she continually pointed out that his views have not changed. In October of 1903, Ellen White referred to Kellogg's views as 'scientific spiritualistic sentiments representing the Creator as an essence pervading all nature', Letter 242, 1903. A year later in August 1904, Ellen White wrote: 'It will be said that the Living Temple has been revised. But the Lord has shown me that the writer has not changed . . . his sentiments do not give a true knowledge of God.' Ellen White, 7 August 1904, SP Series B, 46. Further, in November 1905 she wrote: 'Letters have come to me made by men who claimed to have asked Dr. Kellogg if he believes the testimonies that Sister White bears. He declares that he does, but he does not. He sent a sensible letter to me while I was at Melrose, Mass, saying, "I have surrendered". But he has not spoken or acted as a man who has surrendered.' Ellen White, Ms, 21 1905. In the same letter she referred to the 'spiritualistic representations' of God. It would appear that even after Kellogg's supposed change of view, between 1903 and 1905, Ellen White seemed to maintain a negative reaction to his position on the Godhead. As pointed out, she approached the subject of the Godhead from the trinitarian position. In the same letter she spoke of the 'heavenly trio'. 'The Comforter that Christ promised to send after he ascended to heaven, is the Spirit in all the fullness of the Godhead, making manifest the power of divine grace to all who receive and believe in Christ as a personal Saviour. There are three living persons of the heavenly trio; in the name of these three great powers—the Father, the Son, and the Holy Spirit . . .' Ms 111, December 4, 1905. It must be pointed out that while Ellen White spoke about the 'three living persons' Kellogg saw the Holy Spirit as 'God's life or Spirit or presence as the all-pervading power which is carrying out the will of God in all the universe'.

Conclusion

This chapter has examined Kellogg's understanding of the Godhead and it has explored the influences which fixed Kellogg's mindset on views akin to panentheism. His search for God's immanence reflected the thoughts of classical liberalism and from this stance Kellogg explored the mysteries of God from the hub of universal human experience. In the process, he clothed God's personality with concepts which may be described as abstract, technical and impersonal. Furthermore, his christological reductionism, made no room for Christ as mediator, the eternal son, equal to God, yet a distinct personality. In the process, his views reduced Christ's role to an exempler and a historical figure for reflections and inspiration. Ellen White argued against such views of God and Christ and suggested that Kellogg made them into a nonentity. Further, his lack of reference to the Holy Spirit and overemphasis on the sparks of the divine within man was instrumental in sharpening Ellen White's statements about the relational unity between the Father, Son and the Holy Spirit. It may be suggested that Kellogg's specific view of the Godhead, which Ellen White opposed, helped the church to clarify its understanding of the biblical view of the Trinity.

Appendix
Consensus Statement

Trinity Congress
South Pacific Division
May 1-4, 2008

The Seventh-day Adventist Church has expressed its position on the Godhead in its fundamental beliefs. Paragraph 2 speaks about the Godhead, and paragraphs 3–5 describe each of the three persons of the Trinity.

We, a group of Seventh-day Adventist Christians, theologians, pastors, and administrators, convening in Wahroonga, have been invited by the South Pacific Division to study biblical, theological, and historical aspects of this doctrine.

- On the basis of our study of Scripture we affirm our belief in 'one God: Father, Son, and Holy Spirit, a unity of three co-eternal persons' (Fundamental Belief # 2).
- We understand the eternal pre-existence and full divinity of Jesus and the distinct divine personality of the Holy Spirit to be essential to our belief in the full redemption and atonement in Jesus Christ
- We approach this subject with awe, and we acknowledge that human words cannot fully describe and human minds not fully grasp the mystery of the nature of God. These limitations in understanding and language arise out of God's greatness and majesty and the depth of the divine plan of salvation, particularly of the incarnation of Jesus Christ.
- As we seek to grow in our understanding of God, we recognise the need continually to base our theology on his self-revelation in Jesus Christ, as conveyed to us by the Holy Spirit through the Bible.
- We are grateful that the Holy Spirit has led us in our past history, as the Adventist community has developed a deeper understanding of God through the study of Holy Scripture.

- We pray that God's people will reflect the love and unity of the Godhead as they seek to understand Scripture better and share the good news that God has reconciled the world to himself in Christ.
- May the grace of the Lord Jesus Christ, and the love of God, and the fellowship of the Holy Spirit be with us all (2 Cor 13:14).

Index of Persons and Authors

A
Achtemeier, PJ, 3n.
Ali, AY, 153n.
Allo, E-B, 59n.
Anderson, N, 150n, 156n.
Anderson, PN, 6n, 7n.
Andrews, JN, 165.
Apollinaris, 155, 173.
Aquinas, T, 91, 182.
Arasola, K, 167n.
Arendt, NH, 146n, 149n.
Arius, 3, 26, 33, 39, 44n, 65, 66, 95n, 124, 174.
Athanasius, 33n, 91n, 94n, 174.
Augustine, 91, 118, 119, 184.
Ayres, L, 30n.
Aziz, AY, 154n.

B
Baker, AL, 212n.
Ball, BW, 37n.
Ball, DM, 8n.
Barrett, CK, 20n, 23n.
Bartels, KH, 79n.
Barth, K, 99.
Bates, J, 105, 165, 168, 169, 177, 185n.
Bauckham, R, 41n.
Bauer, W, 140n.
Beatty, M, 37n.
Beeley, CA, 30n.
Berkhof, L, 116.
Beyreuther, E, 79n.
Bickersteth, EH, 132n, 134n, 138n.
Black, M, 21.
Blass, F, 37n
Bletenhard, 79n
Bloiss, S, 167n
Boff, L, 89n,
Bourdeau, D, 165, 171
Bracken, JA, 89n
Bromiley, GW, 204n, 173n
Brown, JP, 21n
Brown, RE, 6, 7n, 8n, 18n, 19n, 23n.
Bruce, FF, 67n, 73n, 76n, 81n, 83n, 86n.
Buchanan, N, 168n.
Bull, M, 172n.
Bulter, GI, 199.
Bulter, JL, 167n, 201n.
Bultmann, R, 7, 19n.
Burdick, DW, 32n.
Burges, SM, 127n.
Burns, P, 89n.

Burt, MD, 168n, 199, 200.
Bushnell, H, 201n, 213n, 215n.

C

Cairns, E, 119n.
Calvin, J, 125, 182.
Canale, FL, 36n.
Canwright, DM, 165.
Carson, DA, 67n.
Carter, W, 12n, 18n.
Cartledge, MJ, 91n.
Cerfaux, L, 60n.
Chadwick, H, 117n.
Charles, CH, 22n.
Clayton, JP, 25n.
Clement of Alexandria, 114–118.
Clouzet, EM, 127n, 133n, 136n, 143n.
Coenen, L, 79n
Conybeare, FC, 3.
Conyers, AJ, 141n.
Cook, JI, 20n.
Coppedge, A, 36n.
Cullmann, O, 21n.
Cunningham, DS, 89n.

D

Damsteegt, PG, 167n.
Daube, D, 8n.
Davey, E, 20n.
Davis, GM, 25n.
de Jong, M, 20n.
Debrunner, A, 37n.
Dederen, R, 36n, 63n, 90n.
Dodd, CH, 8n, 23n.
Donaldson, J, 178n.
Donceel, J, 90n.
Donceel, JD, 105n

Doukhan, J, 52n
Drumwright, HL, 22n
Dulles, A, 98n.
Dunn, JDG, 22n, 59n, 71n, 73n, 74n, 75n, 82n.

E

Edgar, B, 89n, 91n.
Edson, H, 165.
Edwards, BB, 168n.
Edwards, SPS. 208n.
Ehrman, BD, 18n.
Elwell, W, 80n.
Emerson, RW, 170.
English, AC, 115n.
Erickson, MJ, 65, 66n, 80, 90, 92n, 98n, 128n, 208n, 209n, 213n, 214n, 216n, 217n.
Elwell, WA, 218n.

F

Fee, G, 44n, 69n, 71n, 72n, 73, 74n, 75n.
Ferch, AJ, 22n.
Ferguson, E, 117n, 120n.
Feuerbach, 129.
Feuillet, A, 59n.
Fisher, C, 170n.
Fitzmyer, JA, 21n.
Franklin, ST, 217n.
Friedrich, 78n.
Frisbie, JB, 177.
Froom, LE, 165, 168n, 199n, 207, 208.
Funk, RW, 37n.

G

Gane, E, 165, 175n, 179n, 199n.
Gaston, GW, 170.
Geilser, NL, 148n, 157n.
Giles, K, 5n, 30n, 32n, 44n, 90n, 97.
Glassé, C, 145n, 150n.
Gnilka, H, 20n, 22n.
Gonzalez, J, 115n, 121n.
Grant, RM, 39n.
Grappe, C, 51n.
Greenfield, JC, 22n.
Gregg, RC, 94, 95.
Grenz, SJ, 92n, 97n, 101n, 108, 201n, 204, 210n, 213n, 216n, 217n.
Grimal, P, 39n.
Groh, DE, 94, 95n.
Grudem, W, 32n, 80, 130n.
Guder, DL, 105n.
Guelich, RA, 24n.
Guillaume, A, 147n
Gunton, Cm 89n, 100n.
Guthrie, D, 59n, 60n, 67n.
Guy, F, 92n, 172n, 173n, 175n.

H

Hall, CA, 90n.
Hall, CE, 36n, 42n.
Halws, A, 167n.
Harnack, A, 175n, 178n.
Harner, B, 8n.
Harriosn, JFC, 167n.
Hasel, GF, 127n.
Hatton, M, 132n, 133n, 186.
Hawthorne, GF, 103n.
Heine, RC, 122n.
Heinz, D, 148n.
Heinz, H, 148n.
Héring, J, 62n, 64n.
Hezser, Cm 4n.
Hille, R, 130n.
Himes, JV, 168.
Hinson, GE, 201n.
Hippolytos, 176.
Hocken, PD, 127n
Hoffmann, J, 36n.
Holf, R, 165.
Holladay, CR, 65, 73n.
Horn, ID, 213n.
Hudson, WS, 166.
Hull, DW 165, 174n, 177n.

I

Irenaeus, 114

J

Jenson, RW, 102n, 108.
Joest, W, 138n.
Johnsson, WG, 37n.
Judd, WR, 167n.
Jungel, E, 105, 108.
Jungmann, JA, 187n.

K

Kangas, R, 176n.
Kant, I, 89.
Kärkkäinen, VM, 36n, 91n.
Kasarati, J, 169n.
Käsemann, E, 4, 5, 24.
Kasper, W, 57.
Kateregga, BD, 150n.
Keener, CS, 5n, 18n.
Kellogg, JH, 197–221.
Kirschenmann, F, 201n, 213n.

Knight, GR, 167n, 185n, 186n.
Koester, CR, 15n, 16n.
Kohl, M, 90n, 106n.
Köstenberger, AJ, 42n.
Küng, H, 52n.

L

LaCugna, CM, 89n, 98, 99n.
Lamson, A, 116n.
Latourette, KS, 114n, 115n, 118n.
Leenhardt, KF, 57n.
Léon-Dufour, X, 48.
Letham, R, 33n, 36n.
Lincoln, AT, 4n, 25n.
Lindars, B, 22n.
Linden, I, 183n.
Lockahart, K, 172n.
Lohse, B, 121n, 123n, 173n, 177n, 183n.
Loughborough, JN, 165, 173, 174, 178n, 202.
Lund, E, 45n.
Luther , M, 102, 125, 142, 143, 182.

M

MacDonald, MY, 71n.
Mainville, O, 51n.
Maloney, FJ, 21n.
Marguerat, D, 51n.
Marmion, D, 36n.
Martin-Achard, R, 52n, 53n.
Martry, J, 114.
Mastin, BA, 21n.
Maxwell-Hyslop, AR 39n.
McCurry, D, 151n, 156n.
McEnhill, P, 120n.

McGaughey, KJ, 168n.
McGee, GB, 127n.
McGrath, A, 121n, 187n.
McIver, R, 14n.
McPolin, J, 24n.
Mearns, CL, 22n
Meeks, WA, 16n, 17n, 39n.
Melzer, F, 128n.
Metzger, BM, 11n, 18n.
Meyer, R, 49n.
Michaelis, W, 78n, 79.
Miligan, G, 30n.
Millaer, W, 174.
Millard, AR, 4n,
Millard, D, 167n, 168n, 169n.
Miller, W, 167.
Moltmann, J, 90n, 96n, 105n, 106n.
Moody, DJ, 29n.
Moon, J, 36n, 37n, 40n, 80n, 139n, 165, 177n, 178n, 182n, 186n, 194n, 195, 201, 203n, 207n, 208n, 209n, 210, 213n.
Morgan-Wynne, JE, 9n.
Morris, L, 24, 67n.
Moule, CFD, 22n, 24, 25n.
Moulton, JH, 30n.
Mowinckel, S, 12n.
Muller, RA, 140n.
Myers, JM, 22n.

N

Neil, S, 128n.
Nestle-Aland, 81n.
Nestorius, 173.
Newlands, GM, 120n.
Newman, AH, 155n.
Nichol, FD, 7n, 67n, 78n, 79n.

Nieuwenhove, RV, 36n.
Numbers, RL, 167n, 201n, 202.
Nygen, A, 44n

O

O'Brien, P, 44n, 72n, 73n, 75n, 81n, 82n, 83n, 84n.
O'Collins, G, 42n, 82n, 166n.
Olson, RE, 36n, 42n, 90n, 97n, 115n, 119n, 124n, 201n, 204n, 210n, 213n, 216n, 217n.
Olyott, S, 131n, 136n, 137n, 139n, 142n.
Origen of Alexandria, 113, 118–124.
Orr, J, 121n.
Osborne, F, 115n.

P

Pannenberg, W, 105.
Pantaenus, 114.
Patzia, AG, 65n, 67n, 71n, 72n, 75n, 82n, 85n.
Pembroke, N, 99.
Penrer, MB, 92n.
Peppard, M, 30n, 31n, 32n.
Peters, T, 90n, 94.
Pihl, M, 45n.
Pöhler, RJ, 185n, 186n.
Pokorný, P, 73n, 76n, 80n, 82n, 83n.
Pollard, TE, 3, 18n
Prescott, WW, 199
Prigent, P, 59, 60n
Puech, E, 49, 50.

R

Rahlfs, A, 9n
Rahner, K, 89, 90n, 91n, 102n, 105n.
Reid, GW, 36n.
Reeve, JW, 36n, 37n, 139n, 186n, 205.
Reymond, RL, 32n.
Rice, R, 95n.
Roberts, A, 115n, 116n.
Roberts, A, 178n.
Rohleder, A, 136n.
Rusch, WG, 118n, 122n.

S

Saleeb, A, 148n, 157n.
Schaff, P, 184n.
Schantz, B, 152n, 159n, 160n.
Scheck, T, 122n.
Schleiermacher, F, 26n, 101n, 204n.
Schnackenburg, R, 8n, 9n, 23n.
Schnelle, U, 25n.
Schwartz, RW, 197n, 202n, 207n, 212n.
Schweizer, E, 104n.
Schwöbel, C, 90n.
Scragg, WRL, 174.
Senft, C, 61n.
Shelley, B, 201, 203n, 204n.
Shenk, DW, 150n.
Sløk, J, 44n, 45n.
Smith, TL, 166.
Smith, U, 185n.
Spicq, C, 78, 79, 82n.
Stark, R, 176n.
Stephenson, JM, 179.
Stevenson, L, 35n

Stone, ME, 22n.
Swain, SR, 42n.
Sykes, SW, 25n.

T

Talbert, CH, 68n, 74n, 81n, 83n, 85n.
Tarnas, R, 116n, 118n.
Teal, A, 36n.
Tenney, MC, 22n.
Tertulian, 91n, 114, 140, 175n, 176n.
Thompson, MM, 66n, 68n, 73n, 75n, 76n, 81n, 83n.
Tillich, P, 101n.
Tisdall, WS, 156n.
Toom, T, 122n.
Torrance, TF, 90n.
Toom, T, 122n.
Tovey, D, 7n, 13n.
Trench, RC, 136n.
Trillhaas, W, 141n.
Trocmé, E, 49n.
Turretin, 170.

V

Valentine, G, 210n, 211n.
Van Unnik, WC, 12n.
Vanhoozer, KJ, 92n.
Vaughen, C, 22n.
Vermes, G, 21.
Vosloo, R, 99.

W

Waggoner, FJ, 165.
Waggoner, JH, 165.
Walker, W, 114n, 115n.

Walker, WO, 22n.
Walsh, M, 174n.
Whidden, WW, 36n, 37n, 80n, 82n, 85n, 139n, 186n, 205.
White, A, 208n.
White, EG, 110, 129n, 142n, 143, 161n, 165, 171n, 173n, 197n, 198, 201n, 202, 204, 205, 206, 207, 210, 211, 213n, 214, 216n, 218, 219, 220n.
White, J, 165, 169, 172n, 173n, 175n, 185n, 200.
White, WC, 199.
Whitney, SB, 165
Wright, NT, 71n, 81, 82n, 83n, 84, 85n, 128n

Y

Young, FM, 36n
Young, N, 37n

Z

Zizioulas, JD, 90n

Index of Subjects

A

Abode of the dead, 53f.
Absolute monotheism, 146, 148, 150.
Adam, 54, 60, 73, 76.
Adventism, 165f, 185, 188, 199, 210n, 211n.
    epistemology, 184–186.
Alexandrian school of theology, 113–126.
Allah, 145–160.
    and eternity, 147.
    as creator, 146.
    essence of, 145.
    oneness of, 146, 147, 152.
Ancilla theologiae, 125.
Angels, 23, 79, 86, 150, 178, 206n.
Anti-docetic, 25.
Anti-trinitarians, 29, 31n, 33, 37, 38n, 39, 43, 95, 126, 165, 166, 169, 170, 171, 174n, 175n, 177, 179n, 185, 199, 200, 215.
Anti-trinitarianism, 29, 31n, 33n, 37n, 39, 43, 126, 165, 166, 168n, 170, 174n, 177, 179n, 185, 199, 200.
Apologetics, 179n.
Apostolic Christianity, 114, 175, 187, 182.

Apostasy, 172, 174, 185.
Arianism, 65, 66, 94, 95, 170, 182.
Arminian, 125.
Atheism, 105n, 147.
Atonement, the vii, 44, 58, 96, 145, 150, 155, 178n, 179, 206, 219.
Awakening, 51–57.
    Great Awakening, 166.

B

Bible, the, vii, 30, 34, 36, 37, 40, 43, 44, 47n, 51, 53, 57, 91, 118, 120, 128, , 129n, 130, 131, 134, 137, 139, 140, 156, 173, 174n, 176n, 183, 199, 200, 201, 202, 203, 204n, 207, 209, 213n, 215.
Biblical Canon, 187, 188.
Biblical data, 6, 48, 94, 131, 186f, 190.
Biblical first principles, 187–199.
Biblical models of the church, 98, 189.
Biblical monotheism, 30, 40, 42, 43, 187.
Biblical revelation, 39, 62, 68n, 90, 92, 102n, 128n, 130, 162, 176n, 182, 184, 185, 187, 188,

227

189, 190, 191, 198, 199, 219.
Biblical world-view, 183, 186–190, 199.

C

Canons of human reason, 188.
Catholicism, 125, 167.
Chalcedon, 26, 36n, 56, 115n, 155, 156, 187.
Christian community, 5, 6, 56, 90, 91, 93, 98, 99, 102, 101–111, 190, 219.
Christology, 3–27, 41n, 59n, 60n, 66n, 67, 69n, 71n, 73, 74n, 82, 83n, 85n, 94–97, 125, 155, 182, 183, 186, 187.
Christotokos, 173.
Christ's saving act – 1 Corinthians 15:27–28, 47–64.
Church Fathers, the, 30n, 32, 35, 118, 119, 125, 126, 155, 173, 178, 179, 188, 193.
Colossian heresy, the, 66–68, 86.
Conditionalism, 176.
Connexionists, 167, 168, 169.
Constantinople, 33, 119n, 155, 176n, 180.
Conversion, 177, 182.
Cosmos, the, 67, 73, 187.
Creator, the, 40, 44, 53, 65, 67, 71, 72, 73, 74, 82, 83, 85, 94, 120, 134, 146, 147, 158, 159, 160, 161, 206n, 220n.
Creeds, 26, 125, 166, 168, 169, 170, 172–175, 179, 182, 190, 191.
Cross, the, 9, 14, 17, 23, 24, 44, 48, 58, 61, 63, 72, 73, 74, 86, 96, 117, 124, 125, 126, 148n, 162.

D

Darkness, 15.
Defining the divinity of Jesus, 40–41.
Deity, 39, 72n, 82, 85, 105, 114, 116, 120, 122, 145, 151, 152, 154, 157, 162, 185, 186, 187, 192, 194, 210, 211, 215.
Death, 4, 15, 23, 24, 27, 40, 44, 47, 49–57, 59, 61, 62, 72, 73, 84, 96, 103, 106, 114, 124, 126, 134, 145, 149, 152, 162, 197n, 198, 211.
Devil, the, 14, 15, 19, 44, 55 124.
Divine appointment, 188.
Divinisation, 117, 124, 125.
Docetic, 24, 25.
Docetism, 4, 24, 25, 176.
Doctrine, vii, xi, 3, 5n, 32n, 34, 35, 36, 39, 40, 41n, 42, 43, 44, 51, 54, 60n, 65, 67, 80n, 89, 90, 91, 93, 94, 95n, 97, 99, 100, 101, 113, 116n, 119n, 123n, 128, 130, 142, 145, 146, 153, 154, 166, 168n, 169n, 170, 171, 172, 173, 174n, 175, 176, 177n, 178n, 179, 182, 183, 184, 185, 186, 188, 190, 197n, 199, 200, 204, 207, 217n.

E

Eastern Orthodox, 89, 90.
Ecclesiastical magisterium, 185, 186.
Ecclesiology, 98, 109f.
Ephesus, Council of, 155.
Enlightenment, the, 191.
Epistemology, 92n, 184, 185, 187, 191.

Eschatology, 50, 56, 57, 90n, 150, 172n.
Eternal life, 14, 16, 17, 38, 48, 55, 95.
'Eternally Blessed God' (Romans 9:5), 35–45.
Eucharistical context, 56.
Evangelism, 142n, 161n.
Evil, 53, 56, 60, 214.
Exegesis, 44n, 66, 116, 183.
Exegete, 178.

F
First born, the Christological hymn in Colossians 1:15, 65–86.
Freedom, 98, 173.

G
Godhead, the, vii, 33, 42, 43, 85, 93, 105, 121, 129, 136, 140, 141, 145, 153, 154, 162, 171, 175n, 179, 180, 182, 183, 186n, 192, 197f.
Gospel, the, 7, 22, 54, 67, 94, 128.
    Fourth, the, 4, 5, 6, 8, 9n, 10, 11, 12, 13, 14, 15, 16n, 18, 19, 21, 23, 24, 25, 26, 31, 33, 35, 41n, 42n, 44, 78, 95, 106, 136, 137, 154.
    Mathew's, 95, 49.
God, 15, 17, 19, 21, 26, 29, 34, 39, 41, 42, 47, 54, 56, 62, 63, 64, 68, 76, 78, 80, 84, 84, 93, 95, 98, 101, 102, 107, 108, 114, 115, 116, 117, 119, 121, 122, 123, 126, 127, 130, 131, 134, 135, 138, 142, 176, 178.

Angels of God, 23, 86, 150, 178, 202
Biblical God, 44.
Born by God, 31, 32, 77.
Children of God, 32, 95, 107, 204.
Describing God, 42, 184, 205.
Eternally Blessed God, 35–45.
Finger of God, 133.
God and the cosmos, 67, 73, 183.
God and worship of, 128f.
God as intelligent power, 204, 206.
God as suprapersonal power, 210.
God in person, 136, 187, 200, 211.
God is one, 10, 119, 122, 142, 152, 176, 189.
God of the Bible, 56, 120.
God revealed in Scripture, 40, 129, 130.
God, agent of the resurrection, 56, 58.
God, the Creator, 53, 8.
God, one God, 10.
    God, reconciler, 59, 85, 96.
God, supreme ruler, 179.
God, three persons, vii, 42, 43, 90n, 136, 140–143, 145, 180, 181, 182, 188, 218, 219, 220.
God's character, 76, 106, 109, 110, 111, 130, 136, 217.
God's commandments, 175.

God's eternal decrees, 124.
God's gift, 123.
God's glory, 25, 74, 124.
God's immanence, 201, 203, 204, 205, 207, 209, 210, 212, 214, 215, 217n, 221.
God's interventions, 29n.
God's love, 73, 105, 106, 110, 161.
God's nature, 9, 12, 14, 24, 25, 26, 38, 43, 76, 93, 109, 110, 119, 124, 178, 188.
God's people, viii.
God's power, 20, 33, 38, 48, 51, 55–58, 73n, 82n, 83, 103, 116n, 120, 123, 131, 135, 136–139, 143, 144, 185, 192, 203, 204n, 206n, 207–214, 216, 217, 219, 220.
God's transcendence, 97, 115, 145, 213n, 215.
God, the Father, vii, 5, 9, 13n, 17, 18f, 23, 26, 29, 33, 37, 38n, 39, 41, 42, 43, 44n, 47, 48, 57, 61–64, 68, 69, 71–76, 80, 81, 83n, 84, 85, 91, 94, 95, 97, 98, 99, 102n, 104, 106, 107, 108, 115–126, 128–131, 134, 135, 136, 139–142, 144, 145, 151, 154, 155, 157–162, 177–181, 183n, 185–188, 191, 192, 205, 206, 210, 214, 218, 219, 220n, 221.
God's reign, 61.

God's will, 64.
Humanity of God, 109
Image of God, 76, 82.
Inner being of God, 91, 92, 109, 110, 111, 130, 186, 191, 193.
Jesus and God, 18, 20, 62, 65, 104, 136, 154, 161, 182.
Kingdom of God, 16, 57, 75.
Knowledge of God, 67, 75.
Mighty God, 41.
mysteries of God, 26, 27, 129n, 143, 188, 191, 194, 195, 203, 210.
Oneness of God, 26, 41, 43, 92, 94, 169, 183, 186, 188, 190.
Paradox of God, 27.
Revelation of God, 86, 90, 105, 142, 162.
Son of God, 12, 21, 26, 34, 37, 38, 65, 73, 103, 104, 137, 140, 192.
Speaking about God, 30, 31n, 143.
Spirit of God, 130, 132, 133, 139, 159, 177.
Truth of God, 38, 189.
Unity of God, 120.
Will of God, 144.
Wisdom of God, 81.
Gnosis, 117, 123.
Gnostic, 154, 176.
Gnosticism, 66, 117.
Greek mind, the, 9, 51, 113, 115, 137, 172, 191.
Greek Fathers, 32.

H

Hades, 40, 53.
Hadith, the, 147, 148, 149, 159.
Heaven, 4, 10, 11, 15, 16, 17, 18n, 20n, 23, 24, 25, 68, 83, 85, 82, 147n, 149, 153, 154, 158, 161, 166, 179, 180, 182, 183.
Heavenly, 22, 33, 142n, 192, 206n, 218, 219.
Hebrew mind, the, 115, 172, 191.
Hegelian view of the world, 216.
Hellenistic, 39n, 49, 50, 66, 194.
Heresy, 5n, 25, 66, 67, 68, 85, 86, 121, 176, 177, 178.
Heretical, 155, 156, 172.
History, vii, 6, 7, 25n, 35n, 36n, 42n, 45n, 48, 53, 56, 57, 58, 65, 71, 101, 104–106, 109, 114n, 115n, 116n, 118n, 119n, 121n, 123n, 130, 147, 155n, 156, 167n, 168n, 169n, 170n, 171, 172, 173n, 174, 175, 177n, 178n, 182, 184n, 200n, 201n, 202, 203n, 204n, 207.
Holy Spirit, the, vii, viii, 12, 31n, 34, 41, 42n, 43, 48, 58n, 63, 90, 91, 96, 98, 99, 102, 103, 104, 108, 109, 111, 114, 118, 119, 122, 123, 125–144, 145, 150, 151, 159, 161, 162, 178, 180, 181, 183n, 185, 188, 208, 211, 213, 214, 217, 218, 219n, 220n, 221.
    divinity and personality, 127–144.
homoiousios, 173
homoousios, 121, 173.

humanity, 76, 85, 115, 117, 118, 123, 124, 129, 187, 193, 215.
    of Jesus, 23, 24, 25, 123, 192, 209
hypostatic union, 122.

I

'Image of the invisible God', in Colossians 1:15, 75–76.
Immortality, 49, 169, 172.
Incarnation, the, vii, 38n, 60, 63, 73, 93, 105, 117, 123, 130, 145, 160, 181, 186, 187, 188, 191, 192, 195, 215, 216.
Islam, 145–160.
    and Christianity, 152–157, 160–162.
    and the Koran, 157.
    and the Spirit, 150.
    and the ninety-none names for Allah, 158–159.
    prayer and ritual, 152.
Islamic theology, 150, 157.

J

Jesus Christ, vii, viii, 3, 4, 5, 6, 8, 9, 11, 12f, 17–23, 25, 26, 32, 35, 36, 37, 38, 39, 41, 42, 44, 48, 55, 57–64, 65–69, 70, 73, 74, 76, 77, 79–85, 91, 92–98, 102, 103, 105, 106, 108, 116, 119, 123, 124, 130, 135, 137, 139, 144, 145, 148, 149, 150, 151, 152, 154, 156, 157, 159, 161, 162, 173, 178, 179, 191, 192, 205n, 206n, 208, 209, 211, 214, 218, 219.

Jesus-God in person, 36–38.
Johannine Christology, 18–27.
Johannine symbolic universe, 14–18.

K

Katalasso, 85.
Koran, the, 146, 147, 148, 149, 150, 151, 152, 153, 154, 156, 157, 158, 160.
Kosmos, 39.

L

Language, vii, 11, 14, 26, 29, 30, 41, 42, 66n, 115, 116, 118, 119, 120, 122, 128, 142n, 145, 157, 179, 191, 192, 193, 201n, 213, 220n.
Latter Day Saints, 167.
Liberalism, 97, 99, 201, 202, 208, 209n, 213, 222.
Life,
    ascetic, 67, 119, 149.
    earthly, 14, 23, 24, 57, 102, 103.
    eternal, 15, 17, 38, 55, 95.
Light, 11, 14, 15, 30, 82, 84, 118, 130, 148n, 171, 179, 193n, 198, 206, 216n.
Logos asarkos vs *logos ensarkos*, 173.
Logos, 18, 21, 115–118, 120, 121, 123, 154, 173, 178, 187.

M

Mary, 17, 79, 81, 82, 95, 107, 149, 151, 153, 154, 155, 156, 180.

Mediator, 44, 63, 115, 120, 150, 187n, 209, 221.
Messianic, 8n, 13, 14, 78, 80, 82, 191, 192.
    Kingship, 14, 191, 192.
Millerism, 166, 167, 168.
Ministry, 8n, 59n, 73, 99, 102, 103n, 104, 108, 110, 128, 133, 138, 143n, 144, 151, 162, 198.
Modalism, 5n, 41n, 42n, 176, 216.
    modalistic monarchianism, 177–178.
Monogenes, the, 29–34.
Monophysites, 156.
Monotheism, 30, 38, 40, 41, 42n, 43, 146, 148, 150, 169n, 190.
Mystery,
    of God/Allah, vii, 26, 48, 63, 98, 105n, 129, 145, 146, 156, 162, 186, 184, 188, 215.

N

Nature, vii, 9, 12, 14, 24, 25, 26, 38, 43, 58, 64, 66, 72, 76, 85, 93, 97, 98, 101, 106, 109, 110, 116, 118, 119, 121, 122, 123, 124, 127, 129, 130, 131, 141, 142n, 143, 145, 153, 155, 160, 161, 178, 185, 188, 191, 193, 194, 199, 200, 201, 202, 203, 205, 207, 208, 209, 201, 212, 214, 215, 216n, 217, 219, 220n.
Nicaea, 30n, 36n, 114, 118, 121, 124, 125, 126, 155, 176, 186, 189, 191.
Nicene, 26, 121, 126, 180, 191.
Neo-platonism, 115n, 119, 120, 122.

Nestorians, 156.
New,
    Adam, 61, 192.
    body, 54.
    creation, 61, 72n, 73, 76, 82.
        life, 58, 61, 103, 134, 135, 144, 162, 219.
New Testament, the, 3, 5n, 8n, 12n, 18n, 20n, 21n, 22, 24n, 25n, 30, 32, 33, 36, 37, 38, 39n, 40, 41, 43, 53, 54, 55, 56, 58, 60n, 65, 66n, 67n, 68n, 71n, 73n, 74, 77, 78n, 79, 80, 81, 113, 117, 120, 124, 125, 128n, 137, 149, 151, 173, 183, 190, 191, 192, 195, 203n.

O

Old Testament, the, 9, 22, 33, 40, 41, 53, 55, 73, 76, 77, 79, 80, 81, 82, 83, 113, 114, 134, 190, 191, 192, 203n.
Ominpresence, 216.
Omniscience, 216.
Omnipotence, 216.
Origin of the church, 101–104.
Orthodox, 3, 5, 18n, 30n, 89, 90, 94, 95, 96, 119, 123, 125, 155, 156, 157, 165, 170, 201n, 203, 204, 208, 2012, 213, 220n.
Ousia, 173.

P

Paidagogos, 114, 115, 118n.
Pantheism, 197, 208, 214, 215, 217, 219.
Parousia, 54, 63.

Patristic Council, 185.
Patristic era, 125, 185.
Pauline theology, 31, 37, 55, 47–64, 65–86, 96, 103, 131, 134, 135.
    Paul's eschatology, 57–59.
Pentecostal, 90, 127, 167.
Philosophy, 56, 66, 118, 125.
    Greek, 39, 40, 43, 49, 113, 115, 117, 123, 126.
    pagan, 40.
Platonism, Middle, 115, 120.
Polyttheism, 38, 147, 157, 178, 190.
Postmodern challenges, 89–100.
Prayer, 68, 69, 74, 97, 107, 152, 162, 184, 187, 206n.
Preaching, 49, 57, 58, 139.
Profession of faith, 57, 152.
Prophesy, 78, 97, 171, 172, 206n.
Prophetic, 41, 148, 167n, 171, 174, 178, 179, 202n.
Prophet-hood, 148.
Prophets, 13, 30, 44n, 52, 53, 58n, 95, 131, 142n, 146–149, 152, 160, 180, 194.
Proto-Gnosticism, 66.
Prōtotokos, 71, 72, 77–82, 84.
Protestant, 127, 140n, 155, 167, 169, 170, 201, 202n.

R

Reconciliation, 59, 71, 72, 85, 96, 105.
Redeemer, 40, 67, 71, 73, 82, 94, 95, 144, 149.
Reformation, the, 125, 155, 167, 174, 190.
Reincarnation, 49, 54, 55,

Restorationism,
  and creeds, 172–175.
  in early Seventeenth Adventism, 165–184.
  in Trinitarian churches, 169–170.
  theological, 166–169.
Resurrection, the, 4, 11, 17, 24, 47–61, 63, 73, 82, 96, 97, 103, 123, 135, 180, 199, 200, 203.
Revelation, vii, 9n, 39, 58, 63, 68n, 90, 91, 92n, 102, 105, 128, 129, 130, 143, 145, 151, 157, 162, 176n, 186, 188–192, 194, 195, 202, 203, 207, 216.
  science and revelation, 202.
  special revelation, 203.

S

Sabbatarian Adventism, 168, 169, 170, 179.
Sabellianism, 42n, 201, 215.
Salvation, vii, 20, 26, 35, 36n, 38n, 55, 56, 62, 63, 64, 68, 74, 80n, 81, 90, 94, 95n, 96, 99, 104, 105, 106, 109, 110, 115, 117, 123, 124, 125, 126, 130, 133n, 139n, 142, 144, 145, 158, 159, 160, 161, 162, 180, 181.
  and the life of God, 104–106.
Saviour, 35, 37n, 85, 86, 117, 137, 144, 150, 159, 160, 192, 206n, 219, 220n.
Scripture, vii, viii, 5, 18n, 19, 33n, 36n, 38, 39, 40, 58, 78n, 92, 93, 95n, 96, 99, 122, 129, 131, 135, 150, 153, 157, 167, 180, 188, 189, 190, 192, 195, 205n, 210, 217.

Seventh Day Adventist Theology, Consensus Statement, vii–vii.
Sin, 9, 19, 22n, 38, 43, 48, 49, 55, 56, 59, 61, 69, 95, 96, 104, 117, 123, 124, 126, 129, 138, 145, 148, 150, 154, 159, 160, 161, 162, 180, 207, 209, 211, 219.
Sinless, 117, 126, 149, 162.
Soteriology, 90n, 93n, 94, 95, 96, 97, 117, 123, 124, 125, 126.
Soul, the, 49, 50, 51, 55, 116, 117, 118, 120, 123, 150, 172, 182, 199, 200, 203.
Spiritual beings, 123.
Spiritual death, 162.
Spiritual gifts, 123, 162.
Spiritual powers, 86.
Spirituality, 44n, 204n
Subordinationism, 5, 90n, 98, 116, 121, 122, 123, 125.
Sustainer, 67, 72, 73, 83, 84, 120, 146, 147.

T

Tawhid in Islam, 145–162.
Tertullian, 91, 140, 175n, 176.
Theology, vii, 6n, 35, 36, 44n, 89, 90–94, 95n, 97, 101n, 109, 113–116, 118, 119, 121, 122, 124, 125, 150, 156, 167, 170, 172n, 182, 191, 192, 194, 195, 197, 199, 201, 202n, 204.
  biblical theology, vii, 30, 35, 36, 66, 90, 92, 94, 115, 125, 128, 130, 156, 172, 187, 191, 192, 194, 195, 216.
Theosis, 124, 125, 126.
Theotokos, 173.

The title 'Christ' in the Fourth Gospel, 12–14.
The title 'I am' in the Fourth Gospel, 8–11.
Three approaches to Johannine Christological paradoxes, 6–8.
Trinity, the, xi, 5, 33, 34, 35, 36, 41n, 42, 43, 63, 79n, 85n, 89, 90, 91, 92, 93, 94, 96, 97, 98, 99, 100, 105, 106, 108, 109, 113, 114, 115, 118, 119, 122, 128, 129, 130, 132n, 133n, 134n, 138n, 139n, 140, 141, 142, 144, 145, 146, 147, 150, 154, 155, 156, 157, 158, 159, 160, 161, 162, 165n, 166, 168n, 169, 171, 172, 174, 175, 176, 177, 178, 179, 181, 183, 184, 185, 186, 189, 193, 199, 201n, 205n, 207n, 211n, 213n, 217, 221.
    and the Tawhid in Islam, 146–162.
    and the nature of the church, 106–109.
        issue in the Seventh Day Adventist Church, 185–195.
Trinitarian, 30n, 40, 41n, 42, 43, 44, 48, 63, 64, 65, 89n, 91, 93, 94, 96, 98, 99, 100, 101, 109, 110, 114, 118, 119, 121, 122n, 123, 124, 125, 126, 144, 165, 166, 169, 170, 171, 172, 173, 174, 175, 177, 183, 186, 187, 190, 199, 212, 215, 219, 220.

Adventist views on Trinitarian history, 175–176.
ecclesiology, 109–111.
Tritheism, 5, 159, 176, 178.
Truth, 3, 11, 15, 20, 24, 36, 67, 90, 91, 92, 95, 104, 115, 123, 128, 134, 135, 139, 149, 151, 153, 157, 165, 170, 171, 172, 174, 175, 177n, 181, 189, 190, 191, 192, 193, 194, 202, 203, 204, 207.

U

Unitarianism, 167, 169n, 170n.

V

Vulgate, the, 32.

W

Watchtower Society, 167.
World-view, 155, 187, 191, 193, 194, 213, 214.
Worship, 33n, 35–45, 66, 79, 97, 98, 110, 127, 128, 135, 144, 146, 147, 152, 153, 159, 178, 180, 181, 184, 191, 195.

Index of Christian Scriptural References

Genesis		48:18–20	78
1 – 2	39n	48:18	77n
1:2	134	46:8	77n
1:26–27	76	49:3	77n
1:27	76		
2:7	135, 137	Exodus	
2:24	42	3:13–14	10
4:4	77n	4:22	77
6:3	132	6:14	77n
8:11	137	11:5	77n
10:15	77n	12:29	77n
16:11	31	13:13	77n
21:25	41	13:15	77n
22:21	77n	17:7	131
25:1–5	31	22:29	77n
25:1–2	31	34:19	77n
25:13	77n	34:20	77n
25:25	77n		
25:31–34	77n	Numbers	
27:19	77n	1:20	77n
27:32	77n	2	77n
27:36	77n	3:12	77n
35:23	77n	3:13	77n
36:15	77n	3:41	77n
38:6	77n	3:45	77n
38:7	77n	8:16	77n
41:51	77n	8:18	77n
43:33	77n	12	77n
43:37	77n	13	77n

14:11	132	2:42	77n
18:15	77n	2:50	77n
26:5	77n	3:1	77n
40	77n	3:15	77n
41	77n	4:4	77n
45	77n	5:1	77, 77n
46	77n	5:3	77n
50	77n	5:12	77, 77n
		6:13	77n
Deuteronomy		8:1	77n
6:4	41	8:30	77n
12:6	77n	8:38	77n
12:17	77n	8:39	77n
15:9	77n	26:10	78
21:15	77n		
21:16–17	77	2 Chronicles	
21:16	76, 77n	21:3	77
21:17	77n		
32:12	132	2 Esdras	
33:17	77n, 78	13:1–3	22
33:27	134	Daniel	
		3	75n
Nehemiah		5	30
9:20	134	5:2	30
10:37	77n	7	22, 24
		7:9–10	24
Joshua		7:13–14	24
6:26	77n	7:13	23
17:1	77n	8:19	53
		12:2	53
Leviticus		12:4	53
23:10	59	12:9	53
27:26	77n		
		2 Maccabees	
1 Chronicles		6:18–31	50
1:29	77n		
2:2	77n	4 Ezra	
2:13	77n	7:32	50
2:25	77n	7:75–101	50n
2:27	77n		

Index of Christian Scriptural References

2 Baruch		16:10–11	78
50:2–4	50n	20:1	42

Hosea		2 Samuel	
6:1–3	52	3:2	77n
		13:21	77n
Ezekiel		7:8–16	13n
37:1-4	52	7:14	73
37:5	137	7:18	73
37:9	137	19:44	77
37:11	52	23:2	132

Job		Jeremiah	
19:25–27	52n	31:33	131
33:4	134	38:9	77, 78

1 Kings		Psalm	
16:34	77n	2:7	30
17:17–24	52	3:11	50
		3:12	50
2 Kings		8:6	62
3:27	77n	16:10	52
4:32–37	52	16:11	52
13:21	52	17:15	52
		23:1	40
Wisdom		51:11	134
7:22	31	77:51	77n
8:19	49	88:28	77n
8:20	49	88	78
9:15	50	89	78, 78n
		89:3	78
Judges		89:18	81
8:20	77n	89:20	78, 81
13:3–5	103	89:26	81
16:17	103	89:27	81
20:1	42	89:35	78
		89:49	78
1 Samuel		95:6–9	135
8:2	77n	95:8	131
14:49	77n	104:30	134

104:36	77n	Matthew	
110:1	60, 62	1	30
136:10	77n	1:1	13n
139:7	134	1:21	95
143:10	134	1:23	95n
		3:11	137
Isaiah		3:16	137
6:3	136	4:1	103
6:8	131, 136	5–7	96
6:9	131	6:10	75
7:14	95n	6:33	75
8:8–10	95n	9:27	13n
9:6	41	10:8	54n
11:1–16	13n	11:5	54n
26:19	52	12:28	132
40:12–14	134	12:31	138, 144
40:13	134	12:32	138
40:14	134	15:22	13n
40:19–20	75	16:21	54n
40:25	194	16:28	75
41:4	9	17:9	54n
43:10	9, 41	17:23	54n
43:13	41	19:26	133n
44:2	103	20:19	54n
44:6	40	21:9	13n
48:12	41	22:23	54n
51:12	10	22:28	54n
63:10–14	132	22:30	54n
63:10	132, 134, 135	22:31	54n
63:11	132	24:31	55
63:14	132	26:29	75
64:8	134	26:32	54n
		27:51	16
Michah		27:52	54n
6:7	77n	27:53	54n
		27:63	54n
Zechariah		27:64	54n
12:10	77n, 78	28:6	54n
		28:7	54n
		28:19	136, 139

Index of Christian Scriptural References

Mark		8:42	31n
1:14–15	96	8:55	54n
2:5–7	38	9:22	54n
2:27–28	93	9:38	31n
4:41	38	10:21	103
5:42	54n	11:20	132
8:31	54n	12:11	84
9:9	54n	12:12	137
9:10	54n	14:14	54n
10:34	54n	18:33	54n
10:47	13n	18:38–39	13n
11:10	13n	20:27	54n
12:18	54n	20:33	54n
12:23	54n	20:35–37	54n
12:26	54n	20:35	54n
14:28	54n	20:36	54n
15:38	16	20:37	54n
16:6	54n	21:14	54n
16:9	54n	24:6	54n
16:14	54n	24:7	54n
16:38	16	24:46	54n
		24:34	54n
Luke		24:49	133
1:2	8, 84		
1:15	102, 103	John	
1:27	13n	1 – 12	8
1:35	103	1:1–3	74, 83
1:41	102	1:1	15, 18, 21, 25,
1:67	102		37, 95, 157
2:7	79, 79n, 81, 82	1:3	41
2:11	13n	1:4	15
2:25–26	103	1:5	15, 15n
2:26	134	1:6	37n
3:38	192	1:9	15
4	103	1:12	37n, 95
4:1–2	103	1:13–14	31
4:14	139	1:13	31, 32
7:22	54n	1:14	15, 18, 19, 32,
7:12	31n		32n, 157

1:17	11, 13, 134	3:35	20n
1:18	18, 25, 30, 37, 37n, 43n, 76n, 95	4:6	24, 26
		4:25	11
1:19–28	12	4:26	8, 9
1:20	11, 12	4:29	11
1:21	13n	4:26	8, 9
1:25	12	4:34	96
1:29	95	4:42	11n
1:43	41	4:44	13
1:41	11, 12	4:54	8
1:51	23	5:11–18	18
2 – 12	14	5:18	5n, 21, 25
2:11	8	5:19	5
3	16n	5:21–30	26
3:1–21	15	5:21–29	20
3:1	15	5:21	54n, 135
3:2	15, 16n	5:24	8
3:3	16	5:25–29	18
3:4	16	5:26	20, 26, 135
3:5–9	133n	5:27	23, 24
3:5	75	5:29	54n
3:6–7	16	5:30–47	19
3:6	134	5:30	20
3:8	137	5:51	10
3:9	133n	6	24
3:10	16n	6:1–15	11
3:11	16	6:14–16	14
3:12	16	6:14	8, 13, 13n
3:13–14	23	6:20	8, 9
3:13	16	6:22–58	11
3:14–15	23	6:27	23, 24
3:14	17	6:29	20n
3:16	20n, 29n, 30, 95, 153	6:31	17
		6:33	11
3:18	8	6:35	10, 17
3:19–21	15n, 16n	6:37–40	20n
3:24	8	6:37	20, 26
3:28	8, 11, 12	6:41	10, 17
3:31	26	6:42	12n, 17, 24, 26

6:44	20, 20n, 26	8:31–58	19
6:46	17, 20n	8:33	26
6:47	17	8:42	19
6:48	10, 17	8:54	19
6:51	24	8:58–59	41
6:53	23, 24	8:58	8, 9, 10, 25, 41
6:57	20, 20n, 26	8:59	41n
6:62	23, 24	9:1–7	11
6:69	11n	9:4	20n
7	12	9:9	8, 9
7:2	24, 26	9:22	11
7:3	119	9:29	17n
7:15–18	19	9:33	17n
7:16	20, 26	9:35	23
7:25–31	17	10	40
7:26	11	10:7	10
7:27–28	12n	10:9	10
7:27	12	10:11	11, 40
7:28–29	20n	10:14	11
7:28	12	10:24	11
7:29	17	10:25	20n
7:31	12, 13	10:29–30	25
7:38	137	10:30	5
7:39	137	10:31–39	19
7:40–44	17	10:31–33	41
7:40	13	10:31	11
7:41–42	13	10:33	21, 25
7:41	11	10:35	19
7:42	11	10:36	17n
7:50–51	15	10:38	25
8	9	11:5	24, 26
8:12	11n	11:1–44	11
8:16–23	25	11:11	54n
8:16–18	20n	11:23	54n
8:21–29	17	11:24	54n
8:26–27	20n	11:25	11, 135
8:24	8, 9	11:27	11
8:25	9	11:29	17n
8:28	8, 9, 23	11:33	24, 26

11:35	24, 26	14:24	20, 26
11:40	20n	14:26	104, 137
12:1	54n	14:28	17n, 20n, 96
12:9	54n	14:31	20n
12:17	54n	15:1	11
12:17–18	8	15:5	11, 17n
12:23	23	15:12–13	107
12:26	20n	15:21	20n
12:31–32	14	15:23	20n
12:34	11, 23	15:24	137
12:41	25	15:26	20n, 104, 137, 139
12:44–45	20n		
12:49–50	20n	16:8–11	33n
13 – 21	8	16:8	137, 139
13:1–3	19	16:13	134, 137, 139
13:1	17n	16:14	128, 137, 139
13:3	17n	16:15	20n
13:19	8, 9	16:16–17	17n
13:31	23	16:27–30	17n
13:33	17	16:27–28	20
13:34	106	16:27	107
13:35	106	16:33	47n
13:36–37	17	17:1	20, 26
14 – 16	137	17:2	20n
14	136, 136n	17:3	11, 12, 38, 38n
14:2–3	17n	17:5	63n
14:2	20n	17:8	17n
14:6–7	95	17:11	17n
14:6	11, 20	17:20–23	107
14:7–8	20n	17:22–23	98
14:8–9	105	18:5–8	8
14:9	20, 76n, 136	18:5–6	8
14:10	5, 25, 136	18:5	9
14:11	20n	18:6	9
14:12	17n	18:8	8, 9
14:16	136	18:11	20n
14:17	134, 136, 137	18:36	14, 75
14:20–24	20n	19:7	21
14:21	107	19:33–34	24, 26
14:23	107	19:39–40	16

19:11	16	Romans	
19:37	78	1–11	93n
20:17	17, 17n	1:2–4	57n
20:19	54n	1:4	57n, 103, 134
20:22	103		
20:27	24	1:20	75n
20:28	21, 25, 37n	4:17	55n
20:31	11, 12, 21	4:24	55n
21:14	54n	4:25	57n, 58n
27:52	54n	5	60n
		5:10	85
Acts		5:12	57n
1:5	102	6:4	48, 57n, 58n
1:8	102	6:5	55n
1:32	102	6:9	57n
2:3	137	6:23	55
2:4	102, 138	7	61n
5:3	132, 135, 138	7:4	57n
5:4	132, 135	8:9–10	104
5:9	138	8:10	135
5:32	137	8:11	55n, 103, 135
7:51	135, 138	8:15–17	107
7:55	102	8:16	138
8:29	137	8:27	138
8:39	138	8:29	74, 75n, 79, 79n
10:11	84		
10:19	137	8:34	57n
10:20	137	9:4–5	35
10:38	139	9:5	35–45
13:2	138	10:4	48
13:4	138	10:9	56, 57n, 173
13:35	106	11:26	74
15:28	139	11:34	134
16:6–7	138	11:36	83n
17:22–31	113	12:4–5	72n
17:25	137	12:5	72n
28:25–27	131	12–16	93n
28:25	137	13:11	55n
31:52	102	15:12	55n

15:13	139	1:10	67, 68
15:16	138	1:11	68
15:19	134	1:12–15	73
15:30	138	1:12–14	68
		1:12–13	69, 81
Hebrews		1:12	68
1:2–3	74	1:13	69, 73, 74, 85
1:4	37n	1:13b	73
1:6	79, 79n	1:14	68, 69, 74
1:17–18	96	1:14a	73
3:7–11	131	1:15–20	65, 67, 68, 69, 83
3:7–9	135		
3:7	137	1:15–17	73
4:8–9	96	1:15–16	69, 71, 74
5:12	84	1:15	41, 86, 74, 75n, 79, 81
6:2	55n		
7:11	55n	1:16	70, 71, 74, 80, 82, 83, 84
7:15	55n		
9:14	103, 134	1:17	70, 72, 83
10:15–17	131	1:18–20	73
10:29	138	1:18	60, 70, 72, 74, 79, 82, 84, 85
11:17	31, 31n		
11:19	55n	1:18a	71
11:27	75n	1:18b–20	71
11:28	79, 79n	1:18b	71
11:35	55n	1:19	70, 71, 74, 85
12:5	72n	1:20	70, 71 74, 85
12:23	79, 79n	1:21–23	69, 72
		1:22	74, 85
Colossians		1:23	68, 74
1	81	1:24	74
1:1–2	68	1:26–28	67
1:2	81	2:6	68
1:3–14	68	2:7	68
1:5	67, 80	2:8	66, 67
1:6	67	2:9	74, 84, 85
1:7	67	2:10	67, 74, 84
1:9–20	68	2:11	67, 68
1:9	67, 68	2:12	55n, 68

2:13	68	3	132
2:14	74	3:16	132
2:15	60, 74, 84, 85	3:17	132
2:16	67	4:6	129
2:18	66	5:4	57n
2:19	74, 84, 85	6	132
2:20	66	6:14	57n, 58n
3:1	67	6:18–20	98n
3:2–3	67	6:19	132
3:6–15	67	8:4–6	42
3:10	74, 75, 82	8:4	113
3:11	67, 84	8:6	38n, 42, 74
3:15	74	10:7	55n
3:17	74	10:16–17	72n
3:19	67, 74	10:31	98
3:23–24	67	11:3	96, 97
4:3	67	11:26	56
4:11	74, 75	12:11	132, 134, 138
4:15–16	74	12:12	72n
		12:27	72n
1 Thessalonians		12:28	132
1:10	55n	14:4–6	136
4:13	93	15	55
4:18	93	15:3	48, 56
		15:4	48, 55n, 58n
1 Timothy		15:12–17	55n
1:17	75n	15:12	55n, 58n
2:5	45	15:13	55n
		15:14	49
2 Timothy		15:15	48, 57n
2:8	55n, 58n	15:17	48
2:18	55n	15:18	49
3:16	135	15:20–28	57, 58
		15:20–24	60n, 82
1 Corinthians		15:20	49, 54n, 56, 58, 59, 61
2:4	139		
2:10	134, 138	15:21	54n, 56, 57
2:11	134, 138	15:22	56, 57, 60
2:13	137	15:23	59, 60

15:24–28	85	12:9	57n
15:24	47n, 56, 60, 84	13:14	136, 138
15:25	60		
15:25b	60, 61	Galatians	
15:26	61	1:1	55n
15:27–28	47–63	3:21	55n
15:27	61	4:4–7	104
15:27a	61		
15:27b	61	1 Thessalonians	
15:28	56, 60, 61, 62, 96, 97	4:13–18	55
		4:13	93
15:29	55n	4:14	55n
15:32	49, 55n	4:16	54n, 55n
15:35	55n	4:18	93
15:36	55n		
15:42–44	54, 55n	Philippians	
15:42	55n	1:17	55n
15:45	55n	2:4–6	93
15:49	75n	2:5–11	44
15:51–54	61	2:13	126
15:51	54n	3:10	57n
15:52	54, 55, 56n	3:11	55n
15:54	62	3:21	85
15:55	55, 56n	5:14	55n
15:56	55, 56n	12:5–11	44
2 Corinthians		Ephesians	
1:9	55n	1:3	58
1:13	130	1:4	58
3:6	55n	1:13	137
3:17	135	1:20	55n, 57n
3:18	75n	2:16	85
4:4	75n, 76	3:18	130
4:14	54n, 55n	3:19	130
5:15	55n	4:30	138
5:17	103	5:1–2	106n
5:18–21	59n	5:5	37n
5:18–20	85	5:14	55n
5:19	96	6:12	60
6:16	132		

Titus
2:13	37, 37n
3:5	135, 138

1 Peter
1:1–2	136
3:20	132

2 Peter
1:1	37n, 38
1:21	135

1 John
1:3	107
2:1	139
2:19	7n
3:10	106
3:14	106
4:7–9	31
4:7	32
4:9	32
5:6	135
14:16	139

Revelation
1:5	59, 79, 79n, 81
1:10	134
1:17–18	40
3:14	41, 74
7:17	44
8:2	55, 56n
13	75n
14:6–7	98n
20:10	55, 56n
21:6	84
22:13	84

Index of Islamic Scriptural References

Surah			
		10:68–69	153
		12:92	148
2:116	153	14:16	151
2:163	152	15:29	150
3:49	148	16:102	151
4:48	154	17:110	158
4:171	149, 151, 154	19:19	153
		19:16–40	148
4:157	149	33:7	148
4:158	149	48:29	152
4:171	151	50:16	148
5:75	152	59:22–24	146, 158
5:117	154	61:6	148
5:116	153	78:38	150
9:30	153	112:1–4	146
10:37	157		

Lightning Source UK Ltd.
Milton Keynes UK
UKHW010716190719
346411UK00002B/315/P